LIFE CYCLES IN

JEWISH AND CHRISTIAN WORSHIP

TWO LITURGICAL TRADITIONS

Volume 4

Life Cycles in Jewish and Christian Worship

Edited by

PAUL F. BRADSHAW

and

LAWRENCE A. HOFFMAN

University of Notre Dame Press
Notre Dame   London

Copyright 1996 by
University of Notre Dame Press
Notre Dame, IN 46656
All Rights Reserved

Manufactured in the United States of America

*The paper used in this publication meets the minimum
requirements of the American National Standard for Information
Sciences—Permanence of paper for Printed Library Materials,
ANSI Z39.48-1984.*

Library of Congress Cataloging-in-Publication Data

Life cycles in Jewish and Christian worship / edited by Paul F.
Bradshaw and Lawrence A. Hoffman.
    p.   cm. — (Two liturgical traditions ; v. 4)
    Includes bibliographical references and index.
    ISBN 0-268-01307-1 (hard cover)
    1. Occasional services. 2. Rites and ceremonies. 3. Life
cycle, Human—Religious aspects—Christianity. 4. Life cycle,
Human—Religious aspects—Judaism. 5. Judaism—Customs
and practices. 6. Judaism—Liturgy. I. Bradshaw, Paul F.,
1945– . II. Hoffman, Lawrence A., 1942– . III. Series.
BV199.03L54   1995
265—dc20   95-18807
                                           CIP

Contents

Abbreviations

CCAR	Central Conference of American Rabbis
CCSL	Corpus Christianorum, Series Latina. [A series of patristic and medieval texts in Latin.] Turnhout, 1953–.
CSEL	Corpus Scriptorum Ecclesiasticorum Latinorum. [A series of patristic and medieval texts in Latin.] Vienna, 1866–.
PG	Patrologiae Cursus Completus, Series Graeca. Ed. J. P. Migne. 161 vols. [A series of patristic and medieval texts in Greek.] Paris, 1857–1866.
PL	Patrologiae Cursus Completus, Series Latina. Ed. J. P. Migne. 221 vols. [A series of patristic and medieval texts in Latin.] Paris, 1841–1864.
SC	Sources chrétiennes. [A series of ancient Christian texts and French translations, of over 300 volumes.] Paris, 1942–.

Rabbinic References

A. Z.	Avodah Zarah
B. B.	Baba Batra
B. K.	Baba Kamma
B. Ket.	Babylonian Talmud, Ketubot
B. M.	Baba Metsiya
B. San.	Babylonian Talmud, Sanhedrin
B. Sot	Babylonian Talmud, Sotah

B. T.	Babylonian Talmud (Babli)
Ber.	Berakhot
E. H.	Even Ha'ezer
Ecc. Rab.	Ecclesiastes Rabbah
Gen. Rab.	Genesis Rabbah
Git.	Gittin
Ket.	Ketubot
Kid.	Kiddushin
M.	Mishnah
M. Ber.	Mishnah, Berakhot
M. K.	Moed Katan
M. Kid.	Mishnah, Kiddushin
M. M. K.	Mishnah, Moed Katan
M. Meg	Mishnah, Megillah
M. Nid.	Mishnah, Niddah
M. R. H.	Mishnah, Rosh Hashanah
M. San	Mishnah, Sanhedrin
M. Shab.	Mishnah, Shabbat
M. Shek.	Mishnah, Shekalim
Mas. Sof.	Massakhet Sofrim
Meg.	Megillah
Ned.	Nedarim
Nid.	Niddah
O. H.	Orach Chayim
O. H., Y. D.	Orach Chayim, Yoreh De'ah
P. T. Ber.	Palestinian Talmud, Berakhot
P. T. Ket.	Palestinian Talmud, Ketubot
P. T. M. K.	Palestinian Talmud, Moed Katan
P. T. Meg.	Palestinian Talmud, Megillah
Pes.	Pesachim
R. H.	Rosh Hashanah
S. A., E. H.	Shulchan Arukh, Even Ha'ezer
S. A., O. H.	Shulchan Arukh, Orach Chayim
S. A., Y. D.	Shulchan Arukh, Yoreh De'ah
San.	Sanhedrin
Shab.	Shabbat
Sof.	Sofrim

Sot.	Sotah
SRA	Seder Rav Amram Gaon
Suk.	Sukkah
T.	Tosefta
T. Ber.	Tosefta, Berakhot
T. Ket.	Tosefta, Ketubot
T. Kid.	Tosefta, Kiddushin
T. Meg.	Tosefta, Megillah
T. Moed	Tosefta, Moed
T. R. H.	Tosefta, Rosh Hashanah
Tos.	Tosafot
Tos. Pes.	Tosafot Pesachim
Y. D.	Yoreh De'ah

Introduction

Life Cycle
as Religious Metaphor

LAWRENCE A. HOFFMAN

A playwright in a once-upon-a-time Communist bloc country explores the techniques of avant-garde theater, and authorities file a report under "potential dissident activities." A speaker lapses into an embarrassing slip of the tongue, and the Freudian in the crowd smiles over an unresolved oedipal complex. The family next door buys a new car, and neighborhood critics buzz about its purchase of a status symbol. The world is full of activities that mean one thing to those who do them and another altogether to "expert" observers.

How then do we expert observers understand the significance of life-cycle rites that other people do? The very metaphor of a life cycle is an observer construct—and not the only one western thought has concocted to explain the mystery of human biography. Thinking that embryo formation was the first stage in the drying process that converted body fluids like blood and semen into tissue, Greco-Roman medicine pictured human life as one long process of progressive desiccation, going from moist infancy to parched old age and death. Far from a cycle, then, Galen and his peers saw life's journey as a one-way trip toward death, a construction shared by medieval Christian moralists for whom the same odyssey, governed now by the inevitable Fall, culminated in reaching the judgment seat of God. Life as a pilgrimage to God thus dominated European thought, becoming sufficiently pronounced by the fourteenth century to produce poetry on the subject, as well as

1

iconography that portrayed the journey for the first time as a cycle. A wheel of life in a 1339 British psalter displays Christ in the center with spokes radiating out to a circumference composed of medallions, each a stage in the life cycle. A person's life course is equivalent to the annual cycle of time, running inextricably through the seasons from spring to winter, which is to say, from cradle to sepulcher, and then to resurrection, that is, rebirth—hence a cycle![1] Shakespeare's celebrated "seven ages of man" is already a secularized revisionist version of the Christian cycle: it has us moving mechanically from "the infant, mewling and puking in the nurse's arms," to ripe old age, "that second childhood, *sans* teeth, *sans* eyes, *sans* taste, *sans* everything"—it is a cycle then only because old age is infancy revisited.

However much these constructs of a life differ in detail, they are alike in their conflation of the biological and the social. Bodies seen as sponges drying up or as clocks running down are metaphorical constructs of biological processes. Galen's image of the sponge, however, is analogic—like life itself, it lacks precisely differentiated moments when one stage ends and another begins;[2] Shakespeare's time metaphor is digital— we outfit clocks with arbitrary stops at which the minute hand tarries before moving on, as if time jolts along irregularly, stopping and starting through its natural course. Life as a block of time thus requires that we differentiate particular "moments" at which to pause: arbitrary designations like the instant life begins, the day we come of age, the beginning of a marriage, and so forth. Though somewhat rooted in biology, these stations on life's journey are predominantly social constructs, embedded in larger cultural conceits from which they derive their meaning. Even the most patently biological among them, birth and death themselves, are assumed by different cultures to occur at different times, so that what they mean in terms of ethical issues alone—Is abortion murder?—depends on the social construction of a life, not its biological facticity. Moreover, once a culture arrives at its master conception of life's journey, it then posits some social stops that serve purely cultural needs, so are rooted only tangentially (if at all) in biological processes. Marriage, for instance, is as much social as biological; baptism, which varied over time from being a rite for adults to a rite for infants, is obviously tied to the cultural construct of a new life in Christ, not the biological reality of flesh-and-blood infancy; biblical and rabbinic *Pidyon Haben* (Redemption of the First-born) is purely cultural—what biological alteration is there at the prescribed cultural moment of a child's one-month birthday?

The question becomes, then, how to study the arbitrary set of rites that a culture erects to mark the social construct of a life, a construct that is, however, never entirely set free from its biological origins.

The Historical Study of Rites

One obvious response is to attack the problem from the presumed third-person disinterested perspective of historical development. Treated as an independent subject of study, a rite can be traced through time. Kenneth Stevenson, for instance, chronicles Christian marriage with a book that begins with pre-Christian origins and ends with a section entitled simply, "The Future."[3] Alternatively, he and Mark Searle collaborate in presenting the chief documents of that rite, but organizing them historically, with a preface entitled, "An Overview of History."[4] In the Jewish sphere, Hayyim Schauss's classic *The Lifetime of a Jew* sums up earlier scholarship in a popular account that follows each life-cycle event in Judaism back to its biblical and prebiblical origins, and then charts its evolution thereafter.[5] Insofar as the essays in this book delineate the evolution of the various rites under consideration, they remain true to that historicist agenda. We have not, for example, collapsed history in order to analyze a rite in terms of its structural or symbolist "deeper" signification.[6] In each of the chapters that follow, the authors want to know, at least in part, how the rites as we now have them came into being, and how they changed along the way before they reached us. On the other hand, our interest is

more than a mere tracing of liturgical history, even though we
are adamant about the need to retain a firm historical footing to
guard against postulating truths in general about rites that may
not even have existed for more than a few hundred years or
less.[7] Before turning to the additional perspective that we take,
however, let us survey two other options on the horizon, to determine the extent of our indebtedness to them: life cycle as rite
of passage, and life cycle as personal identity.

Life Cycle as Rite of Passage

Unlike the historicists, social scientists have sought to retain
the cultural-biological nexus that makes life-cycle rites what
they are. Uninterested in the kind of ritual history that emerges
from a chronological explication of texts, this approach has
fastened on understanding the role that life-cycle liturgy plays
in the meeting point of human development and social system,
its chief exemplar being the paradigm pursued by Arnold van
Gennep in 1908: life-cycle ritual as rites of passage.[8]

Influenced by the French sociological school of which he
was a part, van Gennep, like another of its members, Emile
Durkheim, pioneered the functionalist school of interpretation,
by which social institutions are to be explained by their service
to the stability of the social group. Van Gennep's emphasis was
on transition, not only across life stages but also between periods of time (a Janus-like new year), from place to place (traversing entrances and exits), and variations in status (the rungs
of a hierarchical ladder). In all such changes, he identified three
elements of rites of passage: separation (from the old), transition (a liminal period, as one crosses the threshold), and incorporation (into the new).

Though van Gennep was careful to follow in the footsteps of
Auguste Comte's positivistic program that denied all reality to
metaphysical speculation, a sort of metaphysical assumption
nevertheless underlies his work. He conceived of society and of
individuals as if they were "systems that become spent and
must be renewed."[9] Hence the particular importance of the

third element in rites of passage, incorporation, which provides rebirth, a new beginning. As regards the individual, van Gennep thus subscribed in part to the same deprivation hypothesis that underlay Freud's equally organic yet mechanistic model of the human psyche. For both, culturally prescribed rites are related to human states of deprivation. Freudian therapy would cure the individual of the need for such things, revealing religious ritual as mass obsessive compulsive neuroses rooted in a primal crime that the prehistoric human horde had committed in killing its primeval father and devouring him.[10] From his Durkheimian perspective, van Gennep argued the reverse. Though rites of passage are indeed responses to the natural crises humans face in our periodic running down and need for regeneration, our natural state is not something from which we can be cured but the grounds for a social contract by which we voluntarily submit to the group and from which we gladly accept the cultural construct that we celebrate as we go from life to death. This is not altogether unlike a second argument advanced by Freud, by which culture is to be explained as a sublimation of personal impulses, part and parcel of the voluntary ceding of individual autonomy to the group's will. But for Freud, the resulting religious ritual is the price of civilization and a heavy price at that, for it renders each of us dissatisfied with instinctual desires that go unfulfilled.[11] For van Gennep, however, as for Durkheim before him, religious ritual is a positive thing, in that it raises us from animals into civilized social beings. Rites of passage are thus the higher-order ways in which humans act out social roles, traverse socially defined spaces, and mark the passage of culturally constructed times.

Rite-of-passage theory has proved remarkably long lived. Its positive evaluation of ritual's function recommended it to researchers of various stamps, including Max Gluckman, whose anthropological thinking at the University of Manchester in the 1950s centered around the thorny problem of social conflict.[12] Orthodox functionalism maintained that social institutions provide social stasis; how then does one account for patent instability, social fission, even civil war? Gluckman's interest was taken over by his student, Victor Turner,[13] who passed on rite-of-passage theory to a generation of students studying with him in Chicago in the '60s and '70s. Turner's interest, however, went beyond rites of passage; he saw van Gennep's model as illuminating ritual in general. As Gluckman's student, Turner too was consumed with the problem of societal change and social conflict. Turner thought that, especially in tribal society, ritual dramatizes grievances and then brings about either a formal break in the status quo or a revolutionary new social order.[14] Human society is thus constantly in process from one stage of stasis to another. Individuals move through stages of life and so too do societies, with ritual laying down the paths that allow for transitions. But Turner valued especially the ideal state that he called *communitas*. Akin to the Judeo-Christian "Reign of God," this was a non-hierarchical state of being where "individuals are not segmented into roles and statuses, but confront one another rather in the manner of Martin Buber's 'I and Thou'."[15] For van Gennep, it was the third stage of passage, incorporation, which mattered most. For Turner, it was the second, the transitional (or liminal) stage, that counted, since it provided a taste of just such *communitas,* by poising individuals uneasily between their status past and future.[16] Ritual's primary purpose became nothing less than social change in the direction of communitarian relations.

This expectation of ritual was rapidly appropriated by Turner's students who applied it to religious rites, including life-cycle ritual in Judaism and Christianity, which was now expected to transform people by providing them with an experience of *communitas.* Anything less was not ritual at all but merely "ceremony," which (by contrast) is not transformational but only confirmatory of the status quo.[17] In the hands of liberation theologians, this neo-Turnerian preference for transformation takes on prophetic power. For Tom Driver, for instance, ritual is the means to human freedom,[18] from which it would follow that if life-cycle rites are truly to fulfill their role as ritual acts, they must transform individuals. Some feminists especially make this claim, as we see from Debra Orenstein, who draws on Marge Piercy's likening of women to "the doorways of life," and adds, "The body of a woman is a physical threshold that each of us crossed when entering the world." No wonder women are attracted to thresholds that men (van Gennep?) simply pass over without thinking about them. Echoing Driver, she adds that ritual and liminality allow feminists "to leave behind our structured hierarchical society and enter a fluid inchoate state [from which there arises] the possibility of transforming gender roles."[19]

The long evolution of life-cycle theory from its founder, van Gennep, to feminists and liberation theologians suggests at least two paradigms that we might apply here. Following van Gennep himself, we might endlessly demonstrate the extent to which each life-cycle rite successfully displays the three stages of separation, transition, and incorporation; or along with Turner, we might attend particularly to the liminal state by which individuals are transformed, asking in the first place if transformation really occurs, or at least studying the uniqueness of that moment which Turner called betwixt and between, and which even van Gennep himself considered a flash of the sacred.[20]

We have eschewed both options here, partly because we are unconvinced that ritual must indeed provide transformation for it to count as ritual. Though any number of ethical proclivities might favor such transformative potential, claiming it *a priori* as necessary would be unfair to the evidence of how life-cycle ritual has in fact operated throughout the centuries. But if life-cycle ritual is to be more than a museum relic studied by historicists, if, that is, it is to retain some functional connection to human society, what might that function be?

Life Cycle as Personal Identity

Some 250 years ago, David Hume wondered how an individual arrives at a single identity, given the skepticism with which we ought to accept the commonsense notion that we are

the same person today that we knew yesterday. Hume's philo-
sophical dilemma has its psychosocial parallel in the work of
Erik Erikson.

The life cycle was a theme to which Erikson returned time
and time again, but never as brilliantly as in his epilogue to
Young Man Luther, arguably the most moving psychological
prose of modern time. Finally transcending his orthodox
Freudian training that posited infancy as the only critical stage
in human development, Erikson set out to provide an overview
of life in its entirety, the ongoing and therefore most difficult
task of which he described as the formation of an ego. As Erikson saw it,

> Society . . . must support the primary function of every individual
> ego, which is to transform instinctual energy into patterns of ac-
> tion, into character, into style—in short, into an identity with a
> core of integrity. . . . At a given age, a human being . . . becomes
> ready and eager to face a new life task, that is, a set of choices and
> tests which are in some traditional way prescribed and prepared
> . . . by society's structure.[21]

In Martin Luther's case, adolescence had been determinative;
for others, it would be other challenges. But everyone pro-
gresses through the same eight stages of life, each of which is
both psychological and sociological, tied at least loosely to biology but dependent on cultural conditioning for its definition.
With each stage, we face new challenges of ego construction,
eventually arriving at the capstone of old age, where we are
asked to attain "integrity," a state akin to the faith one has in the
wholeness of the life one has lived, our sense of ownership of
that life, the opposite of the despair into which we are plunged
if we have failed to claim our life as our own.[22]

Erikson never discusses a single set of life-cycle rites as
ideal, but everywhere he emphasizes tradition as the mediator
of life's meaning: how "success" is defined by the elderly man
or woman looking back on a life in its twilight; or what counts
as "purpose" to the adolescent who must arrive at an ideological context in which life makes sense. As liberation theologians

have seized on Turner, pastoral theologians have therefore favored Erikson, who has been credited, for instance, with providing a necessary critique both of secular culture and of Freudian psychoanalysis, since healthy adult integrity depends on developing an ego that strives for the very ethics of which Christianity (for instance) speaks, and for which, therefore, Christian life-cycle stages are adequate preparation.[23] Others find parallels between Erikson's life-cycle stages and a maturation of the individual's experience of God.[24]

Here too, we might find a model for our use, measuring the competence of Jewish or Christian life-cycle rituals for Erikson's tasks and challenges, or estimating the maturity level of the rites' theological symbolism for the psychological needs entailed by the various stages of human growth. But as with the research program suggested by liberation theology, we have decidedly done neither of these. We are not convinced that we should be limited by a psychological hermeneutic. We do not deny the relevance of Eriksonian concerns, however, and have therefore included chapters (by Marjorie Procter-Smith and Yoel Kahn) that note the relative inadequacy of our inherited life-cycle rites to provide all the ritual passages necessary for the full gamut of men and women who aspire to a healthy old age of integrity and faith.[25]

But Erikson's identity model parallels our own in another way: his insistence that it is *tradition* that tells us what a life is like.[26] We take this task to be theological. Our emphasis here, then, is on the wholeness of a life that is marked by the *religious* metaphors inherent in our life-cycle rites. Seen this way, not every psychosocial stage need be accompanied expressly by religious rites of passage. Not all of them will be seen as equally formative, religiously speaking. While this view of ritual is akin to the deprivation hypothesis, in that we assume ritual serves a human need, a need moreover that will be deadened without the ritual means of satisfying it, we do not explain ritual solely by human deprivation, nor do we hold that ritual is just one means among many by which humans solve their personal problems in growing up. We do suggest, however, that growing up requires some model of what a life is all about, and that mature religious traditions tell us what life is by drawing our attention to theological constructs inherent in the rites we have. Our historical analysis suggests, moreover, that even though the psychological patterns of human growth will not be enough on their own to produce new life-cycle rites, the *inherited* cultural repertoire of ritualized events is insufficient to meet changing human needs. We leave open the possibility that new rites will grow as old ones attenuate, in our time no less than in the past. Our rites will be determined by the intersection of our overall theological construct and our experience of the human developmental pattern.

What follows then is a set of chapters detailing the history and shape of each life-cycle rite within Judaism and Christianity, with some attention to the theological message that each presents. After all the chapters have been presented, we will return to our overall theme, life cycle as theology, to consider briefly how the theologies unique to Judaism and Christianity have determined what aspects of human growth each would emphasize, and how those aspects have been spelled out by the rites that celebrate them.

NOTES

1. All examples taken from Thomas R. Cole, *The Journey of Life* (New York, 1992), chap. 1.
2. See Nelson Goodman, *Languages of Art* (Indianapolis, 1976), pp. 159–64.
3. Kenneth W. Stevenson, *To Join Together: the Rite of Marriage* (New York, 1987).
4. Mark Searle and Kenneth W. Stevenson, *Documents of the Marriage Liturgy* (Collegeville, MN, 1992).
5. Hayyim Schauss, *The Lifetime of a Jew* (New York, 1950).
6. As, for example, Harvey E. Goldberg, "Torah and Children: Symbolic Aspects of the Reproduction of Jews and Judaism," in idem, *Judaism Viewed from Within and from Without* (Albany, NY, 1987).
7. See guidelines laid down in Paul F. Bradshaw, "Ten Principles

for Interpreting Early Christian Liturgical Evidence," and Lawrence A. Hoffman, "Reconstructing Ritual as Identity and Culture," in Paul F. Bradshaw and Lawrence A. Hoffman, eds., *The Making of Jewish and Christian Worship,* volume 1 of this series, Two Liturgical Traditions (Notre Dame, IN, 1991).

8. Arnold van Gennep, *Les Rites de Passage;* trans. Monica B. Vizedom and Gabrielle L. Caffee, *The Rites of Passage* (Chicago, 1960).

9. Solon T. Kimball, introduction to *Rites of Passage* by van Gennep (Chicago ed.), p. viii.

10. Sigmund Freud, *Totem and Taboo* (1913; trans. James Strachey, New York, 1950).

11. Sigmund Freud, *Civilization and its Discontents* (1930; trans. James Strachey, New York, 1961).

12. Max Gluckman, "Les Rites de Passage," in idem, *Essays on the Ritual of Social Relations* (Manchester, 1962), pp. 1–52.

13. On which, cf. Bobby C. Alexander, *Victor Turner Revisited: Ritual as Social Change* (Atlanta, 1991); and Alexander's critic, Don Handelman, "Is Victor Turner Receiving his Intellectual Due?" *Journal of Ritual Studies* 7, no. 2 (1993): 117–26.

14. See esp. Victor Turner, *Dramas, Fields and Metaphors* (Ithaca, NY, 1974), pp. 13–59.

15. Victor Turner, *The Ritual Process* (Chicago, 1969), p. 132.

16. See, esp., his nuanced treatment of liminal/liminoid in Turner, *From Ritual to Theater* (New York, 1982), pp. 20–59.

17. See, e.g., Barbara Myerhoff, *Number our Days* (New York, 1978), p. 225 on true ritual, and pp. 185–86 on ceremony.

18. Tom F. Driver, *The Magic of Ritual* (New York, 1991), p. 106.

19. Debra Orenstein, *Lifecycles: Jewish Women on Life Passages and Personal Milestones* (Woodstock, VT, 1994), pp. 362, 425–26, n. 3. Citation from Marge Piercy, *The Sabbath of Mutual Respect.*

20. Van Gennep, *Rites of Passage,* p. 12.

21. Erik Erikson, *Young Man Luther* (New York, 1958), p. 254.

22. See esp. Erik Erikson, *The Life Cycle Completed* (New York, 1985), pp. 61–66.

23. Joachim Scharfenberg, "Human Maturation and Christian Symbols," in David Power and Luis Maldonado, eds., *Liturgy and Human Passage* (New York, 1979), pp. 27–34.

24. Paul Philibert, "Readiness for Ritual: Psychosocial Aspects of Maturity in Christian Celebration," in Regis A. Duffy, ed., *Alternative*

Futures for Worship, vol. 1 [General Introduction] (Collegeville, MN, 1987), pp. 97–107.

25. This overweighting of youth seems to be universal. See Barbara Myerhoff, "Rites and Signs of Ripening," in David I. Kertzer and Jennie Keith, eds., *Age and Anthropological Theory* (Cornell, 1984), p. 308; cf. p. 313 for bibliographic references to the need for later adult rites in our culture.

26. A theme taken up earlier in this series. See Lawrence A. Hoffman, "What is a Liturgical Tradition?" and Mark Searle, "Two Liturgical Traditions: Looking Toward the Future," in Paul F. Bradshaw and Lawrence A. Hoffman, eds., *The Changing Face of Jewish and Christian Worship in North America,* vol. 2 of Two Liturgical Traditions (Notre Dame, IN, 1991), pp. 3–25, 221–43.

Christian Rites Related to Birth

Paul F. Bradshaw

Strictly speaking, Christianity does not possess any universally practiced rites in relation to the birth of children. We shall see as this chapter unfolds, however, that through a series of historical accidents baptism has come to fulfill the function of a birth rite in many Christian denominations.

Purification/Thanksgiving after Childbirth

In the early centuries of Christianity the only religious ceremony that sometimes seems to have accompanied childbirth was a ritual purification of the mother, inspired by the prescriptions of Leviticus 12, which regarded a woman who had given birth as unclean for forty days in the case of a male child and eighty days in the case of a female and then required her to make a sacrificial offering. It may also have been encouraged by the reference in Luke 2:22f. to the purification of Mary, the mother of Jesus, in accordance with Leviticus 12, although the author confuses it with the redemption of the firstborn in Exodus 13:11–16. The earliest extant reference to the Christian adoption of this custom is in the fourth-century *Canons of Hippolytus* from Egypt, which directs that women who have given birth and the midwives who attended them are to be regarded as impure and are to sit with the catechumens and not receive holy communion until a specified period of time has elapsed (the midwife, twenty days in the case of a male child, forty days for a female; the mother, forty days for a male child, eighty days for a female).[1] Comparable prescriptions, together with rites of purification to mark the end of the period, occur in later eastern Christian liturgical books. So, for example, the Eastern Orthodox Church has a set of three prayers for the mother to be said by the priest in the home on the day of the birth itself, and also a rite for use on the fortieth day after birth when she returns to church with her child.[2]

Ancient western traditions are not nearly so uniform. On the one hand, Pope Gregory the Great did not regard childbirth as rendering a woman impure and hence averred in a letter to Augustine of Canterbury in 597 that "if a woman within an hour of her delivery enters the church to give thanks, she is burdened by no weight of sin."[3] However, although this statement was subsequently quoted with approval by some authorities, others insisted on a period of exclusion from participation in worship. This latter view generally predominated in the later Middle Ages, although there were regional differences over the prescribed length of time.[4]

Gregory's statement suggests that the woman's ritual return to church included an element of thanksgiving for safe delivery as well as purification, and the texts of actual forms of service from the later Middle Ages bear this out. Although varying in form considerably from region to region, the liturgical books include prayers for use immediately before and at the time of the birth, a blessing of the mother in the home after the birth, and a rite for her eventual return to church. This last generally took place at the church door, since the woman was not permitted to enter the sacred building itself until she had been thus purified. Like the blessing after birth, it usually consisted of appropriate psalms (e.g., Pss. 113, 128) and prayers, and sometimes included a sprinkling with holy water.[5] The woman then entered the church to attend the celebration of the eucharist. It was the custom in England for her to wear a veil on this occasion, and the rite was popularly known there as "churching."

Although the equivalent rite is still practiced in eastern churches, it has almost entirely died out among western Christians today, partly as a consequence of changing attitudes towards childbirth and partly as a result of the emergence of alternative rites, to which we shall refer later. In any case, the western version cannot really be described as a birth ritual for the infant, since its focus was entirely upon the mother. Moreover, several texts explicitly presuppose that the baptism of the child will have preceded this occasion, and it is that observance which therefore came to constitute the true life-cycle rite in relation to birth.

Infant Baptism

The custom of baptizing those who were converted to the Christian faith as a sign of their admission into the church can be traced back to New Testament times and may even have been initiated by Jesus himself (see John 3:22; but cf. 4:2). It appears to have been adopted from John the Baptist, who is said to have practiced "a baptism of repentance for the forgiveness of sins" (Mark 1:4), but scholars are divided over the source from which he may have derived the ritual: some have suggested that his action was based on the ablutions of the Essene community at Qumran, others that it arose from the custom of baptizing Jewish proselytes, and yet others that it was influenced by the biblical traditions of ritual purification (see, e.g., Lev. 15:5–13) and/or of prophetic symbolism, which had spoken of God's people being cleansed with pure water in preparation for the advent of the messianic age (see, e.g., Ezek. 36:25–28).

When baptism began to be extended to infants as well as older children and adults is, however, not at all certain. The first undisputed reference to the custom occurs in North Africa at the beginning of the third century in the writings of Tertullian, who disapproves of it.[6] However, some modern scholars, and notably Joachim Jeremias, have argued that infant baptism was not an innovation at this period but a traditional practice going back to the first century. Much depends upon how references to baptisms of a "household" in the New Testament (Acts 16:15; 1 Cor. 1:16) are to be understood: Did that term include very young children or not?[7]

Whatever the answer to that question, early descriptions of baptismal practice and the later texts of the rites themselves show clearly that a profession of faith by the candidates was a central element in the rite. When infants were baptized, therefore, one of their parents or someone else had to say the words for them, but neither the rites themselves nor the most ancient sources offer any real theological justification for allowing some other person to speak on behalf of children too young to speak for themselves. For example, the closest that Cyprian, the third-century bishop of Carthage, came to an explanation was to say that infants' crying constituted their petition to be baptized.[8] Thus it looks as though practice may have preceded doctrine here, perhaps simply as a result of an inchoate desire on the part of Christian parents to have their children share in whatever benefits they believed themselves to enjoy as a result of baptism. Fifth-century sources indicate that a similar action was also taken with adult candidates who had signified their desire for baptism but were too ill to answer for themselves when the time came, a custom which may even have constituted the precedent for the practice with infants.[9]

Only later in the writings of Augustine of Hippo (354–430) did a theological justification for infant baptism first appear that was eventually to become the standard explanation in traditional Catholic theology: belief was not a prerequisite for baptism as it was in the case of an adult, but faith was bestowed on the child through the faith of others in the celebration of the rite itself:

> When, on behalf of an infant as yet incapable of exercising faith, the answer is given that he believes, this answer means that he has faith because of the sacrament of faith. . . . Therefore an infant, although he is not yet a believer in the sense of having that faith which includes the consenting will of those who exercise it, nevertheless becomes a believer through the sacrament of that faith. For as it is answered that he believes, so also he is called a believer, not because he assents to the truth by an act of his own judgment, but because he receives the sacrament of that truth.[10]

What is also clear is that even after the practice of infant baptism was adopted, it did not quickly replace adult baptism as the norm everywhere. On the one hand, in North Africa it seems to have become firmly established at an early date. Thus Cyprian insisted that there was no need to wait until the eighth day after birth to baptize an infant, as some were claiming on the basis of the biblical prescription for circumcision: the mercy and grace of God ought not to be refused to anyone, since all are equal in the gift of grace.[11] On the other hand, we find Gregory of Nazianzus in Cappadocia in 381 advising that children should normally be baptized at about the age of three years, when they are able to answer the baptismal questions themselves and can to some extent understand the Christian faith![12] There are also plenty of examples of people from Christian families in the fourth century who were not baptized until they had become adults. Indeed, there was a widespread tendency to delay baptism as long as possible. Because the forgiveness of sins that baptism was believed to convey was thought to be necessary for salvation, and because repeated opportunities to obtain that remission of sins in other ways did not exist, parents often deferred the baptism of their children at least until after the period of adolescence, when the passions of youth had subsided and there was less chance of them succumbing to temptation. Some adults postponed baptism until much later in life, sometimes even until their deathbed, so as to be more sure of gaining salvation.

By the fifth century, however, those same beliefs began to lead people in the opposite direction: if baptism was necessary for salvation, then in view of the high infant mortality rate in the ancient world it was desirable to baptize children as young as possible, lest they should happen to die and forfeit their opportunity for salvation. This tendency was given strong impetus by the theological reflections of Augustine, who argued that because the church practiced the baptism of infants, babies must therefore be in need of the remission of sins that baptism brings. Since newborn children had not yet committed actual sins, he concluded that they must have inherited the "original sin" of Adam: "What need is there, therefore, for an infant to be conformed to the death of Christ through baptism, if he is not completely poisoned by the serpent's bite?"[13] He was not the first to reason in this way from practice to doctrine. Both Cyprian[14] and Origen[15] in the third century had already drawn similar conclusions from infant baptism, in contrast to earlier Christian theologians who had asserted the purity of newborn children. Augustine not only developed the idea more fully, but he added a powerful motivation for conferring baptism at the earliest possible age, since he argued that children dying un-baptized would inevitably be damned, although he believed that they would receive only "the mildest condemnation."[16]

It was not long, therefore, before infant baptism became more or less universal throughout the Christian church, and people forgot that baptism had originally been connected with adult conversions. Indeed, some western texts from the tenth century onwards offer an amusing illustration of the extent to which infant baptisms came to be considered as normative. They direct that infants are to be held in the right arms of their sponsor and adult candidates are to place their foot upon the foot of their sponsor—the latter apparently an attempt to con-form as closely as possible to what is done in the baptism of in-fants![17] It is also an indication of the extent to which the adoption of infant baptism changed the role of sponsor or god-parent: from being the person who presented an adult candidate for baptism and vouched for the genuineness of the conversion that had already taken place in his or her life, the godparent was now the one who held the baby at the ceremony, made the baptismal renunciation of evil and profession of faith on his or her behalf, and was also charged with the future spiritual up-bringing of the child.[18]

Eventually, baptism came to be associated not just with in-fancy but with birth, as the usual interval between the two events grew shorter, and so it effectively began to function as a rite in connection with birth. Although until the twelfth cen-tury there were theoretically only two regular occasions in the year for the administration of baptism, Easter and Pentecost, in practice most infants were already being baptized soon after their birth because of the high risk of infant mortality. An English directive of 693, for example, ordered all children to be baptized within thirty days of their birth, imposing a fine on parents if this were not done and the confiscation of all their property if the child then died unbaptized. Similar legislation was repeated throughout Europe in later centuries, with the maximum period between birth and baptism being reduced generally to a week, or sometimes even as little as twenty-four hours.[19]

The change in the normal candidacy for baptism from the adult to the infant also profoundly affected the form of the rite. In the writings of Augustine we can already observe one adaptation that was made when infants were baptized. Whereas, when the candidate was an adult or older child, the profession of faith was usually made in the form of a series of direct questions and answers ("Do you believe . . .?" "I believe"), at the baptism of an infant both the questions and the responses made on behalf of the candidate were instead cast in the third person: "Does he/she believe . . . ," "He/she believes."[20] This variation was enough to cause Augustine's theological opponent Pelagius to argue that, if adults and infants were supposed to be receiving the same baptism, then exactly the same words ought to be used in the rite.[21] Although there are signs that this form of the profession of faith was also adopted in Spain and France as well as Africa,[22] apparently it did not affect the liturgy at Rome, and so when the Roman rite eventually supplanted all other local rites in the West during the Middle Ages, the use of the adult formula for infants became universal. This effectively reduced the role of the godparent in the rite to that of a mere ventriloquist, supplying a voice for the silent child.

Later variations, however, had a more lasting effect. They included the substitution of small waist-high fonts for the usually larger baptismal pools of earlier times, into which the candidates had descended naked, and eventually a tendency not to dip the child in the water but to adopt for all infants the provision made from early times for candidates who were sick—merely to pour a small amount of water over the head of the child, who now remained clothed.

Perhaps most profound of all, however, was the effect on the duration of the baptismal process. In the fourth century adults had been required to spend a lengthy period of time as catechumens ("learners") prior to their baptism, during which they were instructed in the faith and their conduct was monitored. According to one pilgrim's account of initiation practice at Jerusalem, for example, "the bishop asks their neighbours questions about them: 'Is this person leading a good life? Does he respect his parents? Is he a drunkard or a boaster?' He asks about all the serious human vices."[23] In the final stage of preparation the candidates were also periodically exorcised in order that all evil spirits might be driven out of them. It obviously did not make much sense for a very young child to go through all the instruction and testing that had been required of adults, and so the catechumenal elements were usually omitted from the process in their case, just as they were when an adult who was in danger of death needed to be baptized immediately.

At Rome, on the other hand, which was particularly conservative in liturgical matters, attempts were made to retain as many of the features of the catechumenate as possible, and for several centuries babies there were still enrolled in the catechumenate and brought to the regular Sunday liturgy during the Lenten season in order to be exorcised and to have token passages from the four Gospels as well as the Apostles' Creed and the Lord's Prayer solemnly read to them and explained before their baptism at Easter.[24] Later western rites, therefore, which were modeled on the Roman pattern, did not abolish the catechumenate entirely but merely compressed it into the first few minutes of the baptismal rite itself. Infants were brought to the door of the church and there admitted as catechumens. Then followed in quick succession all the prayers and exorcisms that had originally been spread over a period of several weeks in the earlier Roman rite, together with the recitation of the Creed and Lord's Prayer and a brief gospel reading (Matt. 19:13–15— where Jesus says, "Let the children come to me . . . for to such belongs the kingdom of God," and then lays his hands on them). After this, the baptismal party then moved inside to the font for the baptism proper.[25]

Another major effect of infant baptism on the form of the rite was the transition from public to private celebration. The whole baptismal process from the enrollment in the catechumenate onwards had originally taken place in the presence and with the active participation of the members of the local church. Although, as we have seen, attempts were made for some time at Rome to continue this practice in the case of infants, later sources indicate that the Lenten prebaptismal ceremonies there were eventually transferred from Sundays to Mondays, presumably so that the babies would not disturb the regular worship of the congregation;[26] and of course the trend to baptize soon after birth eliminated all need for such occasions and often required the baptism itself to take place on a weekday in the presence of only the priest and midwife.

Even the presence of a priest was not absolutely necessary. Because there was always a risk that a new convert to Christianity might die before an ordained minister could be summoned, from early times it had been permitted for baptism to be administered by a lay person in an emergency, and because of the high risk of death soon after birth, this provision became even more widely used when infant baptism became established. Indeed, the late medieval western rites contain rubrics that direct the parish priest regularly to instruct his people how to perform the essential elements of the baptismal rite, which were understood to be sprinkling the child with water or immersing him/her in it while saying the formula, "I baptize you in the name of the Father and of the Son and of the Holy Spirit," either in Latin or in the vernacular. Whenever possible, a lay man, rather than a woman, was to perform the baptism.

Baptism and Naming

A popular belief emerged during the Middle Ages, and has persisted widely ever since, that baptism is the time when a child is given his or her name. Such a view is not surprising when one considers that until recent centuries in most countries the church's baptismal register was the only way in which any birth was formally recorded. But features of the rite itself also encouraged this interpretation of it. In the early church, when adult converts sought baptism, their names were publicly recorded in a book at the beginning of the period of their final preparation, and they were often referred to by name in the various prayers and formularies that were spoken over them during the ceremonies in the catechumenal process. No doubt at this time some who had names that were intimately connected with pagan religions would have taken a new "Christian" name.

Relics of this practice persisted in the medieval period, when the final period of preparation had been absorbed within the baptismal rite itself. Here it was necessary for the priest or other minister to ask what the name of each child was before proceeding to use that name in the various formularies of the rite, and because this now occurred so soon after birth, it naturally gave rise to the idea that this rite was the occasion when a child actually received his or her name. Indeed, the rubrics in some baptismal rites explicitly say that the priest "gives the name" at the first occasion when he asks what it is and uses it. An eleventh-century Spanish rite, for example, gives the following direction: *"He signs him upon the forehead and gives him his name in this exorcism: he asks his name and says to him as follows*: N., receive the sign of the cross. . . . "[27] And we can see a similar assumption operative in the directive given by John Peckham, archbishop of Canterbury 1279–1292, that the clergy should not allow improper names to be conferred upon infants at their baptism, especially on those of the female sex.[28]

Baptism and the Reformation

The sixteenth-century Reformation in western Christianity brought with it a challenge to the now traditional practice of infant baptism. While the mainstream Reformers did not question its legitimacy, those on the more radical wing of the Reformation did, arguing that the New Testament sanctioned only the baptism of true believers and not of uncomprehending and unresponsive infants. Because of this, they were called Anabaptists ("Re-baptizers") by their opponents. Among their number were Thomas Müntzer and the Zwickau Prophets who appeared in Wittenburg in 1521; the Swiss Brethren who emerged in Zurich in 1525; the Moravian Brethren, under the leadership of Jacob Hutter, who are also known as Hutterite or Hutterian Brethren; those influenced by Melchior Hoffmann (1498–1543) and so known as Melchiorites or Hoffmanites; and the Mennonites, organized in the Netherlands by Menno Simons (1496–1561). This last group also influenced John Smyth (c. 1554–1612), who at the beginning of the sixteenth century baptized himself (consequently being called the "Sebaptist") and founded a Baptist church in Amsterdam. From this sprang other Baptist congregations, first in London and then throughout Britain and in the American colonies.

In their opposition to the Anabaptist position, many of the leaders of the Reformation churches developed an understanding of baptism as being the Christian equivalent of circumcision under the Old Covenant. This was not a complete innovation: for example, St. Paul linked baptism with circumcision in Col. 2:11–12,[29] and this idea was taken up by several early Christian writers.[30] Moreover, as we have seen earlier, Cyprian in the third century knew of those who wished to baptize infants on the eighth day after birth in line with the Jewish prescription concerning circumcision. But the parallel was never developed strongly until the Reformers needed a defense against the Anabaptist exegesis of the Bible. They argued that baptism was intended to be the sign of the covenant God had made with Christians, just as circumcision was the sign of the covenant that God had made with the Jews, and that therefore it was right to baptize infants as early as possible and so bring them into that covenant relationship.[31]

Since one of the principal tenets of the Reformation was the doctrine of justification by faith alone, one might expect that the practice of baptizing infants, who apparently did not possess conscious faith, would have caused some difficulty for the Reformers. However, they solved this problem in different ways. Martin Luther, for instance, appears somewhat inconsistent in his defense of infant baptism. On the one hand, and in contrast to his views elsewhere on the necessity of faith on the part of the recipients of the sacraments,[32] he seems to have accepted the sufficiency of vicarious faith:

> Here I say what all say: Infants are aided by the faith of others, namely those who bring them for baptism. For the Word of God is powerful enough, when uttered, to change even a godless heart, which is no less unresponsive and helpless than any infant. So through the prayer of the believing church which presents it, a prayer to which all things are possible [Mark 9:23], the infant is changed, cleansed, and renewed by inpoured faith.[33]

On the other hand, the actual baptismal rites that he drew up retained the traditional medieval arrangement of the interrogations being addressed directly to the infants,[34] while in his *Large Catechism* he appears to regard all prior faith as unnecessary:

> Further, we are not primarily concerned whether the baptized person believes or not, for in the latter case Baptism does not become invalid. Everything depends upon the Word and commandment of God. . . . For my faith does not constitute Baptism, but receives it. . . . We bring the child with the purpose and hope that he may believe, and we pray God to grant him faith. But we do not baptize him on that account, but solely on the command of God.[35]

Another Reformer, Martin Bucer, adopted a quite different approach to the question of faith and infant baptism. Since he believed that it was the faith of the parents and godparents that was requisite in the case of infants, he insisted that the questions in the rite should be put to them about their own beliefs and not vicariously about the beliefs of the child.[36] Yet another approach was taken in the Church of England: the questions answered by the godparents were thought of as promises for the future being made by the infants through the godparents as their "sureties," in much the same way as a contract might be made by a parent or guardian on behalf of a minor.[37]

Through ways like this, infant baptism was able to retain its place in the majority of the Reformation churches and to continue to function there just as it did in the Roman Catholic tradition as the principal rite for children born into a Christian culture. Whatever may have been its "official" meaning in the eyes of the various ecclesiastical authorities, as far as most parents were concerned baptism gave their children a name, ensured that they would not go to hell if they died young, and opened up access to the sacraments and other ministrations of the church, especially a Christian wedding and funeral service. The "private" and familial (as distinct from ecclesial) character of the event was further encouraged in later centuries when most Reformation churches abandoned their original insistence upon the celebration of baptisms only during the Sunday worship of the congregation and allowed them to take place at other times with just the child's family and their friends present. Only in the last few decades has this practice been challenged and begun to be reversed in both Catholic and Protestant traditions.

Infant Blessing/Dedication

In addition to the provision for the purification of women after childbirth in eastern Christian traditions, there is also a rite for use on the eighth day after the birth, in which the child is brought to church, given a name, and prayed for.[38] We have no way of knowing how old the custom is, since the earliest extant liturgical texts are medieval, but the choice of the eighth day seems to imply that this was intended to supply a Christian counterpart for the biblical injunctions about circumcision.

As we have seen, baptism itself came to fulfill the function of a naming ceremony for the child in the medieval West.

However, the abolition of infant baptism among the sixteenth-century Anabaptists meant that something else was required to meet that particular need, and so rites of infant dedication begin to emerge in that tradition. Both Pilgrim Marpeck (1495–1556) and Balthasar Hübmaier (c. 1485–1528) are known to have produced such forms.[39]

It is often argued that English Baptists adopted this practice only in the nineteenth century in conjunction with the Sunday School movement, and that it then spread from there to Baptists in the United States during what is known as the Second Great Awakening. However, at least one late-eighteenth-century Baptist minister's manual from the American colonies already included a rite of infant dedication, suggesting that the practice was derived directly from continental Anabaptists.[40]

More recently, interest has also been shown in the idea of such a rite of blessing and/or dedication by some Christians from traditions that do practice infant baptism, and this for a variety of different reasons. Some are motivated by increasing discomfort with the custom of baptizing babies at all in the light of the apparent emphasis in the New Testament on the connection between personal faith and church membership, and want to offer parents an alternative rite.[41]

Others, while not unhappy with infant baptism as such, are disturbed by the longstanding tradition of what they see as indiscriminate baptism within their particular church, whereby all children who are presented for baptism are willingly baptized, without any enquiry being made as to the faith commitment of their parents or other members of their family. These Christians want to meet the pastoral needs of non-churchgoing parents while reserving baptism itself for the children of those who are committed members of the church. Still others simply want to separate the function of a rite for newborn babies or the celebration of a birth or adoption from the process of becoming a Christian, which has no necessary connection with any particular point in the biological cycle, so that the true meaning of baptism as commitment to Christ and entry into the church may be more clearly seen. Another variation of this has been a desire to return more closely to what is perceived as the practice of the early church, by admitting infants to a catechumenate and allowing them to grow in the Christian faith before baptizing them at a later age.[42]

In other cases, the motivation has been not so much a concern to protect the integrity of baptism as a disquiet with traditional forms of the churching of women: rejecting the emphasis on the need for the ritual purification of women from the uncleanness of childbirth as being incompatible with a belief in the goodness of God's creation, these reformers have sought to produce rites that focus instead upon the child and the family, in thanksgiving for the birth and in prayers for their future life.

Such attempts have not so far always met with very great success. Although many Christians today have abandoned the Augustinian view that babies who die unbaptized will not enter heaven, this belief still persists in the folk traditions of many countries and drives many parents (or grandparents) who have little or no other contact with Christianity to continue to seek the baptism of infants and to be dissatisfied with the alternative rites offered. Moreover, the custom of the churching of women had all but died out in a number of cultures before the new rites of thanksgiving/blessing for a new child were introduced, and so in those situations there was little by way of a living tradition on which these renewed observances might build.

NOTES

1. Canon 18: see Paul F. Bradshaw, ed., *The Canons of Hippolytus,* Alcuin/GROW Liturgical Study 2 (Nottingham, 1987), p. 20.

2. For an English version, see *Service Book of the Holy Orthodox-Catholic Apostolic Church,* rev. ed., trans. Isabel Florence Hapgood (Englewood, NJ, 1983), pp. 266–70. See also Alexander Schmemann, *Of Water and the Spirit* (Crestwood, NY, 1974), pp. 131–38, 141–47; and Miguel Arranz, "Les sacrements de l'ancien Euchologe constantinopolitain (3): IIème partie: Admission dans l'église des enfants des familles chrétiennes («Premier catéchuménat»)," *Orientalia Christiana Periodica* 49 (1983): 284–302. Arranz,

however, treats the rite on the fortieth day as primarily the "church-ing" of the child, based on the presentation of Christ in the Temple, and maintains that the prayers for the mother are not as ancient; but this ignores the comparative evidence provided by other eastern traditions.

3.   Bede, *Historia ecclesiastica* 1.27 (PL 95:63).

4.   See Pierre J. Payer, "Early Medieval Regulations Concerning Marital Sexual Relations," *Journal of Medieval History* 6 (1980): 366.

5.   For examples of medieval texts for all these occasions, see Adolph Franz, *Die kirchlichen Benediktionen im Mittelalter* (Freiburg im Breisgau, 1909; reprint, Graz, Austria, 1960), 2:186–240. See also Walter von Arx, "The Churching of Women after Childbirth: History and Significance," in David Power and Luis Maldonado, eds., *Liturgy and Human Passage* (New York, 1979 = *Concilium* 112), pp. 63–72.

6.   Tertullian, *De baptismo* 18.4–5 (CCSL 1:293). See also David F. Wright, "How Controversial Was the Development of Infant Baptism in the Early Church?" in James E. Bradley and Richard A. Muller, eds., *Church, Word, and Spirit: Historical and Theological Essays in Honor of Geoffrey W. Bromiley* (Grand Rapids, MI, 1987), pp. 47–50.

7.   See Joachim Jeremias, *Infant Baptism in the First Four Centuries* (London, 1960), and *The Origins of Infant Baptism* (London, 1963); and for an opposing view, Kurt Aland, *Did the Early Church Baptize Infants?* (London, 1963). See also the contributions to the debate by Everett Ferguson, "Inscriptions and the Origin of Infant Baptism," *Journal of Theological Studies* 30 (1979): 37–46; and David F. Wright, "The Origins of Infant Baptism—Child Believers' Baptism?" *Scottish Journal of Theology* 40 (1987): 1–23.

8.   Cyprian, *Epistola* 64.6 (CSEL 3:721).

9.   See Council of Hippo (North Africa, 393 C.E.), canon 36; First Council of Orange (France, 441 C.E.), canon 12; Cyril of Alexandria, *Commentaria in Joannem* 11.26 (PG 74:49); Fulgentius, *Epistola* 11.7 (PL 65:387); Gennadius of Marseilles, *De ecclesiasticus dogmatibus* 52 (PL 58:993).

10.   Augustine, *Epistola* 98.9.10 (PL 33:364). English translation from Philip Schaff, ed., *A Select Library of the Nicene and Post-Nicene Fathers* 1 (Buffalo, NY, 1886), p. 410. See also Augustine, *Sermo* 294.12 (PL 38:1342).

11. Cyprian, *Epistola* 64 (CSEL 3:717–21).

12. Gregory of Nazianzus, *Oratio* 40.28 (PG 36:400).

13. Augustine, *De peccatorum meritis et remissione* 1.61 (PL 44:145).

14. Cyprian, *Epistola* 64.5 (CSEL 3:720–21).

15. Origen, *Homiliae in Leviticum* 8 (PG 12:496); *Homiliae in Lucam* 14 (PG 13:1835–36); *Commentaria in Romanos* 5.9 (PG 14:1047).

16. Augustine, *De peccatorum* 1.21 (PL 44:120). See also Wright, "How Controversial?" pp. 52–63.

17. See J. D. C. Fisher, *Christian Initiation: Baptism in the Medieval West* (London, 1965), p. 26.

18. For a detailed study of the role of the godparent, see Joseph H. Lynch, *Godparents and Kinship in Early Medieval Europe* (Princeton, NJ, 1986); and for recent developments within the Roman Catholic Church, see Mark Searle, "From Gossips to Compadres: A Note on the Role of Godparents in the Roman Rite for the Baptism of Children," in E. Carr et al., eds., *Eulogema: Studies in Honor of Robert Taft, S.J.* (Rome, 1993), pp. 473–84.

19. Fisher, *Christian Initiation: Baptism in the Medieval West,* pp. 82, 86–87, 109–19.

20. See Augustine, *Epistola* 98.7 (PL 33:363); *Sermo* 294.12 (PL 38:1342).

21. See Augustine, *De gratia Christi et de peccato originali* 1.32.35; 2.1.1; 2.21.24 (PL 44:377, 385, 397).

22. See J. Ch. Didier, "Une adaptation de la liturgie baptismale au baptême des enfants dans l'Église ancienne," *Mélanges de science religieuse* 22 (1965): 79–90.

23. *Itinerarium Egeriae* 45.3; English translation from John Wilkinson, *Egeria's Travels* (London, 1971), p. 145. Similar questions are also found in the ancient church order known as the *Apostolic Tradition*: see chap. 20 in G. J. Cuming, *Hippolytus: A Text for Students,* Grove Liturgical Study 8 (Nottingham, 1976), p. 17.

24. Fisher, *Christian Initiation: Baptism in the Medieval West,* pp. 3–12.

25. Ibid., pp. 158–79.

26. Ibid., pp. 5–6.

27. M. Férotin, ed., *Liber Ordinum,* Monumenta Ecclesiae Liturgica 5 (Paris, 1904), col. 26; English translation from E. C.

Whitaker, ed., *Documents of the Baptismal Liturgy,* 2d ed. (London, 1970), p. 117.

28. *De baptismo,* in D. Wilkins, *Concilia Magnae Britanniae et Hiberniae* (London, 1737), 2:53.

29. "In him [Christ] also you were circumcised with a circumcision made without hands, by putting off the body of flesh in the circumcision of Christ; and you were buried with him in baptism, in which you were also raised with him through faith in the working of God, who raised him from the dead."

30. See, for example, Justin Martyr, *Dialogus cum Tryphone* 43 (PG 6:565–70): "And we, who have approached God through him [Christ] have received not carnal but spiritual circumcision, which Enoch and those like him observed. And we have received it through baptism . . ."; Cyril of Jerusalem, *Catechesis* 5 (PG 33:514): "And then, following upon our faith, we receive like him [Abraham] the spiritual seal, being circumcised by the Holy Spirit through baptism, not in the foreskin of the body, but in the heart, according to Jeremiah. . . ."

31. For examples, see J. D. C. Fisher, *Christian Initiation: The Reformation Period* (London, 1970), pp. 27, 35, 36–37, 39, 46, 78, 88, 115, 120. See also Hughes Oliphant Old, *The Shaping of the Reformed Baptismal Rite in the Sixteenth Century* (Grand Rapids, MI, 1992).

32. See Martin Luther, "The Babylonian Captivity of the Church"; English translation from *Luther's Works* 36 (Philadelphia, 1959), p. 66: "Thus it is not baptism that justifies or benefits anyone, but it is faith in that word of promise to which baptism is added. This faith justifies, and fulfills that which baptism signifies. . . ."

33. *Luther's Works* 36, p. 73.

34. See *Luther's Works* 53 (Philadelphia, 1965), pp. 99, 108–9.

35. Theodore Tappert, ed., *The Book of Concord* (Philadelphia, 1959), pp. 443–44. See also "Concerning Rebaptism," in *Luther's Works* 40 (Philadelphia, 1958), pp. 242–44.

36. See, for example, the *Pia Deliberatio* of Hermann von Wied of Cologne (the section on baptism was drawn up by Bucer), and Bucer's *Censura* xiv; English translation of both in Fisher, *Christian Initiation: The Reformation Period,* pp. 54–69, 102–3.

37. Fisher, *Christian Initiation: The Reformation Period,* pp. 92–93.

38. An English translation of the Eastern Orthodox rite is in Hapgood, *Service Book,* p. 267. See also Schmemann, *Of Water and the Spirit,* pp. 138–41.

39. See Rollin Stely Armour, *Anabaptist Baptism: A Representative Study* (Scottdale, PA, 1966), pp. 23, 132.

40. Morgan Edwards, *The Customs of the Primitive Churches* (Philadelphia, 1774), pp. 96ff., cited in Keith Wimmersberger, "Infant Dedication: A Rite of Community Renewal for Baptist Congregations," *Foundations* 20 (1977): 245–48. For a modern version, see Max Thurian and Geoffrey Wainwright, eds., *Baptism and Eucharist: Ecumenical Convergence in Celebration,* Faith and Order Paper 117 (Geneva/Grand Rapids, MI, 1983), pp. 71–73.

41. See, for example, Neville Cryer, *By What Rite?* (London, 1969).

42. See Geoffrey Wainwright, "The Need for a Methodist Service for Admission of Infants to the Catechumenate," *London Quarterly and Holborn Review* (January 1968): 51–60.

Rituals of Birth in Judaism

LAWRENCE A. HOFFMAN

People imagine that always and everywhere, religious rituals must mark birth as the beginning of the life cycle. But
that is not necessarily the case. Whether cultures choose to
post official notices for even the most obvious biological
changes that their members experience remains a cultural
option. And as often as not, the changes a culture marks
with ceremony are skewed culturally, with gender implications in particular. North Americans, for instance, have at
various times and places celebrated such things as "sweet
sixteens" and "debutante coming out" for girls but not for
boys. Judaism too has emphasized some aspects of biological change at the expense of others, overlaying even what is
common to men and women with gender implications. Thus
to the extent that classical Jewish ritual celebrates birth at
all, it can be said that through the ritual of circumcision
(*brit milah*), it is the birth of boys, not girls, that receives
attention. And within the category of "male," a further ritual
("redemption of the first-born" [*Pidyon Haben*]) emphasizes
the dichotomy between being "born into priestly stock" and
"born as an ordinary Israelite." This chapter analyzes these
two traditional practices, asking what they implied to the
Rabbis. It surveys also an unofficial custom known to rabbinic society, but about which the Rabbis themselves had
relatively little to say: *Shavua Haben* (for boys) and *Shavua
Habat* (for girls).

32

1. Brit Milah *("The Covenant of Circumcision")*

Reaching well back into pre-rabbinic times, male circumcision is well attested in the various strands of Hebrew Scripture. Israel's narrative is organized so that it virtually begins when Abraham circumcises Isaac (Gen. 21:4), after circumcising himself and Ishmael and all the other male members of his retinue (Gen. 17: 23–27). Thereupon, the Bible presents circumcision as a custom that is taken for granted as normative for all Israelite men. Jacob's sons, for instance, tell Chamor and Shechem that no Israelite woman can have uncircumcised husbands, since an uncircumcised condition for males is "a disgrace among us" (Gen. 34: 13–16). When Israel leaves Egypt, God instructs Moses to prepare a Passover offering, of which only the circumcised may eat (Exod. 12:44, 48). With Leviticus 12:3, circumcision enters Israel's legal regulations for all time.

Circumcision thus winds like a twisted thread through the biblical narratives. Zipporah circumcises Moses' son when his uncircumcised condition threatens him with danger (Exod. 4: 24–26), and Joshua assures a circumcised state for all males before entering the Promised Land (Josh. 5: 2–8).

But the biblical editor's carefully orchestrated presentation of circumcision as a covenantal custom stretching back endlessly and without change from Abraham on is not without lacunae. Deuteronomy presents Moses' final charge to Israel as if the covenant and circumcision have nothing to do with each other. It knows a covenant involving the gift of the Land, which the Israelites will enjoy if they follow all of God's Torah, but as for circumcision, it records only the metaphoric vision that "God will circumcise your heart" (Deut. 30:6), a usage picked up a century later by Jeremiah (Jer. 9:25).

If we survey the biblical narrative according to the probable date at which its several interwoven strands were composed rather than the canonical chronology imposed by the final editors, it becomes clear that even though Israelite men were indeed circumcised from a very ancient time, it was only in the

post-exilic period that circumcision was associated with covenanthood. As for circumcision, abundant evidence prior to the
destruction of the first temple associates it not with covenant at
all, but with the belief that circumcised males would prove more
fertile.[1] And as for covenant, the same sources (Deuteronomy
and the pre-exilic prophets) posit covenanthood as the condition
by virtue of which Israel has been deeded God's chosen Land,[2]
but having nothing directly to do with circumcision at all. The
covenanted people must choose life over death, blessing over
curse, says Moses in his final peroration (Deut. 30). Nowhere
does he stipulate that they must choose also to be circumcised.
The early account of the Abrahamic covenant given in Genesis
15 thus emphasizes landedness, but overlooks circumcision entirely.

After the exile, however, and under theocratic hegemony,
circumcision was reinterpreted theologically to be the sign of
the covenant. Genesis 15 was thus recast in Genesis 17 to picture circumcision of Israelite men as the normative condition
on which the covenant depends, and Leviticus—newly composed as the middle and ideologically central chapter in Israel's
narrative—portrayed circumcision as a foundational cultic responsibility. By contrast, Jeremiah's metaphoric image of a circumcised heart was ignored until Christian exegetes used it to
support the arguments of those within the early church who denied the necessity of circumcision.

If we accept a fifth-century B.C.E. date for the final canonization of Torah, we thus have some seven hundred years between
the time at which our sources present circumcision as the
covenant's *sine qua non* and the time when our first rabbinic
document, the Mishnah, comes into being. The biggest change
in those seven centuries is the rise of a rabbinic ritual script to
accompany the physical operation.[3]

The ritual featured five liturgical parts, all of which are present today as well.[4]

1. The circumciser, known as a *mohel,* recites an opening
blessing: "Blessed art Thou, Lord our God, King of the uni-

verse, who has sanctified us by your commandments and commanded us concerning circumcision."

2. The father, on whom Jewish legal responsibility to circumcise his son devolves, says, "Blessed art Thou, Lord our God, King of the Universe, who has sanctified us by your commandments, and commanded us to admit him [the child] to the covenant of Abraham our father."

3. Those in attendance respond, "As you have brought him into the covenant, so may you admit him to the study of Torah and marriage." Eventually, this response was altered in two ways. First, to "study of Torah and marriage," the phrase, ". . . and to good deeds" was added. A midrashic fragment from Ecclesiastes Rabbah suggests that the addendum was a response to a folk belief that good deeds, a prophylactic against early death, should be sought at the moment of circumcision when demonic forces threaten to cut short a child's life.[5] In addition, mentioning good deeds may have played a polemical role in the Jewish-Christian debate on the efficacy of works over faith.

4. The *mohel* adds, "Blessed art Thou, Lord our God, King of the universe, who sanctified the beloved one [Abraham] in the womb. He [God] set a statute in his [Abraham's] flesh, and he [Abraham] stamped his descendants with the sign of the holy covenant. Therefore, as a reward for this, O living God, our Portion and our Rock, command [the imperative, or "commanded," the past tense] that the beloved of our flesh shall be delivered from the pit. Blessed art Thou, Lord, who make a covenant."[6]

The struggle with early Christianity is evident throughout this blessing, which polemicizes in favor of the salvific character of circumcision, in contrast to the Pauline epistles, and even uses identical language to Paul's *sphragis,* that is, terminology indicative of a seal or signet ring demonstrating ownership.[7] For Paul, the seal of circumcision was a sign of Abraham's faith, so that ever after, it was faith that mattered, while circumcision was allowed to lapse. For the Rabbis, circumcision remains the eternal sign of the covenant.

5. There is reason to believe that the early ritual also contained a naming prayer.[8] John was named at his circumcision (Luke 1:59–63). The absence of any prayer ritual in that account may indicate only its authors' lack of concern with whatever blessings people normally said; or it may be that the liturgy in question postdates Luke's account, and must be dated only in the second century—after Luke but before the Mishnah's codification. In either case, however, we know at least that names were bestowed at the circumcision, that we have a naming prayer in today's ritual, and that such a prayer may go back to the tannaitic record. True, naming prayers are unattested in tannaitic literature. But neither Mishnah nor Tosefta (our two exemplary tannaitic works) contains comprehensive records of tannaitic ritual, and at least one medieval witness says he saw a prayer similar to today's version in his edition of the Palestinian Talmud.[9] Moreover, the naming prayer as we have it functioned also as a petition for the health of both mother and child, and *Seder Rav Amram* (c. 860 C.E.) contains a parallel prayer,[10] the Palestinian Aramaic of which suggests that it was a much earlier alternative to the version that eventually became customary with us. We may conclude, therefore, that the early ritual ended with naming the child and praying for his health and that of his mother.

Of greatest interest here is Ezekiel 16:6, which is cited prominently in today's prayer,[11] but which occurs also in second-century sources, again within the context of anti-Christian polemic: "I passed by you and saw you wallowing in your blood, and I said to you: In your blood, live; I said to you: In your blood, live." Its significance in the context of the debate on the efficacy of works over faith is evident from the following second-century midrashic citation, which reads the biblical text as saying, "*By* your blood, live"—that is, "You shall live by virtue of the blood shed in circumcision."

Rabbi Matia ben Heresh used to say, "Behold it says 'I passed by you and looked at you and saw it was a time of love' [Ezek. 16:8]. This means the time had arrived for God's vow to Abraham to be fulfilled, namely, that He would save his children. But as yet they had no commandments to perform, by virtue of which they might merit redemption, as it says, 'Your breasts were fashioned and your hair had grown, but you were naked' [Ezek. 16:8]—meaning that they were naked of all commandments. God therefore assigned them two commandments: the sacrifice of the paschal lamb, and circumcision, which they were to perform so as to merit being saved, as it says: 'I passed by you and saw you wallowing in your blood, and I said, "By your blood live . . . By your blood live"' [Ezek. 16:6]. . . . *One cannot obtain reward except by deeds.*"[12]

As the Ezekiel exegesis demonstrates, blood became the central symbol of the circumcision ritual. Regularly, therefore, we find reference not only to the salvific nature of the rite in general, but more specifically, to the saving merit of circumcision blood. Nowadays, a blessing accompanies the symbolic placing of some wine on the lips of the baby boy just after the circumcision wound has been cauterized. It is virtually certain that wine once symbolized blood.[13] The blessing over the wine was probably added at a later time when the original symbolic value of the wine as blood had been forgotten. Originally, no blessing was recited here, since the wine was never meant to be consumed as such, certainly not by the adult participants; it was instead regarded as an oral transfusion of wine (= blood) for the child. In a nutshell: blood escapes the system; wine as blood enters it.

At any rate, the symbolic value of circumcision as an act of salvation is evident throughout our second-century sources. It is the sign of the covenant that saves. The blood drawn in the act is equivalent to the blood of the paschal lamb that Israelites smeared on their doorposts to warn off the angel of death on the night the first-born Egyptians were slaughtered. It is the paradigmatic salvific example of a good work, practiced in every generation from Abraham onward. As such, it has commanded the universal allegiance of Jews throughout history.

Medieval Jews added to the symbolic prism through which circumcision's merit was perceived. Following the Crusades and paralleling Christian expectations of an imminent second coming of Christ, Jewish ritual began evoking Elijah's presence in happy anticipation of messianic deliverance.[14] In Italy, at least, the child was welcomed as if he might be the messiah himself born into the world. He was seated on a chair, first mentioned in a geonic midrash, but later universally known as *kisei eliyahu,* "Elijah's chair."[15] Haggadah art of the time merges the figure of the messiah and of Elijah, his harbinger.[16] So too, the ritual of circumcision among Italian Jews unites both Elijah and messiah in the person of the eight-day-old baby boy.

Originally, mothers had carried their sons to their circumcision, holding them during the operation. John's mother is therefore portrayed as being present in the account of Luke, and mothers drink wine and are prayed for in the ninth-century *Seder Rav Amram.* By the thirteenth century, however, Rabbi Samson bar Tzaddok of Germany complains on behalf of his deceased teacher, Meir of Rothenberg (known as Maharam), that mothers should be removed from the ceremony because it is unseemly for women to mix with men, especially in the synagogue (where the ceremony occurred in his day), and all the more so during morning worship (when the rite was usually scheduled).[17] A spiritual descendant of the strict pietism that dominated post-Crusade Germany, Maharam became the most influential leader of his generation, so that within a century, his opinion prevailed: women were henceforth excluded from the rite, and a newly developed ritual role of *sandek* (related to the Christian term for godfather) evolved in the mother's place.[18] Now the *sandek,* always a man, held the boy on his lap for the operation.

In time, his role was further understood according to sacrificial symbolism—his knees were likened to the temple altar, and the circumcision was compared to a sacrifice, especially the near sacrifice of Isaac on Mt. Moriah. The fourteenth-century German master Jacob Moellin (known as Maharil), clearly the leading exponent of German Jewish thought after

Maharam, thus held that acting as a *sandek* "is greater than the commandment performed by the *mohel*, since his knees are likened to an altar as if he were offering incense to heaven."[19]

The sixteenth-century Polish savant, Moses Isserles, quoted Maharam further, summing up the development of several centuries:

> Thus a woman may not serve as a *sandek*, because that would constitute brazenness [*pritsut*], although she may help her husband take the boy to the synagogue where the man takes him from her and becomes the *sandek*. However a man may do the whole thing without a woman; that was the Maharil's practice.[20]

By the nineteenth century, some Jews were having second thoughts about the circumcision rite. European boys were not universally circumcised, so that Jewish practice stood out as unusual, possibly even primitive, given the mores of the period. Particularly embarrassing, for German Jews intent on demonstrating that they were worthy of being granted citizenship and civil rights, was the fact that the sanitary bureau of Frankfort had been investigating some cases of infant fatality said to be traceable to the operation.[21] When members of a lay society announced their intention of jettisoning the age-old rite on the grounds that it no longer represented the essence of Mosaic faith, they encountered universal condemnation by German rabbis, even the liberals, some of whom personally opposed circumcision themselves but were loath to say so publicly. The rite therefore continued despite reservations that many had about its spiritual efficacy.

Again in our time, the issue has been joined, this time on different but related grounds. Nineteenth-century opposition was rooted in evolutionism, the assumption that a mature Judaism could safely pare away the ritual remnants of its youth. Today's objections come in part from feminist circles where this very masculine rite is seen as reinforcing outmoded notions of a covenant solely with men. Objections emerge also from the perception that the rite may entail sexual mutilation.

Supporters of the rite champion its age-old centrality in Jewish consciousness, mentioning especially the fact that in times
of persecution, Jews have willingly died rather than give up
the sign of the covenant. They deny the charge of mutilation,
noting that the operation may even be in the child's best interest for other than religious reasons (medical opinion goes
back and forth on this score). Liberal Jews have thus tended to
retain the rite, but to do so in a way that mutes its objection-
able features. A local anesthetic does away with any pain for
the child, and a revised ritual script emphasizes the theological status of covenanthood into which boys and girls are now
equally inducted. The blessing structure of the rite is thus recited for both sexes, and the actual operation attendant upon it
and relevant only to boys is relegated to a background event
hardly noticed as the liturgical (and egalitarian) script proceeds.[22]

For many, therefore, circumcision now is hardly the central
act of faith that it once was. Almost no one is aware any more
of the salvific symbolism it once contained. No one at all re-
members the symbolism of blood as salvific, the parallelism
between circumcision blood and blood of the paschal lamb, the
very real hopes once invested in the child as potential messiah,
or the cultic symbolism of sacrifice that once dominated centuries of rabbinic thought. But the rite still maintains its hold on
the popular imagination, at least in most circles, and since most
baby boys in North America are systematically circumcised
anyway, Jews who advocate Jewish circumcision as a religious
responsibility are at least sheltered from the need to justify
their own practice in the light of a contrary cultural trend, such
as Germany presented a century and a half ago.

2. *Redemption of the First-born* (Pidyon Haben)

Since first-born male Israelites were saved from destruction
in Egypt, they are said by the Bible to belong ever after to
God. (First-born is defined as the first to "open the womb" of
the mother). The Bible therefore provides for redemption of the

first-born, *Pidyon Haben*,[23] through a monetary payment to the priests.[24] By tannaitic times, the monetary exchange was accompanied by its own liturgy, which, however, is first reported only in an addendum tacked onto the end of a tractate of the Babylonian Talmud.

> Rabbi Simlai happened to be at a Redemption of the First-born. They asked him, "It is obvious that . . . the father must recite the blessing, '[Blessed are Thou . . .] who has sanctified us with your commandments and commanded us concerning the redemption of the first-born.' But should it be the priest or the father who says, 'Blessed art Thou . . . who has given us life, sustained us, and brought us to this time'? Should the priest say this, in as much as he receives benefit from the occasion [the child is redeemed for silver pieces, which become his possession]? Or does the father say it, since he is fulfilling a commandment?" He [Rabbi Simlai] could not answer the question, so he posed it at the academy, and was told, "The father says both blessings."[25]

Clearly, in that early time, the rite already called for (1) a blessing affirming the commandment to redeem the first-born, and (2) in some places, a further benediction known as *Shehecheyanu* or *Birkat Hazeman,* "the blessing of time," meaning a blessing that welcomes the return of sacred times or specific natural events in the annual cycle, with praise to God for "giving us life, sustaining us and bringing us to this time [of year]." Clearly also, a priest officiated at the event, and received some silver pieces as redemption money for the child.

The Babylonian Talmud's question is a polemic against rival practice in Palestine, where the priest, not the father, said the benediction over redeeming the child; in Babylonia, the father said it. Also, the Palestinians did not say the *Shehecheyanu* benediction at all, whereas the Babylonians did.[26]

Predictably, contemporary custom[27] follows Babylonian precedent, in that it includes the *Shehecheyanu* and entrusts the blessing over the commandment to the father, not the officiating priest. The ritual script features the father presenting his first-born son at the latter's month-old birthday along with five silver coins to a *kohen,* a Jewish male who claims priestly descent from Temple times. Testifying that this is indeed his first-born, the father cites the biblical verses that oblige him to redeem his son. The priest asks which the father prefers to have: his child or the redemption money. After affirming his preference for his son, the father recites the blessing over the commandment of redemption ("who has commanded us to redeem the first-born son") and the *Shehecheyanu.* The priest accepts the money and passes it over the child's head three times, reciting "This instead of that," each time. He then prays for the child's welfare and blesses him, first with Jacob's blessing of his grandsons Ephraim and Manasseh (Gen. 48:20), and then with the priestly benediction from Numbers (6:24–26). Not all Jews who consider themselves *kohanim* (the plural of *kohen,* "priest") officiate at such a rite, but those who do so generally consider it a religious privilege for which they accept no remuneration; the silver pieces are donated to charity.

Throughout the ages, the redemption rite has grown but little. In fact, it was once fuller than it is today. The geonic era involved the mother as well as the father, since technically, her testimony was necessary to determine if the child being redeemed was actually a first-born at all—she alone would know if she had ever had a child by another father, or, for that matter, aborted a fetus old enough to have already counted as opening her womb. Rabbinic attitudes toward women eventually downplayed the mother's role, removing her active presence in the rite altogether. But until the early Middle Ages, she held the child, testified to his status as first-born, and along with the father, recited the blessing affirming that she too bore the obligation to redeem her son—even though technically, Jewish law invests that responsibility in the father alone, so that her required liturgical avowal constituted a flagrant violation of rabbinic legislation. Early texts say clearly, "The mother says, 'This is my first-born son, for God opened the doors of my womb with him. We are obligated [*nitchayavnu*] to give the priest five selahs as his redemption.'"[28]

In addition, we find a blessing, now long gone, which provides a rare view of rabbinic embryology:

[The priest] says, "Blessed art Thou who sanctified the fetus in its mother's womb [*bim'ei imo*]. From the tenth day on, He [God] apportions 248 bodily parts, and after that breathes a soul into him, as it says [Gen. 2:7]: 'He breathed a living soul into his nostrils and the man became a living being.' He clothes him with skin, and intertwines him with bones and sinews, as it is written [Job 10:1]: 'You have clothed me with skin, and intertwined me with bones and sinews.' Through the miracle of his wonders, He feeds him with food and drink, honey and milk, to make him rejoice, and summons his angels to watch over him in his mother's womb, as it is written [Job 10:12]; 'You granted me life and favor, and your command sustained my soul.' "[29]

Another fragment from the geonic era gives us the rationale behind the ritual. Rabbinic cosmology insisted on mapping things by domains (*reshuyot*; sing., *reshut*). Sabbath law, for instance, depends on the distinction between *reshut hayachid* and *reshut harabim*, private domain and public domain. On the Sabbath, you may carry anything you want in your own private domain, without fear of doing "work." Work is defined as transporting goods, but only from one domain to the other.[30] This "geography of domains" is extended even to the metaphysical level of the universe as a whole. The Rabbis warn us against saying *modim, modim* ("We acknowledge [God], we acknowledge [God]")—saying the word twice, that is—lest it be imagined that we believe in the existence of two *reshuyot,* two "domains".[31] The particular breach of conduct involved is usually translated as "We give thanks, we give thanks,"[32] but *modim* here connotes more than "to give thanks"; it means "to acknowledge," in this case, to acknowledge God. We are warned not to acknowledge the deity twice, lest we be suspected of acknowledging the existence of two domains, one for each of two heavenly forces.

Now the Rabbis do not systematically call every domain a *reshut,* but they do establish the general principle of there being a place for everything, and everything in its place, as well as the corollary that things belonging to one place can be moved to another through ritual.[33] For the Rabbis, then, liturgical ritual transforms things from being an instance of one domain into being an instance of another.

Redemption is such a rite of transfer.[34] By scriptural mandate, first-born sons of ordinary Israelites belong to God and must therefore be redeemed. But redemption is not required for first-born sons born to priests or Levites. The reasoning is obvious. For first-born priests or Levites, there is no category conflict. Unlike adult Israelites who are neither of levitical nor of priestly stock, adult priests and Levites are themselves sacred. Their first-born sons are thus holy as priests and Levites, and holy also as first-born sons. But Israelites are not dedicated to Temple service (and therefore to God) the way priests and Levites are. They cannot perform the daily or festival sacrifices, enter the court where sacrificing occurs, live on items sanctified to Temple use (*hekdesh*), and so forth. An Israelite male who is at the same time a first-born thus lives in two conflicting worlds, the world of the everyday (insofar as he is an Israelite), and the world of the sacred (insofar as he is an unredeemed first-born). It is this category conflict that rabbinic thought cannot abide. So it conceives a liturgical rite to transform the status of the anomalous first-born Israelites, moving them metaphysically (insofar as they are first-born) from the domain of the sacred (*kodesh*) to the domain of the everyday (*chol*), where (as everyday Israelites) they can proceed with their lives.

In the parallel medieval Palestinian rite, the father actually stipulates that the money for which he exchanges the child is not holy, but "everyday." The "everyday" money thus becomes holy as it enters the domain of the priest, while the holy child becomes "everyday" as he passes out of the priest's (that is, God's) domain.[35] One manuscript fragment actually describes the change in domain being effected.

> They bring money and gold and florins and he [the priest] asks, "Is this your first-born, and do you redeem him?"

He [the father] says, "Yes."

He [the priest] says, "When you were in your mother's womb, you were in the *domain of your creator* [*reshut bor'akha*], and now you are in *our domain* [*reshutenu*]: you are holy, as the Torah says, 'Sanctify unto me all the first-born, whatever opens the womb [among the children of Israel, whether man or beast. It is mine].' But these goods, the silver and the gold, are profane [*chulin*]. Your forefathers have accepted upon themselves to redeem you with them, and with the five silver pieces, as the Torah says, 'Their redemption money—from a month old you shall redeem them.' *You have gone out from our domain* [*reshutenu*] *to the everyday, to the domain of your father, and these goods with the five selahs enter in your place as your redemption price into our domain* [*reshutenu*]."[36]

Nowadays, Redemption of the First-born is common only among Orthodox Jews, and to some extent, Conservative Jews too, though it may turn up unexpectedly among Reform Jews as well from time to time. Technically, nineteenth-century Reform Judaism abolished the rite of redemption along with its underlying class hierarchy that distinguished priests and Levites from Israelites. Practically speaking, modern Reform Judaism permits it, should people request it, but does not recommend that it be done, and as a result, it rarely finds its way into the homes of liberal Jews.

3. Shavua Haben/Habat

Strictly speaking, we might do better not linking either circumcision or the redemption of the first-born to the general category of "birth ritual," since on the one hand, not every child born undergoes either rite, and on the other, the two rites are applied systematically to various classes of adults, who can be said to be "reborn" only in the strictly metaphoric sense. Thus male converts of any age are circumcised, and first-born males who were not redeemed as children may undergo redemption as adults. For that matter, rabbinic law calls for some children who die before circumcision to be circumcised prior to their burial. It seems unwieldy at best to speak of birth rituals when we have practices that may take place at any time in life, even after death, and that under the best of circumstances are performed only at stipulated intervals after birth (eight days, and a month, respectively) and only for some of the population, but not all. The other side of the debate sees circumcision but not redemption as a genuine birth ritual, at least in biblical Israel, where the eight-day stipulation may correspond to the time at which a woman who had given birth emerged from her confinement outside the camp (Lev. 12:1–2).[37] If so, circumcision would be a ritual of birth that eventually becomes also a rite of of covenantal initiation, with birth being culturally defined as male birth only, and the importance of males being identified as carriers of the covenant.

In any case, by the rabbinic era, to describe circumcision as a birth ritual is to miss the point; by then it is clearly a rite of initiation. Birth, an act of nature, has been overshadowed by covenant, a cultural construct. As a result, yet another rite emerges, this one a celebration of the natural phenomenon of birth and scarcely touched by cultural associations. Tannaitic texts call it a *Shavua Haben*, literally, "A week[-long celebration] of a boy." As we shall see, rabbinic Jews knew also a parallel *Shavua Habat* for girls. But these two events remained within popular culture, not rabbinic legislation.

Rabbinic society featured a synagogue and a Temple as foci of religious life—these are well known to us. But in addition, the Rabbis frequented an institution known as the *chavurah* (plural: *chavurot*), best translated as a "tableship" group, either *ad hoc* or ongoing in membership, but in either case, a place where the sacred calendar and moments of personal sanctity were marked in the ambience of sacred meals.[38] Our sources thus describe *chavurot* in Jerusalem convening for a ceremony known as *Shavua Haben*.[39] Almost universally, and going all the way back to a medieval exegetical tradition,[40] this ceremony has been assumed to be an all-night vigil on the eve of a boy's circumcision, a rite known elsewhere as *Yeshua Haben*, and *Sholom Zakhor* as well.[41] But this can hardly be the case. As one talmudic commentator of note explains:

> It is difficult to identify *Shavua Haben* as the exact day of circumcision, since circumcision falls on the eighth day, [not the seventh, whereas the word *shavua* comes from the Hebrew for "seven," appearing to refer to the whole week between the boy's birth and his circumcision]. The [talmudic] sources themselves do not indicate [that it was circumcision day], so that the purpose of the *Shavua Haben* may have been to let people know that a son had been born.[42]

Shavua Haben was a real birth ceremony. It lasted for a week, concluding only on the eve of a boy's circumcision. Hence the confusion that it was related to circumcision. By the Middle Ages, that confusion was widespread, so that in the case of boys, the last night of the *Shavua Haben* took on its own independent ritual life, and became known as *Yeshua Haben,* an all-night party on the eve of circumcision day.[43] In the earlier period, however, Jews knew only *Shavua Haben,* which they marked with a week-long celebration, and which they probably borrowed from a parallel Greek custom of celebrating a child's birth for a whole week, a custom that continued among the Arab population, and could still be seen among Jews in Arab lands at least as late as the nineteenth century.[44]

Of interest, then, is a medieval version of an ancient tannaitic text, which adds the following rule to the inherited store of data regarding *chavurah* celebration etiquette. "If one has to choose between a *Shavua Habat* and a *Shavua Haben, Shavua Haben* takes precedence."[45] *Ben* means "son." *Bat* means "daugher." *Shavua Habat,* "the *Shavua* rite for a daughter," can hardly be connected to a circumcision! But neither was *Shavua Haben,* the parallel rite for a boy. Both must have been parallel week-long celebrations marking a child's birth.

So unofficial rabbinic culture did have birth ceremonies for girls and for boys. But these were largely lost as time passed and texts were copied with selective attention to their wording. In the rules of the *Shavua* celebration, the clause regarding girls was omitted altogether, so that the very term *Shavua* was linked only to the male *ben* but not the female *bat*. As the week-long celebration waned in importance, only the last night was retained, and only for boys because it was associated with the circumcision that was to occur the next day, and for which it was seen as preparatory; it thus emerged with a new name, *Yeshua Haben,* or various vernacular equivalents (like *Wachtnacht,* the vigil or night of watching that anticipates the redemptive act of circumcision).

4. The Triumph of Redemptive Imagery

The term *yeshua* (from *Yeshua Haben*) means "salvation, deliverance, redemption," and alerts us to the triumph of redemptive imagery in all three rituals under discussion here. As we saw above, circumcision became completely immersed in associations with redemption, the blood of circumcision being linked symbolically to the blood of the paschal lamb that had redeemed the Israelites in Egypt. Performing the operation of circumcision on a child was metaphorically equivalent to slaughtering the lamb. But that is not all; as we saw, the image of a child being (or almost being) slaughtered on an altar recalls the binding of Isaac (the *akedah*). Late strata of the circumcision ritual thus emphasize the sacrificial nature of circumcision and the parallelism between the boy being circumcised, on one hand, and both Isaac and the paschal lamb, on the other. Borrowing on late medieval imagery, today's rite prays,

> Creator of the Universe, may it be your will that this child be considered and accepted positively by You, just as if I had brought him before your throne of glory. In your great mercy, send by means of your sacred messengers [angels] a holy and a pure soul to this circumcised child. . . . May his heart be open to your holy Torah like the opening of the doorway to the Temple hall.[46]

The final image, "the doorway to the Temple hall," immediately evokes the master metaphor of sacrifice, as does the verb "as if I had brought him" [*hikravtihu*], which more properly means "as if I had offered him up as a sacrifice." The double entendre goes back to the medieval notion that Isaac really did die at the hand of his father. But God intervened and sent him a new soul that revived him. Thus here, the child is Isaac; the father, who is supposed ideally to circumcise his own son, is Abraham; the place on which the circumcision takes place is an altar. The child sheds his blood which is now sacrificial, and he, as it were, dies just as any sacrifice does. But his death is momentary; he is revived immediately, resurrected even without the saving gift of his blood which has been shed on the altar.[47]

By the fifteenth century, as we already saw, this sacramentalization of the circumcision ritual reached its high point, as the boy was circumcised on the knees of the *sandek*.[48] Like the Christian godfather who offered his ward for baptism, the *sandek* offered the boy to the circumciser, holding him in place during the operation. No wonder Maharam (d. 1293), whom we have already encountered, took the step of proclaiming the *sandek*'s role as a religious commandment rather than mere custom, complaining in that regard about women who "snatch away the commandment from the men."[49] No wonder also that Maharil (1360?–1427) likened circumcision to the ancient sacrificial cult with the *sandek* as priest,[50] a theological lesson reiterated by Isserles, who reported in his sixteenth-century legal glosses:

> The *sandek* takes precedence over the *mohel* in being called to the Torah, since a *sandek* is likened to someone who offers incense at the altar.[51]

So by the sixteenth century and the codification of Ashkenazic attitudes into the law of the *Shulchan Arukh*, the most significant ritual of all three we have surveyed here was clearly circumcision. And it had become thoroughly sacramentalized.

But the sacramentalization of circumcision drew increasing attention to the night of watching that preceded it. The Talmud

itself refers both to *Shavua Haben* and to *Yeshua Haben*. We
have already looked at the former and identified it as the birth
celebration that lasted a week after a child was born. We saw
too that the latter was a feast that became associated in the
Middle Ages with circumcision. We can now be more precise
as to the time and place of such a feast. The talmudic citation of
Yeshva Haben attracts commentary from the two medieval exegetes, Rashi and Rabbenu Tam, neither of whom yet associate
it with circumcision. Rashi (d. 1105) is explicit about its being
the feast attendant upon a Redemption of the First-born.[52]
Rabbenu Tam (France, d. 1171) knows it cannot be that, but is
himself unclear about what it might be.

> *Yeshua Haben*: Rashi explains that this means "Redemption of the
> First-born" and so too does the *Arukh* [an 11th-century talmudic
> lexicon, composed in Italy]. But that interpretation is difficult to
> hold. . . . Rabbenu Tam explains it by saying that when a boy is
> born, he is saved from his mother's womb, as it is written [Isa.
> 66:7], "She has delivered a male child." Thus the Talmud uses a
> term meaning "saved = delivered." It was their custom to hold a
> feast.[53]

Rabbenu Tam's etymology aside, his ignorance of any pre-
circumcision watch-night is striking. We should therefore date
the *Yeshua Haben* as the circumcision watch-night in the period following, namely, the time of the Chasidei Ashkenaz
(after the First Crusade), the very people who sacramentalize
the ritual of circumcision in the first place. It was then that the
operation as a whole came to be sacramentally significant. It
was then also that a new genre of *piyyut* dealing with the saving
power of Isaac came into being, largely as a result of the massacre of German Jewry by Crusaders.[54] In the new view, deliverance was attendant upon martyrdom, in which Jews like
Isaac had been slaughtered. Thus an emphasis on Isaac, a
sacramentalization of circumcision as a sacrifice, and an old
parallel between the blood of circumcision and the blood of the
paschal lamb came together to make the night prior to circumcision similar to the night of the Passover seder.

Following Exodus 12:42, this latter event had long been known as a watch-night. Ashkenazic Jews had thus outfitted *seder* night with a poem similar to the Easter vigil's *Exultet,* in which various salvific events in Israel's history were all collapsed as having occurred at the same time on the same auspicious midnight of 14 Nisan.[55] We may be justified, then, in seeing the *Yeshua Haben* as another watch-night, it too being the night prior to the sacrificial event whence the blood of salvation would result.

NOTES

1. Howard Eilberg-Schwartz, *The Savage in Judaism* (Bloomington, IN, 1990), pp. 141–76.

2. See Harry M. Orlinsky, "The Biblical Concept of the Land of Israel: Cornerstone of the Covenant Between God and Israel," in Lawrence A. Hoffman, ed., *The Land of Israel: Jewish Perspectives* (Notre Dame, IN, 1986), pp. 28–55.

3. For full treatment of all rabbinic sources and a broader history of what is merely sketched here, see Lawrence A. Hoffman, *Covenant of Blood: Circumcision and Gender in Rabbinic Judaism* (Chicago, 1995).

4. For today's ritual, cf. Hyman E. Goldin, *Hamadrikh: the Rabbi's Guide* (New York, 1939, 1956), pp. 33–37; Philip Birnbaum, *Hasiddur Hashalem: Daily and Sabbath Prayer Book* (New York, 1977), pp. 741–44.

5. Ecc. Rab. 3:1.

6. Our current version differs somewhat, containing redundant material added through the ages; the designation of the subject— given here in brackets—follows my own reconstruction, based in part on medieval exegetes, Rashi and Tosafot (to Shab. 137b, d.h. *yedid*). Cf. *Orchot Chaim,* ed. M. Schlesinger (Berlin, 1902), p. 10; Saul Lieberman, *Tosefta Kifshuta,* vol. 1 (New York, 1955), p. 114.

7. Romans 4:11.

8. The prayer used today reads, in part, "Our God and God of our fathers, sustain this child to his father and to his mother, and let his name in Israel be (so-and-so, son of so-and-so, his father). Let the father rejoice in what has come forth from his loins, and let the mother

be happy with the fruit of her womb, as it is written: 'Let your father and mother rejoice, and let her that bore you be happy' (Prov. 23:25); And it is said, 'I passed by you and saw you wallowing in your blood, and I said to you: In your blood, live; I said to you: In your blood, live' (Ezek. 16:6)."

9. Eliezer ben Joel Halevi (c. 1140 – c. 1225), *Ravyah* 1:360.

10. *Seder Rav Amram,* p. 169.

11. Ibid.

12. *Mekhilta Bo,* chap. 5.

13. Cf. Lawrence A. Hoffman, "How Ritual Means: Ritual Circumcision in Rabbinic Culture and Today," *Studia Liturgica* 23, no. 1 (1993): 78–97; *Covenant of Blood.*

14. See, Lawrence A. Hoffman, *Beyond the Text* (Bloomington IN, 1987), pp. 43–45.

15. The original term is *moshav kavod;* see *Pirkei deRabbi Eliezer,* chap. 29 (end). For *kisei eliyahu,* we have to wait until the Italian literature of the thirteenth century—see, e.g., *Shibbolei Haleket, Hilkhot Milah,* section 8.

16. Joseph Gutmann, "The Messiah at the Seder," *Raphael Mahler Jubilee Volume* (Israel, 1974), pp. 29–38.

17. *Tashbetz,* #397.

18. For details, see Hoffman, *Covenant of Blood.* The term *sandek* appears in the eleventh century *Arukh,* whose author, Nathan of Rome, saw it in the *Midrash on Psalms.* Thereafter, the term is used by Eleazer of Worms [d. 1238], Peretz of Corbeil [d. 1295], and others. The parallel Greek term (used in the East, and hence known to the Mediterranean author of the *Midrash on Psalms* collection, as well as to Nathan in Rome) was *anadekomenos,* from *anadekomai,* meaning "one who undertakes, promises to do, or stands surety for," and was used as such by John Chrysostom (d. 404) in Constantinople and by Theodore of Mopsuestia (d. 429), one hundred miles or so outside of Antioch.

19. *Sefer Maharil, Hilkhot Milah.*

20. S.A., Y.D. 265:11.

21. See literature cited by Michael Meyer, *Response to Modernity* (New York, 1990), pp. 423–24, n. 86.

22. For further discussion, see below, pp. 272–73.

23. For current ceremony, see Goldin, *Hamadrikh,* pp. 51–54; Birnbaum, *Daily and Sabbath Prayer Book,* pp. 749–52.

24. Numbers 18:15; c.f. Numbers 3: 40–51, 8:16, and Exodus 13:2.

25. Pes. 121b.

26. See "Addendum" by Israel Ta-shema, in Mordecai Margoliot, *Hilkhot Eretz Yisra'el min Hagenizah* (Jerusalem: Mossad Harav Kook, 1973), p. 32.

27. For today's rite, cf. Goldin, *Hamadrikh,* pp. 52–53; Birnbaum, *Daily and Sabbath Prayer Book,* pp. 749–52.

28. B. M. Lewin, *Otsar Hageonim,* vol. 3 (Jerusalem, 1931), p. 130, citing *Tsedah Laderekh,* but cited elsewhere also by many Rishonim, and available now in genizah form accredited to Hai Gaon. See Ta-Shema, "Addendum," in Margoliot, *Hilkhot Eretz Yisra'el,* pp. 34–37, for variants.

29. Ibid.

30. M. Shab. 1:1.

31. M. Ber. 5:3; B.T. 33b.

32. Cf. Herbert Danby, ed., *The Mishnah* (London, 1933), p. 6; Jacob Neusner, ed., *The Mishnah* (New Haven, CT, 1988), p. 8.

33. See, e.g., Samuel Cooper, "The Laws of Mixture: An Anthropological Study in *Halakhah,*" in Harvey E. Goldberg, ed., *Anthropology Viewed from Within and from Without* (Albany, NY, 1987), pp. 55–74.

34. See below, esp. p. 130.

35. For extended treatment, see Lawrence A. Hoffman, "Life-Cycle Liturgy as Status Transformation," in E. Carr et al., eds., *Eulogema: Studies in Honor of Robert Taft, S.J.* (Rome, 1993), pp. 161–77. Primary texts of the Palestinian order of service can be found in Ta-Shema, "Addendum," in Margoliot, *Hilkhot Eretz Yisra'el,* pp. 32–36.

36. Margoliot, *Hilkhot Eretz Yisr'ael,* p. 29. I reproduce the text as Margoliot has reconstructed it. See discussion of ceremony by Israel Ta-Shema, in "Addendum" to Margoliot's book, pp. 32–36.

37. See Eilberg-Schwartz, *Savage,* pp. 174–76.

38. See Lawrence A. Hoffman, "Tempel, Synagoge, Chawura," in Andreas Nachama, Julius H. Schoeps, Edward van Voolen, eds., *Jüdische Lebenswelten: Essays,* (Berlin, 1992), pp. 33–49.

39. T. Meg. 3:15; cf. P.T. Ket. 1:6; B. San. 32b., B.K. 80a.

40. Cf. Rashi to B.K. 80a, B.B. 60b, San. 32b, *Arukh,* s.v. *sheva.*

41. The author of *Arukh,* however, knew the two ceremonies differed, although he incorrectly thought that *Shavua Haben* was the watchnight prior to the circumcision, and *Yeshua Haben* was the first night after a boy's birth, when people came "to congratulate the father on the good news that a male child had been born to him." For

present customs, see *Encyclopedia Judaica,* s.v. "circumcision: folk-lore," vol. 5, p. 576. See also what did become a celebration of the eve of a boy's circumcision, described in detail in Elliott Horowitz, "The Eve of Circumcision: a Chapter in the History of Jewish Nightlife," *Journal of Social History* 23 (1989): 45–69.

42. Saul Lieberman, *Tosefta Kifshutah,* vol. 5, p. 1186.

43. Called also *Veglia* and *Wachtnacht,* on which, see Judah Bergman, "Shebua Haben," *Monatschrift für Geschichte und Wissenschaft des Judentums* 76 (1932): pp. 465–70. Actually, Bergman quotes yet earlier studies by Leopold Löw (1811–1875) and Samuel Krauss (1866–1948).

44. Bergman, "Shebua Haben," p. 465.

45. Cf. *Sha'arei Simchah* of Rabbi Isaac Giat, ed. Isaac Dov Halevi Bamberger (Fürth, 1861), *Hilchot avel,* p. 38; Nachmanides' *Torat Ha'adam,* vol. 2, p. 109; *Massekhet Semachot,* ed. Michael Higger (New York, 1931), p. 231.

46. Goldin, *Hamadrikh,* p. 36.

47. See especially Jon D. Levenson, *The Death and Resurrection of the Beloved Son* (New Haven, CT, 1993).

48. See note 18 above.

49. See note 17 above.

50. See note 19 above.

51. See note 20 above.

52. Rashi, s.v., *Yeshua Haben,* B.K. 80a.

53. Tos. to B.K. 80a, s.v., *levei yeshua haben.*

54. See Yoel Kahn, *The Martyrological Akedah: the Relationship Between Religious Ideology and Ritual* (unpublished ordination thesis, Hebrew Union College, New York, 1985).

55. *Az rov nisim,* originally part of a Yannai *kerovah* for *Parashat Bo,* but adopted for Passover in Ashkenaz. Cf. Israel Davidson, *Otsar Shirah Vehapiyyut,* vol. 1 (1924: reprint, New York: Ktav, 1960), p. 102; E. D. Goldschmidt, *Haggadah Shel Pesach Vetoldoteha* (Jerusalem: Bialik, 1960), p. 96.

Christian Rites of Adolescence

Ruth A. Meyers

In its earliest stages, Christianity did not have any rituals specifically for adolescents. Eventually in western Christianity the rite of confirmation came to fill this role, but eastern Christian traditions have developed neither a separate rite of confirmation nor any other ritual to mark adolescence.

The origins of confirmation in western Christianity lie within the rite of baptism. As the original unity of the baptismal rite disintegrated, not only confirmation but also admission to communion came to function as rituals of adolescence.

The Emergence of "Confirmation"

By the fourth century, baptism had developed into a complex rite of Christian initiation, giving symbolic expression to the multifaceted theological dimensions of entrance into Christian faith and life. The normative candidate was an adult, although from at least as early as the end of the second century, the children of believers, including infants, were incorporated into the Christian community by the same rite. Baptism culminated in the celebration of eucharist, and no further rite was considered necessary to complete Christian initiation.

One element of this complex initiatory rite was an anointing of the head immediately following the immersion in water. This is first attested by Tertullian in North Africa in the early third century;[1] and by the fifth century had become a nearly universal feature of baptismal rites.[2] The baptismal rite of the city of Rome and of the small dioceses of central Italy, however, was unique in including, in addition to this postbaptismal anointing by a priest, a second anointing on the forehead by a bishop, associated with the bestowal of the Holy Spirit.[3] In cases where a bishop was unable to be present for the initiation rite, this final anointing could be readily supplied within a short period of time. For example, someone in imminent danger of death would be immediately baptized by a priest. If that person then recovered, it would not be difficult to travel to the bishop to receive the second anointing at the next convenient opportunity. This arrangement effectively preserved a role for the bishop in Christian initiation.[4]

Quite different circumstances prevailed in the larger dioceses in other parts of Europe. Owing to their size and the difficulty of travel, bishops could not be present at most celebrations of Christian initiation. Instead, a priest administered the whole rite, including the single postbaptismal anointing and culminating in the eucharist, and this was viewed as full initiation.

When in the late eighth century the rites of Rome were imposed by the emperor Charlemagne on dioceses outside Rome, the Roman initiatory rite with its second postbaptismal anointing administered by a bishop gradually became the standard initiatory rite of western Christianity. However, in these other European dioceses the rite did not function nearly as well. The problem of geography was in itself a significant obstacle: dioceses were large, roads were poor, and travel was especially hazardous in the winter months, making both the journey by candidates to the bishop's church and episcopal visitations difficult, and often resulting in a significant lapse of time before the final anointing could be administered. Adding to this difficulty, bishops did not always make visitations for the purpose of confirming a priority in their work. Some bishops were frequently preoccupied with affairs of state, while others simply neglected many of their duties. Even where bishops attended to their responsibilities of visitations, parents were often negligent in bringing their children to receive anointing by the bishop. Since baptism afforded full communicant membership and was understood to convey the

Holy Spirit, many parents did not see the necessity of bringing their children to receive a further ceremony which seemed
to add nothing to the baptism they had already received. Likewise, parish priests were often unable to explain to parents the
significance of this additional rite and so could not convince
parents of its necessity.

In order to encourage the practice of confirmation, local ecclesiastical councils adopted legislation setting maximum ages
by which children should be confirmed and providing penalties
for parents who did not comply. For example, the Council of
Worcester in 1240 ordered that children should be confirmed
by the age of one "provided they had access to a bishop, or it
was well known that he was passing through the vicinity," and
directed that parents not complying should be denied entry into
the church until they had remedied the omission. Other councils set three or seven as the age by which a child should be
confirmed.

While such legislation set *maximum* age limits, eventually
these came to be seen as *minimum* ages for confirmation. The
Council of Cologne in 1280, one of the first councils to legislate in this manner, set the age of confirmation as seven years
but acknowledged that candidates might be ten or older. By the
end of the Middle Ages numerous councils prohibited confirmation until children reached a minimum age, often set at
seven. Nonetheless, until the sixteenth century, there is evidence that confirmation of infants was still a possibility in
some places, though rare in practice. One well-known example
is that of the princess Elizabeth, daughter of Henry VIII of
England, who in 1533 was baptized, confirmed, and admitted
to communion at the age of three *days.*

As confirmation developed into a separate rite, often administered several years after baptism, a theological rationale for
the rite was sought. An important source for this theological
development was the *False Decretals,* a collection of papal
pronouncements and conciliar decisions purporting to have
been made by Isidore, Bishop of Seville from 600 to 636. Their
authenticity was first questioned in the fifteenth century and

contemporary scholars generally date them to about 850, but for several centuries they were accepted as genuine and widely cited by leading theologians. Among the documents was an excerpt from a sermon attributed to the fourth-century pope Melchiades but now generally ascribed to Faustus of Riez in the late fifth century. In an oft-quoted fragment, the preacher explained the necessity of confirmation:

> Therefore the Holy Spirit who comes down upon the waters of baptism with his saving descent confers in the font all that is needed for innocence, in confirmation he provides an increase in grace. . . . In baptism we are regenerated to life, after baptism we are confirmed to combat. In baptism we are washed, after baptism we are strengthened. . . . Regeneration [baptism] by itself saves those who are presently to be received into the peace of the world of bliss [those who would die soon after birth], but confirmation arms and equips those who are to be reserved for the contests and battles of this world.[5]

In the thirteenth century, Thomas Aquinas drew upon the *False Decretals* to defend the necessity of confirmation and distinguish the grace bestowed there from that bestowed at baptism. While not insisting that confirmation was necessary for salvation, Aquinas argued that the sacrament should be received by all who lived beyond infancy because confirmation conveys spiritual maturity. To support this position, Aquinas interpreted the letter of pseudo-Melchiades, defining confirmation as an "increase" in grace, as meaning "growth" in the sense of spiritual growth or maturity. The impulse toward growth in Christian life, first bestowed at baptism, is increased or "perfected" by confirmation.[6] According to Aquinas, confirmation supplies grace for growing and maturing in holiness, providing spiritual strength for battle against the enemies of the faith. Thus the sacramental character imparted at baptism corresponds to spiritual childhood, while the character of confirmation is that of spiritual maturity.[7] Aquinas compared baptism to human conception and birth, and likewise made the analogy between confirmation and human maturity:

"Confirmation is to baptism as growth to birth."[8] Yet he also insisted that this spiritual maturity is not necessarily related to chronological age, but reflects the limitless transformative power of grace.[9]

Aquinas thus provided a theological rationale for the delay of several years between baptism and confirmation, a delay that had become customary by the thirteenth century but had been rare in the ninth century when the *False Decretals* were compiled. His understanding of confirmation dominated theological reflection for several centuries and became an important factor in confirmation becoming a Christian rite of adolescence.

While confirmation gradually came to be administered several years after baptism, up until the twelfth century infants continued to be communicated at the time of their baptism, and the reception of communion was considered necessary to their salvation. However, a doctrine of sacramental realism, emphasizing that in the eucharist the bread and wine actually become the body and blood of Jesus, began to emerge in the ninth century. By the eleventh century doubts began to arise about the propriety of communicating infants, lest they desecrate the sacrament by spitting up the host. To reduce this risk, infants began to be communicated with wine only. But by the thirteenth century, this same sacramental realism resulted in the withdrawal of the chalice from the laity, lest drops of the precious blood be spilled, and so infants ceased to be communicated at all. Beginning with the fourth Lateran Council in 1215, legislation restricted communion to those who had achieved the age of discretion, variously defined as age seven or age ten. Nonetheless, there is evidence that the communion of infants continued in at least some circumstances until the Reformation.[10]

Another significant medieval regulation, affecting both confirmation and admission to communion in England, resulted from a Council of Lambeth, held under Archbishop John Peckham in 1281. Concerned that many persons had reached an old age without receiving confirmation, the council declared that no one should be admitted to communion until confirmed. The intent was not to discourage communion, but rather to encourage parents to bring their children for confirmation.[11]

Thus by the sixteenth century the unified initiatory rite had disintegrated into a process comprising baptism, an anointing by the bishop called "confirmation," and admission to communion. Baptism was usually administered within eight days of birth, while confirmation and admission to communion came at later ages.

Reformation Developments

Once it became customary to administer confirmation at the age of discretion, the idea of catechesis, or instruction, prior to confirmation began to develop, and confirmation and admission to communion became more firmly established as rites of adolescence. While this practice came to full flower only with the Reformation of the sixteenth century, the seeds of this concept were already evident in the late fourteenth-century writings of John Wycliffe and then more fully developed by Jan Huss and his followers, the Bohemian Brethren. Wycliffe denounced the medieval practice of confirmation as "frivolous," not derived from scripture but introduced "at the prompting of the devil to this end that . . . the dignity and necessity of bishops should be the more accepted."[12] Drawing upon Wycliffe's ideas, the Bohemian Brethren provided a period of instruction for those baptized in infancy who had now come "to years of discretion." This was concluded by a profession of faith accompanied by the laying on of hands, which seems to have been regarded primarily as a solemn blessing rather than as a sacramental bestowal of grace akin to confirmation.[13]

The importance of postbaptismal catechesis followed by a profession of faith was also emphasized by the Christian humanists of the Renaissance. Erasmus, in an appendix to his *Paraphrase on St. Matthew's Gospel* (1522), proposed that boys (*pueri*) baptized in infancy should at puberty receive instruction in the meaning of their baptismal commitment.[14]

Following this instruction, they were to be examined in private and, if they responded satisfactorily, ratify their baptismal promises. They would then renew their profession of faith at a solemn public ceremony, which would have greater authority if it were performed by a bishop. While Erasmus did not identify this public ceremony as confirmation, his proposal influenced the Protestant Reformers in their approach to catechesis and confirmation.[15]

Martin Luther vigorously attacked confirmation on the grounds that it lacked a clear warrant in the New Testament and that it had been devised to "embellish the duties of bishops, lest they be entirely without function in the church." Although he referred to the rite as "monkey business," Luther conceded: "I allow that confirmation be administered provided that it is known that God has said nothing about it, and knows nothing of it, and that what the bishops allege about it is false."[16]

While Luther saw no use for confirmation as practiced in the Roman church, he saw great value in catechesis and in this context was willing to accept a form of confirmation: "We do not find fault if every pastor examines the faith of the children to see whether it is good and sincere, lays hands on them, and confirms them." Luther himself never composed a rite of confirmation, but his Longer and Shorter Catechisms called for those baptized in infancy to receive instruction in the faith before they were admitted to adult membership in the church and began to receive communion.[17]

Like Luther, the Reformer John Calvin strongly denounced the medieval practice of confirmation, which he called an "idle ceremony," lacking foundation in scripture and detracting from baptism. However, Calvin erroneously believed that the ancient rite of confirmation was an imposition of hands confirming a profession of faith by those baptized in infancy:

It was an ancient custom in the church for the children of Christians, after they were come to years of discretion, to be presented to the bishop in order to fulfil that duty which was required of adults who offered themselves to baptism. . . . [T]hose who had

been baptized in their infancy, because they had not then made
such a confession of faith before the church, at the close of childhood or the commencement of adolescence, were again presented
by their parents, and were examined by the bishop according to the
form of the catechism which was then in common use. That this
exercise . . . might have the greater dignity and reverence, they
also practised the ceremony of imposition of hands. Thus the
youth . . . was dismissed with a solemn benediction.[18]

Although Calvin viewed this profession of faith and imposition
of hands as the authentic practice of the early church, he did
not attempt to "restore" such a confirmation rite at Strassburg
or Geneva. Rather, he provided a catechism, *The Manner of ex-
amining children before they are admitted to the Lord's Supper*
(1533), with the intent that children would present themselves
to the church, profess their faith, and respond to questions.[19]

Calvin was not alone in his belief that confirmation was
originally a rite whereby those baptized in infancy, after appropriate instruction, professed their faith before the church. Martin Bucer expressed a similar view in the *Consultation,* or *Pia
Deliberatio* (1543), drawn up for Hermann von Wied, the reforming archbishop of Cologne.[20] However, unlike Calvin and
Luther, Bucer developed rites for adolescents to confess their
faith and make a public commitment to the church. His ideas
were first put into effect in 1538, when the Landgrave Philip
summoned Bucer to Hesse to assist in reforming the church
there. Under Bucer's direction, the Ziegenhain Order of
Church Discipline was drawn up with provisions for postbaptismal catechesis and a rite of confirmation in which young
people made a confession of faith.[21]

In this provision, Bucer was apparently influenced by Erasmus. But Bucer went beyond the proposals of Erasmus in associating this catechetical confirmation with admission to
communion. Arthur Repp notes that "this is the first formal association of the rite of confirmation with the Lord's Supper."
Furthermore, Bucer required of the youth not only catechetical

instruction, but a vow of obedience to the discipline of the churches. The Ziegenhain Order of Church Discipline was not widely used, but its provisions were incorporated in the 1539 Church Order of Cassel and from there influenced later public rites of confirmation in the Lutheran Church.[22]

In the Church of England, Thomas Cranmer, considered the chief architect of the 1549 and 1552 Prayer Books of the Church of England, held a view of the origins of confirmation similar to that of Calvin and Bucer, that confirmation was meant to be a rite of profession of faith by those baptized in infancy.[23] Nevertheless, the first (1549) Prayer Book of the Church of England retained a rite of confirmation markedly similar to the medieval rite. This rite was to be administered by a bishop and included the prayer for the sevenfold gifts of the Spirit, albeit with the imposition of hands and signing the forehead with the sign of the cross rather than an anointing.[24]

The 1549 Church of England confirmation rite was prefaced by "a catechism for children" and required children to learn the responses to this catechism as well as the Creed, the Lord's Prayer, and the Ten Commandments. The rubrics directed that the curate of every parish provide instruction in some part of the catechism at least once every six weeks. Children who came to the "years of discretion" were expected "openly before the church [to] ratify and confess the same [the promises made at their baptism]," although no ritual form was provided for this profession of faith. Confirmation was to be administered as soon as children could recite the Creed, Lord's Prayer, Ten Commandments, and the responses to the catechism.[25]

Although the Reformation emphasis on postbaptismal catechesis is apparent in the rubrics of the 1549 Anglican confirmation rite, Bucer objected that the provisions for catechetical instruction every six weeks were inadequate. In his *Censura,* responding to the 1549 *Book of Common Prayer,* Bucer expressed his concern that children should not only be able to recite catechetical responses from memory, but also demonstrate in their lives their understanding and adherence to the faith:

I would wish . . . that adolescents and all young people, male and female, should attend the catechizing until they are so proficient in the doctrine of Christ that they may be excused from the requirements of this rubric [attendance at catechetical instruction]. Nor are those somewhat few words, which are prescribed in the Book, to be asked and answered to as if they were the entire catechism of Christ: but catechumens ought to be placed in various classes, and all the mysteries of Christ which it is necessary to believe should with such method, diligence, and power be explained and elucidated, commended and instilled into them, as will enable each to make the quicker and fuller progress and to observe whatever the Lord has commanded.[26]

Influenced by Bucer, the concluding rubrics of the confirmation rite in the 1552 *Book of Common Prayer* called for the clergy to provide instruction on Sundays and holy days, presumably meaning all such days, in contrast to the 1549 provision for catechesis every six weeks. Furthermore, the revisions of the ritual text emphasized strengthening with the Holy Spirit rather than an objective conferral of the Spirit at the moment of confirmation, thus diminishing or eliminating an interpretation of confirmation as a sacramental rite bestowing the Holy Spirit.[27] However, it was only in the 1662 revision of the *Book of Common Prayer* that an explicit profession of faith was added to the Anglican confirmation rite.

It is also to be noted that the Church of England, beginning with the 1549 rite, retained the requirement of confirmation before admission to communion introduced at the 1281 Council of Lambeth. This effectively made admission to communion as well as confirmation rites of adolescence contingent upon catechesis.

While the Anglican tradition provided a rite of confirmation beginning with the first (1549) Prayer Book, the Lutheran and Reformed traditions developed such rites only gradually. Most Lutheran churches in the sixteenth century had no formal rites of confirmation or of admission to communion, although catechesis was provided before a child was admitted to communion. During the seventeenth and eighteenth centuries, patterns of catechesis and rites of confirmation and/or admission to communion developed in different ways, owing to a diversity of social, political, and ecclesiastical contexts for the Lutheran churches.[28] In churches of the Reformed (Calvinist) tradition, children would be instructed in a special class led by the pastor, and then approved for admission to communion. After this the children's names would be read to the entire congregation, who then joined in prayers for God's blessing upon the children. While rites for admission to the Lord's Table were first developed during the sixteenth century, confirmation rites involving a public profession of faith were introduced into continental Reformed churches only in the eighteenth century.[29]

In sum, while the Anglican tradition linked catechesis with a revision of the medieval confirmation rite, the Lutheran and Reformed traditions emphasized postbaptismal catechesis for children and only subsequently developed formal rites of admission to communion and confirmation. The concern for instruction, evident in the proliferation of catechetical materials in the sixteenth century, reflected the Reformation desire to provide members of the church with a firmer foundation in the essentials of the faith, in order to restore the spirit of the early church and to build the reformed church of the future.[30] This intensive attention to the education of children may also be linked to an emerging concept of childhood fostered by the sixteenth-century humanists. Medieval art and literature suggest that children were viewed as miniature adults. Although some provisions had been made for the religious instruction of children during the later Middle Ages, educational reform and renewal during the sixteenth century gave new attention to the importance of children as distinct from adults.[31]

The concern for catechesis advanced by the Protestant Reformers was acknowledged as well in the Roman Catholic tradition. A 1563 declaration of the Council of Trent required that on Sundays and holy days children were to be taught "the rudiments of the faith and obedience toward God and their parents." However, this instruction was not tied to confirmation, admission to communion, or a public profession of faith.[32] Instead, responding to the Reformed and Lutheran repudiation of the medieval doctrine of confirmation, the Council of Trent in its seventh session (1547) defended the sacramental character of confirmation:

> If anyone says that the confirmation of those baptized is an empty ceremony and not a true and proper sacrament; or that of old it was nothing more than a sort of instruction, whereby those approaching adolescence gave an account of their faith to the church: let [it] be anathema.[33]

The Catechism of the Council of Trent (1566) affirmed the necessity of confirmation and, citing pseudo-Melchiades, described it as a sacrament of spiritual growth and strengthening for battle. However, the catechism asserted that administration of confirmation was "inexpedient" until children attained the age of reason, and hence if not postponed until the age of twelve, it was to be deferred at least to the age of seven.[34] Likewise, with regard to admission to communion, the Council of Trent in 1562 declared that children below the age of reason were under no obligation to receive the eucharist, and pronounced anathema upon any who insisted that children required communion before they reached the age of discretion.[35] These conciliar decisions established for the Roman Catholic Church that confirmation and communion were rites to be administered only upon attainment of the age of reason, if not at the beginning of adolescence.

Thus in the Roman Catholic as well as the Lutheran, Anglican, and Reformed traditions rites of adolescence emerged during the sixteenth century. In the Roman Catholic tradition, the decrees of the Council of Trent were the final stage in the late medieval separation of confirmation and admission to communion from baptism. By contrast, the Lutheran and Reformed traditions abandoned entirely the medieval rite of confirmation and emphasized instead instruction in the essentials of the faith, including learning the Creed, Ten Commandments, and

Lord's Prayer, followed by reception into adult membership in the church and admission to communion. The Anglican reform, with a rite of confirmation by a bishop subsequent to postbaptismal catechesis, included elements of both traditions.

In contrast to the Protestant and Roman Catholic traditions which maintained infant baptism and provided postbaptismal catechesis and rites of adolescence, the Anabaptist tradition abolished infant baptism altogether, developing instead a practice of believers' baptism.[36] This eliminated the need for a separate rite of confirmation or profession of faith for those baptized in infancy. Instead, joining the fellowship through baptism and admission to the Lord's Supper became for the Anabaptists rites recognizing both physical maturity and spiritual regeneration. For most Anabaptists, therefore, baptism became the primary rite of adolescence (although the followers of Hans Hut believed that candidates for baptism must be thirty years of age, the age at which Jesus was baptized).[37]

While the Anabaptists believed that infants were incapable of faith, they gave careful attention to child rearing in order to develop in their children the characteristics of obedience and understanding necessary for faith and baptism. This Anabaptist perception of childhood was influenced by the same sixteenth-century humanist traditions that influenced the Protestant Reformers. However, in developing their educational systems the Anabaptists were particularly attentive to children's stages of growth. This allowed them to inculcate the attitudes of obedience appropriate to the child's age and development, with baptism as the final goal of education and child rearing.[38]

The Anabaptist concern for education and Christian commitment was a factor in Bucer's development of a rite of confession of faith for adolescents who had been baptized in infancy. In his disputes with the Anabaptists at Strassburg, Bucer vigorously defended the doctrine of infant baptism, but he also recognized the validity of the Anabaptist insistence upon instruction and explicit faith. This interchange with the Anabaptists helped form the ideas about adolescent profession

of faith that Bucer later put forth in the Ziegenhain Order
of Church Discipline.[39]

The Age for Confirmation

   While the attainment of a certain age became necessary for
confirmation and admission to communion in the Anglican,
Lutheran, Reformed, and Roman Catholic traditions, the actual
age varied widely. Medieval legislation variously defined the
age of discretion as age seven, or ten, or twelve, a range of ages
adopted in Reformation practice. The Council of Trent thus
provided for admission to communion at age seven, the age of
reason, and recommended that confirmation be postponed to
age twelve, or at least to age seven. The Lutheran church orders
used an expression such as "when the children have come of
age" to identify readiness for first communion, rather than
specifying one age. During the sixteenth century, children as
young as six or seven were admitted to communion in Denmark, while elsewhere in Lutheran churches the age for confirmation was rarely higher than twelve.[40] The rubrics of the
Church of England *Book of Common Prayer* directed that confirmation be administered to those "of perfect age," again not
identifying a particular age. Other documents of the sixteenth
century indicate that in some places confirmation was administered as early as age seven, while elsewhere age twelve or thirteen was deemed suitable.[41]
   During the centuries following the Reformation, the age of
confirmation was raised in both the Lutheran and Anglican traditions. In the Lutheran churches under the influence of Pietism
during the seventeenth and eighteenth centuries, which stressed
inner spiritual experience, confirmation came to be seen as a
subjective renewal of one's baptismal covenant. Because the
confirmand was required to make a personal affirmation of
faith, rather than simply having a rudimentary understanding of
doctrine and being able to "discern" the Lord's body and blood,
the customary age for confirmation became fourteen, and in
some places it was set as high as age sixteen. As Rationalism

emerged during the seventeenth and eighteenth centuries, the intellect was emphasized over emotions and experience. This too required a more advanced age, fourteen to sixteen, to permit the completion of a child's education. In many places on the European continent, confirmation marked the completion of education and became associated with the attainment of civic and economic privileges. Thus confirmation, linked with admission to communion, became in continental Lutheran churches a rite marking the end of adolescence and the acceptance of more adult responsibilities.[42]

In the United States, pioneer conditions in the eighteenth and nineteenth centuries were such that most Lutherans had much looser associations with the church. Contact with pastors was often limited to traveling missionaries, and education was frequently neglected as families struggled for existence. Hence the age for confirmation varied widely, ranging from thirteen to as high as thirty-two. Confirmation was still associated with education and profession of faith, necessitating a certain minimum age, but the rite was not as closely tied to adolescence. As the country became more settled, confirmation once again became primarily a rite of adolescence, usually administered at age fourteen or fifteen.[43]

In the Anglican communion, bishops played an important role in determining the age for confirmation, although many bishops gave some measure of discretion to parish clergy. As in the Lutheran churches, the customary age for confirmation increased to age fourteen or sixteen during the eighteenth and nineteenth centuries. However, unlike the continental Lutheran churches, confirmation was widely neglected in England during the seventeenth and eighteenth centuries and hence had little practical significance as a rite of adolescence. It was only during the nineteenth century that confirmation was administered more regularly in England. By the late nineteenth century there was pressure for confirmation at a younger age, before children completed their schooling and began work, a development suggesting that confirmation came to be given some importance as a rite of adolescence.[44]

In the United States, confirmation would have been impossible for most Anglicans during the colonial period because there were no bishops in the colonies. Only during the nineteenth century, after the Episcopal Church was established and significant missionary efforts began, did confirmation begin to be widely administered. As was true in the Lutheran Church, it is likely that a certain minimum age was required, to ensure adequate instruction, but adults as well as adolescents would have been presented for confirmation.

The situation is more complex in other Protestant churches in the United States, not all of which maintained a rite called "confirmation." For example, John Wesley retained much of the Anglican baptismal rite but eliminated confirmation. Methodists in the nineteenth century introduced a rite for the reception of members, with a probationary period for baptized persons, but only in the 1960s was the term "confirmation" introduced. In churches influenced by the revivalism of the eighteenth and nineteenth centuries, the emphasis was on the subjective experience of conversion rather than catechesis. Conversion was often an adult experience rather than a coming-of-age event, and this experience was frequently viewed as distinct from the sacramental or ritual expressions of baptism, confirmation, or other rites of profession of faith. As liturgical patterns stabilized in these churches, Sunday school instruction became a means to prepare children for conversion. Such instruction generally concluded with a rite of adolescent commitment, either baptism (among Baptists and Disciples of Christ) or a subsequent profession of faith or rite of membership (among other Protestant churches). Responding to the revivalist emphasis on conversion, the Congregationalist Horace Bushnell, in *Christian Nurture* (1861), urged a careful program of education for children, concluded by a rite of profession of faith akin to the Lutheran rite of confirmation.[45]

In the Roman Catholic Church, an increase in the age for first communion is evident in the decree *Quam singulari*, issued in 1910 by the Sacred Congregation of the Sacraments under Pope Pius X. According to this decree, in many places the customary age for first reception of communion had become age ten or twelve, or even fourteen or older, in effect making admission to communion a rite of adolescence. The decree reaffirmed that the age for first communion was the age of reason, understood to be age seven and further defined as the age at which a child could distinguish eucharistic bread from ordinary bread. While *Quam singulari* did not discuss confirmation, it had the effect of reversing the sequence of sacraments: first reception of communion began to precede confirmation. A statement issued by the Sacred Congregation on the Sacraments in 1932 asserted the appropriateness of the traditional sequence, confirmation followed by communion, with confirmation administered at age seven. Hence the official stance of the Roman Catholic Church was that confirmation and first communion were not associated with adolescence but with the initial development of a child's ability to reason.[46]

Yet, despite the official declarations of the Roman Catholic Church, confirmation was not universally associated with the age of reason. In Spain and Portugal, confirmation was customarily administered to infants, while first eucharist was given at the age of reason. In Mexico, infants are usually confirmed soon after baptism, a practice that arose when the first missionaries there obtained permission to confirm infants because bishops were scarce. Furthermore, it has always been permissible to administer confirmation to a young child in imminent danger of death.[47] These are, however, exceptions to the general norm.

In African countries where Christianity has been introduced only in more recent centuries, confirmation may be particularly significant as a rite of puberty. Cultural rites of passage, initiating boys and girls into manhood and womanhood, are of especial importance in these countries. The customary administration of confirmation in adolescence provides a readily apparent equivalent to these indigenous non-Christian rites, and, at least in some Anglican churches, the cultural importance of puberty rites has been a factor in the significance attached to confirmation.[48]

Contemporary Revisions

During the twentieth century, the age for confirmation has
been the subject of extensive debate in major western Christian
traditions. This may reflect the emergence of a more extended
developmental period of adolescence, a psychological concept
described by G. Stanley Hall in a 1904 work entitled *Adolescence.* Hall viewed adolescence as a turbulent period of change
marking the transition from childhood to adulthood, and described confirmation in various Christian traditions as a religious rite of passage in which "the young become members of
the religious community as well as of the home, and parents
seek divine and ecclesiastical cooperation in the further nurture
of their offspring."[49]

This phenomenon of a prolonged adolescence has its origins
in the complexities of modern industrial society, in which
childhood is a time devoted to education and psycho-social development rather than a period of apprenticeship for adult
labor. Subsequent studies of human development by psychologists such as Jean Piaget, Erik Erikson, Lawrence Kohlberg,
and Carol Gilligan have provided further insights into the dy-
namics and stages of growth, and the work of James Fowler has
applied these insights to faith development.[50]

Additional pressure for a rite of personal commitment arises
in the transition to a post-Christian or post-Constantinian world
view, in which Christianity no longer dominates social discourse and the establishment of societal norms. Increasingly in
the twentieth century, life in the church is no longer seen as
continuous with life in society, and being Christian may at
times set one apart from or against society (a perspective already evident in the Anabaptist sects of the sixteenth century).
In this world view, the need for rites to establish a distinctively
Christian identity is heightened.[51]

By the mid-twentieth century, Christian educators, theologians, liturgists, and pastors in the United States were actively
debating the most appropriate age for an adolescent profession
of faith and its accompanying rites. The religious education

movement which swept the country after World War II led to increasing awareness of the difficulties inherent in an adolescent profession of faith. Some argued that instruction should continue throughout adolescence, with a confirmation rite administered at age seventeen or eighteen, or even later. But because confirmation was also associated with admission to communion, others argued that it should be administered at a much earlier age, since it was inappropriate to deprive adolescents of the grace of communion.[52]

In the Anglican churches, the 1968 Lambeth Conference (an international conference of Anglican bishops) commended two possible lines of experiment: infant baptism, admission to communion after an appropriate course of instruction, and confirmation for young people ready to assume adult responsibility; or infant baptism and confirmation, admission to communion after appropriate instruction, and a service of commissioning for young adults ready to make a responsible commitment.[53] These are in effect the same process, providing admission to communion at an age akin to the age of reason in the Roman Catholic Church and a rite of commitment at the end of adolescence. The primary difference is whether confirmation is understood as a sacramental rite completing baptism and hence administered at the time of baptism or rather is interpreted as a catechetical rite of commitment appropriate in late adolescence, as a transition to adulthood.

The revisions in the Episcopal Church's 1979 *Book of Common Prayer* are based upon the latter view, that the rite of confirmation is a mature affirmation of baptismal vows. It is no longer required for reception of communion, and in many places communion of infants has become normative, so that admission to communion has ceased to serve as a rite of adolescence. Confirmation tends to be administered at a later age, with an emphasis on maturity rather than puberty. Furthermore, the rite of confirmation includes as well formulas for "Reaffirmation of Baptismal Vows" and for "Reception" (from another Christian denomination), suggesting that a rite of commitment is appropriate not only at the time of adolescence for those baptized as infants but also in the course of the adult life of faith.

The pattern adopted by the Episcopal Church has influenced revisions in other North American Protestant churches. The *Lutheran Book of Worship* (1978), the *Book of Alternative Services* (1985) of the Anglican Church of Canada, the United Methodist *Book of Worship* (1992), and the Presbyterian *Book of Common Worship* (1993) include rites of affirmation of faith appropriate for a variety of occasions, including an adolescent rite of commitment as well as adult affirmations of faith and reception of baptized members from other Christian traditions. The Lutheran rite no longer links first communion with confirmation, but rather permits admission to communion at an earlier age.[54]

In the worldwide Anglican Communion, a 1991 liturgical consultation described confirmation as a pastoral rite of affirmation or renewal of faith, appropriate for use on more than one occasion in a Christian's life but not a prerequisite for admission to communion. Here the emphasis is not on an adolescent rite of commitment but on an individual renewal of faith.[55] Practice continues to vary outside North America: in some Anglican churches, all the baptized are admitted to communion, and confirmation functions as a rite of adolescence; in other churches, admission to communion occurs after baptism but several years before confirmation, so that first communion and confirmation mark separate stages in Christian development; in still other Anglican churches, confirmation remains a prerequisite for communion and both rites are rites of adolescence.

Debates about the age for confirmation have affected practice in the Roman Catholic Church as well. Official documents continue to place confirmation and first reception of communion at the age of reason. But since the 1970s a practice of delaying confirmation beyond age twelve and as late as age seventeen has spread in the Roman Catholic Church in the United States and in other countries, owing to the desire of religious educators, catechists, and others to provide appropriate formation in faith and encourage commitment by adolescents.

This in effect ritualizes commitment in a manner similar to that encouraged by Erasmus and by the Protestant Reformers of the sixteenth century. While not denying the sacramental nature of confirmation, many Roman Catholics who advocate adolescent confirmation emphasize the necessity of personal commitment for full Christian initiation and describe confirmation as the culmination of an extended process of initiation for those baptized in infancy.[56]

The Future of Christian Rites of Adolescence

Confirmation and first reception of communion have their origins in the practice of initiation into the Christian community and are only secondarily rites of adolescence. As these rites were gradually separated from baptism during the Middle Ages, theological reflection came to identify confirmation as a sacrament of growth. But it was primarily the sixteenth-century Reformation emphasis on instruction and Christian commitment that established rites of adolescence. Churches that continued to practice infant baptism developed rites of profession of faith and admission to communion, in some cases called "confirmation," while in churches which instituted believers' baptism, the rite of baptism came to function as a rite of adolescence for children of believers.

Contemporary liturgical reforms of these rites have taken two primary directions. On the one hand, Anglican and Protestant churches that practice infant baptism have begun to identify and ritualize multiple occasions for a reaffirmation or recommitment to faith, rather than a single occasion at some point in adolescence. Some Roman Catholics are also proposing that confirmation should not be limited to a single occasion but rather should be permitted at several stages of human growth throughout adulthood.[57] Such developments reflect the complexities of modern western culture, in which adulthood may be marked by several significant transitions.

On the other hand, some recent proposals and experiments are attempting to provide rituals of adolescence separate from more traditional Christian rites. For example, amongst American Hispanic Catholics the cultural tradition of a *quince años* ("fifteen years") celebration, marking passage into the adult community upon the fifteenth birthday, is being Christianized as a rite of adolescence involving faith commitment.[58] John Westerhoff, an Episcopalian, points to the complexities of adolescence in contemporary society and argues that confirmation, as a rite of maturity, is inappropriate for adolescents. He proposes instead two rites of adolescence, one at about age twelve to mark the transition from childhood into adolescence, and the other in the twelfth grade or at about age eighteen to signify the beginning of adulthood.[59]

These emerging trends reflect the continuing need for Christian ritual to respond to the contemporary cultural situation. Lacking rituals specifically intended as rites of adolescence, Christians over the centuries have interpreted and adapted initiatory rituals in response to pastoral needs, a process that continues. In more recent liturgical revision, new rituals are being devised with less explicit connection to initiatory rites. These rituals draw upon the insights of religious educators and developmental psychologists in an effort to provide a Christian response to the perceived need for ritualization of the transition from childhood to adulthood, a transition which in late twentieth-century western culture extends over a period of several years.

NOTES

1. Tertullian, *De baptismo* 7, in E. C. Whitaker, *Documents of the Baptismal Liturgy,* 2d ed. (London, 1970), p. 8.

2. See Leonel L. Mitchell, *Baptismal Anointing* (London, 1966), for a study of the origins and development of anointing in eastern and western rites of Christian initiation.

3. See Whitaker, *Documents,* pp. 188, 203–4, 229–30; J. D. C. Fisher, *Christian Initiation: Baptism in the Medieval West* (London, 1965), pp. 17–27.

4. Fisher, in *Christian Initiation: Baptism in the Medieval West,*

the standard text on the subject, discusses the dissolution of Christian initiation and the origins of confirmation. His work is summarized in this essay. Further discussion can be found in Nathan D. Mitchell, "Dissolution of the Rite of Christian Initiation," in *Made Not Born: New Perspectives on Christian Initiation and the Catechumenate* (Notre Dame, IN, 1976), pp. 50–82; Gerard Austin, *Anointing with the Spirit: The Rite of Confirmation* (New York, 1985), pp. 3–37. Aidan Kavanagh, *Confirmation: Origins and Reform* (New York, 1988), proposes that confirmation developed out of a postbaptismal dismissal. He does not dispute Fisher's understanding of the medieval disintegration of Christian initiation, but his theory about the origins of the rite gives Kavanagh a different perspective on medieval developments.

5. Text in J. D. C. Fisher, *Christian Initiation: The Reformation Period* (London, 1970), pp. 161–62. Discussion in Austin, *Anointing with the Spirit,* pp. 14–15; Fisher, *Christian Initiation: Baptism in the Medieval West,* pp. 125–27. E. H. Davenport, *The False Decretals* (Oxford, 1916), discusses the history, authorship, and dating of *The False Decretals* but does not discuss the texts related to confirmation.

6. Thomas Aquinas, *Summa Theologica,* Part III, Ques. 72, Art. 1.

7. Ibid., Part. III, Q. 72, Art. 5.

8. Ibid., Part III, Q. 72, Art. 6.

9. Ibid., Part III, Q. 72, Art. 8. For discussion of Aquinas' theology of confirmation, see Austin, *Anointing with the Spirit,* pp. 26–27; Fisher, *Christian Initiation: Baptism in the Medieval West,* pp. 129–30; Nathan Mitchell, "Dissolution of the Rite of Christian Initiation," pp. 59–69.

10. Fisher, *Christian Initiation: Baptism in the Medieval West,* pp. 101–6.

11. Ibid., p. 124.

12. Fisher, *Christian Initiation: The Reformation Period,* pp. 165–66.

13. Ibid., pp. 166–69.

14. Erasmus apparently made no parallel recommendations for the instruction and examination of girls. The Latin word *pueri* may have meant both boys and girls. In his discussion of the passage, John Payne, *Erasmus: His Theology of the Sacraments* (Richmond, VA, 1970), pp. 172–74, refers to "youths" but does not discuss the translation of the Latin *pueri*.

15. Text in Fisher, *Christian Initiation: The Reformation Period,* p. 169. Discussion in Payne, *Erasmus,* pp. 172–74, 179–80; Leonel L. Mitchell, "Christian Initiation: The Reformation Period," in *Made Not Born,* pp. 84–85.

16. Texts in Fisher, *Christian Initiation: The Reformation Period,* pp. 171–72. Discussion in Arthur C. Repp, *Confirmation in the Lutheran Church* (St. Louis, 1964), pp. 15–17.

17. Text in Fisher, *Christian Initiation: The Reformation Period,* p. 173. Discussion in Repp, *Confirmation in the Lutheran Church,* pp. 17–20.

18. Calvin, *Institutes of the Christian Religion,* IV.19.4 (1543 edition), in Fisher, *Christian Initiation: The Reformation Period,* p. 258.

19. John M. Barkley, *The Worship of the Reformed Church* (London, 1966), pp. 115–16.

20. Fisher, *Christian Initiation: The Reformation Period,* p. 194.

21. Ibid., p. 179.

22. Repp, *Confirmation in the Lutheran Church,* pp. 32–37.

23. See Fisher, *Christian Initiation: The Reformation Period,* p. 234.

24. Ibid., pp. 241–42.

25. Ibid., pp. 236–43.

26. Ibid., p. 249.

27. Ibid., pp. 252–53.

28. Repp, *Confirmation in the Lutheran Church,* pp. 21–93.

29. Barkley, *The Worship of the Reformed Church,* pp. 116–17.

30. Philippa Tudor, "Religious Instruction for Children and Adolescents in the Early English Reformation," *Journal of Ecclesiastical History* 35 (1984): 301–4.

31. Richard L. DeMolen, "Childhood and Sacraments in the Sixteenth Century," *Archiv für Reformationsgeschichte* 66 (1975): 49–51.

32. Decree Concerning Reform, Chapter IV, Twenty-fourth session of the Council of Trent, 11 November 1563, in *Canons and Decrees of the Council of Trent,* trans. H. J. Schroeder (St. Louis, 1941), p. 196.

33. Canons on Confirmation, canon 1, Seventh Session of the Council of Trent, 3 March 1547, in *Canons and Decrees,* pp. 54–55.

34. *Catechism of the Council of Trent,* trans. John A. McHugh and Charles J. Callan (New York, 1934), pp. 199–210.

35. "The Doctrine of Communion under Both Kinds and the Communion of Little Children," Chapter IV, and Canons on Communion under Both Species and that of Little Children, canon 4, Twenty-first Session of the Council of Trent, 16 July 1562, in *Canons and Decrees,* pp. 134–35. (Fisher, *Christian Initiation: Baptism in the Medieval West,* p. 107, mistakenly identifies this as the session of 16 July 1552, instead of 1562.)

36. See above p. 23.

37. Rollin Stely Armour, *Anabaptist Baptism: A Representative Study* (Scottdale, PA, 1966), pp. 55, 61, 95.

38. Hillel Schwartz, "Early Anabaptist Ideas about the Nature of Children," *Mennonite Quarterly Review* 47 (1973): 102–14; L. L. Mitchell, "Christian Initiation: The Reformation Period," pp. 95–96.

39. George Huntston Williams, *The Radical Reformation* (Philadelphia, 1962), pp. 450–51; Repp, *Confirmation in the Lutheran Church,* pp. 29–30.

40. Repp, *Confirmation in the Lutheran Church,* pp. 56–57.

41. W. Lockton, "The Age for Confirmation," *Church Quarterly Review* 100 (1925): 57–60.

42. Repp, *Confirmation in the Lutheran Church,* pp. 75, 81–82, 182–83.

43. Ibid., pp. 95–99, 125–29, 184–85.

44. "The Age for Confirmation," *Church Quarterly Review* 23 (1886): 52–58, 75–83; Lockton, "The Age for Confirmation," pp. 63–64.

45. Robert H. Fischer, "Confirmation outside the Anglican Tradition," in *Confirmation: History, Doctrine, and Practice,* ed. Kendig Brubaker Cully (Greenwich, CT, 1962), pp. 45–49; Lawrence H. Stookey, *Baptism: Christ's Act in the Church* (Nashville, 1982), pp. 128–30.

46. Paul Turner, *Confirmation: The Baby in Solomon's Court* (New York, 1993), pp. 86–87, 147–49.

47. Ibid., pp. 102–3, 148–50.

48. Themba Jerome Vundla, "Traditional Initiation Rites among the Ngunis and Their Relationship to Christian Initiation," in *Growing in Newness of Life: Christian Initiation in Anglicanism Today,* ed. David Holeton (Toronto, 1993), pp. 211–12; "Walk in Newness of Life: the Findings of the International Anglican Liturgical Consultation," ibid., pp. 248–49.

49. G. Stanley Hall, *Adolescence: Its Psychology and Its Relations to Physiology, Anthropology, Sociology, Sex, Crime, Religion and Education* (New York, 1904), 2:262. Hall provides an extended description of Jewish and Christian rites and continues with a lengthy chapter entitled "The Adolescent Psychology of Conversion." He does not, however, display accurate knowledge of the origins of confirmation, and his descriptions may not be wholly reliable. Hall is most significant as the primary early figure in the identification and study of adolescence as a unique stage of human development.

50. James W. Fowler, *Stages of Faith: The Psychology of Human Development and the Quest for Meaning* (San Francisco, 1981), discusses the work of Piaget, Erikson, Kohlberg, and Gilligan in developing his thesis.

51. See, for example, the discussion of Daniel Stevick, *Baptismal Moments; Baptismal Meanings* (New York, 1987), pp. 27–34.

52. "A Symposium: The Proper Age for a Declaration of Faith," *Religious Education* 58 (1963): 411–42; "Symposium: The Proper Age for a Declaration of Faith," *Religious Education* 60 (1965): 290–302, 313.

53. *The Lambeth Conference 1968* (New York, 1968), p. 99.

54. Stevick, *Baptismal Moments; Baptismal Meanings,* pp. xv–xvii; Frank C. Senn, "Lutheran and Anglican Liturgies: Reciprocal Influences," *Anglican Theological Review* 64 (1982): 59–60; Lawrence H. Stookey, "Three New Initiation Rites," *Worship* 51 (1977): 42–48.

55. "Walk in Newness of Life," in *Growing in Newness of Life,* pp. 229, 240–48.

56. Turner, *Confirmation,* pp. 85–121; *Confirming the Faith of Adolescents: An Alternative Future for Confirmation,* ed. Arthur J. Kubick (New York, 1991).

57. Craig Cox, "Rethinking Confirmation: Possible Ways Forward," in *Confirming the Faith of Adolescents,* pp. 165–77.

58. See, for example, Angela Erevia, *Quince Años: Celebrating a Tradition* (San Antonio, 1985).

59. John Westerhoff, "Confirmation: An Episcopal Church Perspective," in *Confirming the Faith of Adolescents,* pp. 160–63.

Jewish Rites of Adolescence

Debra R. Blank

The traditional rite[1] of adolescence for a Jew is bar mitzvah (literally, son of the commandment), celebrated at the age of thirteen years and one day.[2] Technically, it is a rite of initiation into adulthood, for which the boy prepares by a period of study. On the day itself, usually a Sabbath, he is extended the privileges of adulthood: he will receive his first *aliyah* (being called to recite the requisite blessings over the reading of Torah and to stand by the reader as the scroll is recited); he will be assigned the liturgical responsibility of reading the Haftarah (the weekly lectionary from the prophetic books); and he will have the right to deliver a talk, a *Devar Torah* (literally, a "word of Torah") or homily, varying in length and erudition according to the child and the community. His new responsibilities can also include leading services and reading the Torah before the assembled congregation; no longer a child, he will hereafter be counted among the ten adults—traditionally, male only—required for a *minyan* (a prayer quorum). Through the public occasion of his coming of age, designated popularly as "his" bar mitzvah, the boy is expected to display the fruits of his learning and his maturity, and have his entry into the cult[3] of Torah recognized by the community. The father of the boy marks the occasion by the public recitation of a liturgical formula which acknowledges his son's newly found adulthood by praising God for having relieved him of parental responsibility. The event is celebrated by an obligatory meal sponsored by the father.

81

In modern times girls have celebrated this same ceremony (known as bat mitzvah,[4] "daughter of the covenant"), albeit in varying degrees according to the community's norms (e.g., in more conservative circles, she might choose to study and deliver a talk, but not be allowed to receive an *aliyah,* or to read from the texts). Mothers too may be extended greater acknowledgment and participate in varying degrees along with fathers.

Though bar/bat mitzvah has emerged in North America as perhaps the most well-known Jewish rite, it differs from the vast majority of Jewish holidays, life-cycle celebrations, practices, and liturgies in that it cannot be traced to the biblical or even the rabbinic period (ending with the closing of the Talmud, approximately 550 C.E.). As we shall see, the earliest reference to the ceremony of bar mitzvah dates only from the fourteenth century.

This essay reviews the historical evidence for the ceremony of bar mitzvah, as well as two other ceremonies which were part of the background out of which bar mitzvah seems to have developed. Finally, we will review the modern developments of the bar mitzvah ceremony—its waning in importance, the success of nineteenth-century German Jewish Reformers in replacing it with a confirmation ceremony, its subsequent resurgence in popularity, and its adaptation to girls in the bat mitzvah celebration.

The well-known scheme provided by van Gennep posits a ritualized transition from childhood into adulthood, marked by relatively discrete and largely successive stages of separation, liminality, and incorporation.[5] So in our case, the child "separates" from childhood by being engrossed in a prolonged period of study, undergoes transition by the ritualized public demonstration of success in that preparation, and is incorporated into the adult community by being awarded the ritual perquisites of Jewish adulthood, including being counted to make up the symbolic community at prayer. But this scheme, while helpful, is limited. There is more to our story of the bar mitzvah.

Rites express the ultimate values of a society. A coming-of-age ceremony initiates children into those activities reserved as highly valuable for a society's adults. Torah is the ultimate value of rabbinic Jewish society, so the bar mitzvah ceremony celebrates and effects the initiation of the adolescent into the circle of those who must officially bear the responsibility of studying Torah. A boy who reaches the age of majority is thus now able to be called up as a participant in the public reading of the Torah, and will preach a homily based upon it. Predictably, the boy has prepared for these honors by studying that very Torah.

The value placed upon Torah is expressed within the life-cycle rites that span the age from birth to marriage. At the circumcision of the eight-day-old, the celebrants cry out, "Just as he has entered the covenant, so may he enter into Torah, marriage, and good deeds!" [Eds. note: see above, p. 35]; at adolescence, the child is formally initiated into ritual practices associated with Torah; and at marriage, a man stands prepared to generate the next generation of Torah-adherents.[6] The traditional understanding of the Jewish male's life-line, so centered on the Torah and its study, finds expression in the Mishnah: "At five years old [one is ready] for the [study of] Scripture, at ten years for the Mishnah, at thirteen for [the fulfilling of] the commandments, at fifteen for the Talmud, at eighteen for marriage."[7]

But bar mitzvah is just part of a larger cultural whole, in which the study and celebration of Torah are ubiquitous elements.

Simchat Torah—The Children's Holiday

Bar mitzvah can be understood fully only as the culmination of a childhood dedicated to Torah. The autumn holiday of Simchat Torah (literally, "Joy of the Torah") and the spring festival of Shavuot (Festival of "Weeks," corresponding to the Christian Pentecost) link the theme of Torah to children.

Simchat Torah celebrates the completion of the annual cycle of the reading of the Torah (the first five books of the Bible) and inaugurates the beginning of the cycle again; on this day the last two chapters of Deuteronomy are read followed by Genesis 1–2:3. Shavuot recalls the giving of the Torah at Sinai. While children's initiation ceremonies have tended to be celebrated on Shavuot (see below, *Confirmation*), the special relationship of children to Torah is acknowledged also on Simchat Torah, the final day of a nine-day celebration of which the first seven are Sukkot (Tabernacles) and the eighth, Shemini Atseret (The Eighth Day of Assembly). (In Israel and among most Reform Jews, the observances of Shemini Atseret and Simchat Torah occur together on the eighth day, not the ninth.)

On Simchat Torah, a child's connection to the Torah is affirmed, in that children participate together then in a group *aliyah.* We saw above that individuals are first called to the Torah as adults when they reach their age of majority. Throughout the year, in fact, upon all occasions of the public Torah reading, adult members of the community are given this honor; their name is called, they "come up" to stand next to the reader for a designated portion of the reading, and they recite the special blessings that introduce and conclude the reading. Depending upon the day, there will be as few as three *aliyot* (plural), or as many as seven. But on Simchat Torah everyone present who is of majority age (traditionally, only males; modern communities with egalitarian leanings afford the honor to women too) receives an *aliyah.* And on that day also, a "practice run," so to speak, occurs for children as well. Upon completing the last reading of Deuteronomy, they join together for the annual children's *aliyah,* generally regarded as an especially joyous highlight of the holiday which is already marked by its festivities.[8] The children thereby experience the promise of what adulthood will bring.

This *aliyah* of the children, called *kol ha-na'arim,* varies by region: the children go up one by one, group by group, or all at once; with an adult or without an adult; part of the day's Torah reading is read (thus it is a legitimate *aliyah*) or only Genesis 48:16 ("The angel who has redeemed me from all harm, bless the children. In them may my name be recalled, and the names of my fathers Abraham and Isaac; and may they be teeming multitudes upon the earth");[9] "The angel" is actually read from the Torah in addition to the regular reading, or it is just recited from memory or from a printed text by the congregation; the children say the *aliyah* blessings, an adult does so for them, or an adult says them word by word with the children repeating afterwards.

The popular reason usually given for this special *aliyah* is the need to educate children in the commandment to read Torah and to impress upon them the love of this commandment. Certainly this *aliyah* for children provides a taste of an adult Jewish prerogative: the right to be called up to the Torah as a full member of the community. Presumably, the lure of this privilege encourages the proper study on which its award will depend. Scholarly speculation links the practice further to the biblical commandment (Deut. 31:10–12) to gather for the public reading of the Torah on Shemini Atseret (The Eighth Day of Assembly) at the end of the Sabbatical year; the text states specifically that children are in attendance. This ceremony, and its explanation according to Deuteronomy, are first described by Rashi (northern France, late eleventh century),[10] and thereafter appear in many sources with different degrees of detail and numerous variations.

The official rationale may or may not be correct, but regardless, what is significant is that a primary privilege of adulthood—*aliyah* to the Torah—is extended to children on Simchat Torah. The reasons are unabashedly Torah-centered: to educate them about the commandment of Torah reading and to foster their love for the Torah. Ashkenazic circles also apparently sought to ward off the evil eye through the recitation of "The angel," for the children gathered on Simchat Torah are the next generation of Torah-transmitters, and must be protected from harm if Torah is to pass beyond the current adult generation. In some locales we find a final symbol, the *tallit* (prayer shawl),

which is spread above the children during their *aliyah* as a
harbinger of marriage, for the *tallit* may be used in the same way
to form the *chuppah* (the canopy) over the heads of the bride and
groom. Thus this ceremony even looks forward to the following
generation of Torah adherents, the future children who will
come into being when these children are married.

Even in those areas where the custom of the children's
aliyah is not practiced, for example, among Jews who do not
trace their heritage to Europe, the holiday nevertheless has special significance for children, involving them in the public
ceremonies as does no other holiday. Here too the emphasis remains on the Torah. As part of the holiday, huge processionals
occur amid communal dancing and singing, during which
everyone—children included, generally—takes a turn holding
a scroll of the Torah. Occasionally children even lead the
processionals. Sometimes too, the processionals circle the children, who are grouped in the center, thereby symbolically
equating them, through this focusing and centering, with the
Torah which is otherwise the center of attention. Other customs abound: placing the crown of the Torah scrolls upon babies' heads (thereby identifying these newest inheritors of the
Torah with the Torah that they will inherit); throwing fruit to
the children (a common theme of associating sweets with the
study of Torah); saying a special blessing for the entire congregation, in which the children are specifically mentioned.
When Yemenite Jews bring to synagogue for the first time a
child who has just learned to stand, they dress him up and the
father gives a party, as a sign that the child will become a
student of Torah.[11]

Shavuot: Rite for Induction of a Child into Torah

Like Simchat Torah in the fall, Shavuot in the spring (seven
weeks after Passover) is closely associated with Torah. Though
biblically a harvest festival, the Rabbis converted it into a celebration of the giving of Torah on Mt. Sinai.

Literature from thirteenth-century Germany and northern
France describes Shavuot as the time for ritual induction of

boys into the study of Torah.[12] No absolute, arbitrary chronological age is set for this ceremony, but most likely it occurred
when the child displayed readiness for formal education, probably between the ages of five and seven.

On the day in question, the child is washed, nicely dressed,
and covered up with a cloak as he is carried to the schoolhouse
or synagogue. Once there, the teacher presents him with a
board or slate on which the letters of the Hebrew alphabet are
written forwards and backwards, along with some biblical
verses. The teacher reads the letters and verses which the child
repeats after him. The child is taught to sway back and forth
while studying. After this the board is covered with honey and
he is told to lick it. He is then fed three honey cakes (which
were prepared by a young girl), and cooked eggs, upon which
biblical texts are written. Then he is covered up and carried
home.

The thirteenth-century literature explains the details of the
foregoing rite with a metaphorical reference to revelation at
Sinai.[13] Biblical texts, largely from the Exodus account of the
revelation of Torah, are combined with popular lore to justify
each piece of the ceremony. We learn, for example, that this
ceremony introducing a child to Torah study occurs on
Shavuot, because the Torah was revealed on that day. But when
the first set of tablets was given, there was great fanfare, the
angels became jealous, vengeful Satan came, and the tablets
were broken. The second time, therefore, the Torah was given
quietly, that it might endure forever. In like fashion, so as to
prevent the evil eye, the child is covered up on his way to
school. Similarly he is washed and dressed in clean clothes, to
prepare as the Israelites did when the Torah was given to them.

Other analogies follow. The child is carried in the arms of a
teacher because Moses was told to "carry them in your arms,
as a nurse carries the sucking child" (Num. 11:12). The licking
of the honey-covered board is from Ezekiel, who was told,
"Eat this scroll which I am giving to you" and who "ate it and
it was as sweet as honey" (Ezek. 3:3). The child is taught
to sway while studying because when the Israelites were at
Sinai, "they were shaken" (Exod. 20:15). The three cakes are a

reminder of the three delicacies which Israel enjoyed in the desert: the well, the manna, and the quails. A young girl must knead the pastry because her ritual purity (as a not-yet menstruant) corresponds to that of the innocent child—just as the Israelites were in a state of ritual purity when they received the Torah.

According to the thirteenth-century accounts, after the alphabet and verses, the book of Leviticus is the next item of Torah study for the child. The reason given is that the ritual purity of the sacrifices described in Leviticus corresponds to the purity of the sinless child. The literature compares the animal whose fat and blood are sacrificed to the child whose fat and blood [i.e., strength] are diminished by the study of the Torah. The child is fed after his intellectual exertions because he is so physically spent.

The entire rite echoes Sinai: Mount Sinai is the metaphor for the schoolhouse, the teacher is Moses, and the child (a potential progenitor of the next generation) represents the entire people of Israel. The letters of the alphabet are taught just as the Torah was revealed; the child ingests the letters just as the people received the Torah. In short, the child's journey to the schoolhouse and his experience there echo the journey of the ancient Israelites to Sinai and their experience at the mountain. The child's mundane experience is given a cosmic, spiritual, and theological dimension. The literature gives the reason for this rite: so that the Torah will be upheld for the generations.

Most striking of all is the merging of identities between the child who studies and the Torah which is studied. We saw that on Simchat Torah the Torah's crown is placed on the baby's head, and the people dance around the children, who thus become the Torah, the normal focus of attention. Here too, at the Shavuot rite, the child is identified as the Torah: just as the enduring Torah was given quietly, without fanfare, so too the child is introduced quietly, under wraps. The child is thus first of all Israel, but also Torah itself. In addition, he is likened to a sacrificial victim,[14] offered up, as it were, to the cult of Torah study: his physical being is diminished in service to study of

God's word, thereby renewing the covenantal relationship. In this there is a parallel to circumcision: entrance into the covenant results in the loss of the child's strength. In both cases the blood of the child (actual in one case, metaphorical in the second) is viewed as a sacrifice to God.

This formal induction into the cult of Torah study is the culmination of the wish extended the infant on the occasion of his circumcision when the bystanders called out, "Just as he has entered the covenant, so may he enter into Torah, marriage, and good deeds!" Now they bless him again, saying, "Just as you have entered into the covenant and the Torah, may you enter into *chuppah* (marriage) and good deeds!" By this variation on the blessing at circumcision, the people pair the child's entrance into the covenant of circumcision with his entrance into Torah study; he will later enter into *chuppah*. Each of these stages represent increasing degrees of entry into the cult, into Jewish society.

By the fourteenth century this ceremony appears to die out—precisely when we begin to see references to a ceremony associated with becoming bar mitzvah.[15]

Bar Mitzvah as Age of Majority: Becoming an Adult

While the age of majority is not designated as such in biblical literature, the age of twenty seems to be the standard for purposes both of taxation (e.g., Exod. 30:14) and conscription (e.g., Num. 1:3, 24). This age seems to apply equally to males and to females (see Lev. 27:4–7), albeit only for taxation.

The age for moral responsibility seems to be the same. In Numbers, God distinguishes those of age twenty and above, guilty of mutinous, faithless complaints, from "your little ones" and "your children," who alone will arrive in the Land of Israel as promised (Num. 14:26–35). So the age of twenty marked the transition to adulthood in the biblical period; but no rite marking the transition is recorded there.

In rabbinic literature (primarily the Mishnah and Babylonian Talmud, with respective editorial dates of approximately

200 C.E. and 550 C.E.), the ages of twelve years and one day for girls and thirteen years and one day for boys—the ages widely regarded traditionally as the threshold of adulthood—begin to take on significance.[16] This change from the biblical age of majority may reflect outside influence.[17] At this point a thirteen-year-old boy is obligated to participate in public, religious fasts.[18] Likewise any vows he might make are to be regarded as valid.[19]

Two criteria are given for this chronological marker for boys: physical maturation and moral discernment. The first is reflected in the assumption that at about that age pubic hair appears. "A boy who has grown two [pubic] hairs is subject to all the commandments in the Torah."[20] But physical signs are not enough. He must attain a certain age as well. "From the point of his birth until he is thirteen, he is called a boy or a baby. Even if within this period he grows a couple of [pubic] hairs, these are not considered evidence [of maturation], but [only] a mole [with hairs]."[21]

However, thirteen is not an arbitrarily determined transition point based solely upon its being associated with a boy's physical coming of age. Moral maturation also occurs at this point, as the midrashic collection Avot deRabbi Natan indicates: "The evil inclination . . . grows with and accompanies the child from the moment it comes forth from the mother's womb. A child who begins to violate the Sabbath is not deterred; a child about to take a life is not deterred; a child about to commit an immoral act is not deterred. After thirteen years, however, the good inclination is born in him. If then he is about to violate the Sabbath it warns him."[22]

Rabbinic literature appreciates this process as a gradual movement into adulthood rather than a sudden, absolute, and singular moment of transition. So while a thirteen-year-old boy's vows are accepted as binding, his testimony regarding real estate negotiations is not, because though he is thirteen and a man for some purposes, for others he is still only a boy, lacking in sufficient knowledge to be held liable.[23] Moreover, thirteen is not an absolute beginning just as it is not an absolute end to the maturation process; thus, upon examination, a boy's vows even from the age of twelve and one day will be accepted.[24]

In keeping with this apparent appreciation for the individual pace of maturity of each child, education and intellectual readiness are emphasized. Preparation for the responsibilities inherent in Torah comes in the form of education, which begins long before the age of majority: "'Teach these [commandments] to your children' (Deut. 11:19). Based on this they said that when the baby begins to speak, his father speaks to him in the holy language [Hebrew] and teaches him Torah. If he does not speak to him in the holy language and does not teach him Torah, it is as if he has buried him."[25]

The Talmud provides a further example of early education in ritual matters:

> A minor who knows how to shake the *lulav* (the palm branch associated with the festival of Sukkot) is subject to the obligation of the *lulav*; if he knows how to wrap himself with the *tallit* he is subject to the obligation of the *tallit*; if he knows how to take care of *tefillin* [phylacteries: a wooden box containing scripture, attached to leather straps that are wrapped around the left arm and forehead as a morning devotion—following Deut. 6:8, "You shall bind them for a sign upon your hand and they shall be frontlets between your eyes."] his father must acquire *tefillin* for him; if he is able to speak, his father must teach him Torah and the reading of the *Shema*.[26]

Moreover, it is clear that in the Mishnaic period (before the year 200 C.E.), reading from the Haftarah and the Torah, two of the significant ritual actions that today typically mark the occasion of bar mitzvah, were permitted to minors as well.[27] A minor could even be called up for an *aliyah* in some circumstances,[28] and was counted when necessary to make a prayer quorum.[29] Thus the *lulav, tallit, tefillin,* and the public reading of scripture as well as adult status for prayer, were once dependent upon knowledge and ability, not age. True, minors were not deemed eligible actually to lead the public obligatory prayers; these were legally binding on adults, and only an adult could fulfill the obligation of leading an "adult" public liturgy for an "adult" congregation; but other than that, it seems that the synagogue enforced no sweeping distinction in role based simply on the age at which a child was held to become an adult.

Thus most of the major cultic activities associated today with the entry into the age of majority—*aliyah,* reading from the sacred texts, donning *tallit* and *tefillin,* being counted in the quorum—were all permitted the minor in rabbinic times, apparently without ceremony. How then did Jewish culture move to a point where a boy begins doing these things only upon turning thirteen, usually celebrated with a ceremony?[30]

Bar Mitzvah as Rite: Coming of Age Ritually

While the term "bar mitzvah" occurs in the Talmud to describe one who is subject to the commandments,[31] early rabbinic literature provides no reference to an occasion or rite under that name. However, there is some suggestion that the thirteenth birthday did not pass unnoticed, for it was marked by a blessing.

> Rabbi Phinehas said in Rabbi Levi's name: They [Jacob and Esau] were like a myrtle and a wild rose-bush growing side by side; when they reached the age of maturity, one displayed its fragrance, and the other grew its thorns. So for thirteen years both went to school. But after turning thirteen, one went to the study hall and the other to idolatrous shrines. Rabbi Eleazar ben Rabbi Simeon said: A man is responsible for his son until the age of thirteen; thereafter he must say, 'Blessed is He who has now freed me from the responsibility of this boy.'[32]

We have therefore an early and distinct reference, in a midrash collection usually dated no later than the fifth century, to a blessing that was associated with a boy's coming of age. However there is no evidence that actual recitation of this blessing ever occurred, at least not in any public forum whence it would have received some form of official recognition in legal literature that customarily records such things as obligatory. No further reference to this blessing can be found until the fourteenth century when Aaron ben Jacob Hakohen of Provence wrote:

> It is written in Genesis Rabbah . . . that he whose son reaches the age of thirteen must say the blessing, 'Blessed is He who has now freed me from the responsibility of this boy.' There are those who say it the first time that the boy receives his *aliyah* to read the Torah. The [eighth-century] Gaon Rabbi Yehudai rose in the synagogue and said this blessing the first time that his son read the Torah.[33]

This fourteenth-century source provides us with our first reference to a public occasion marking a boy's reaching the age of majority, claiming, however (whether accurately or not), that the precedent extends back some six centuries.

By the seventeenth century, the Polish commentator and jurist, Abraham Gumbiner (1635–1683), tells us,

> Nowadays it is customary to say the blessing at the point at which the youth prays or reads on the first Sabbath [after his thirteenth birthday] such that it will be publicly known that he is a *bar mitzvah*. In such a case, the father says, 'Blessed is He who has now freed me from the responsibility of this boy.' "[34]

The customary understanding of this blessing, according to Gumbiner, is that "up until now, the father has been punished when the son sinned because he had not educated him [as it is assumed that it is the father's responsibility to teach the child]."[35]

Because this blessing is mentioned not in the Talmud, but only in the midrashic literature, which is held to be of secondary legal importance, there is some discussion about whether or not it has legal standing. Hence the question is asked whether or not the full blessing formula which includes the name of God (*Barukh atah adonai, eloheinu melekh ha'olam*) should be used, or whether an abbreviated version of the formula without this formal address should suffice. The first reference to this question appears in Moses Isserles' comment (sixteenth-century Poland): "It is good to say [the blessing] without the [formula containing God's] name and sovereignty."[36] The question regarding its legality may actually have arisen because of a larger ambivalence. Originally just an age of majority status, bar mitzvah had become a ritual ceremony, which in Isserles' time was likely a recent innovation. Since people were now saying the blessing in a public ritual setting, authorities worried about its propriety. Generally today the form of this blessing is established by local practice,[37] some saying it in its longer form and some preferring the truncated version. In either case—in the fourteenth-century claim about an eighth-century practice, as well as today—it is said when the son reads from scripture, at precisely that point when he enters (tangibly) into the cult of Torah.

Closely connected to the ceremony of bar mitzvah is a ritually obligatory meal, the *se'udat mitzvah,* which we encounter first in Gumbiner's legal commentary as well as the *Be'er Heteiv,* a marginal gloss to the *Shulchan Arukh,* by Judah Ashkenazi (1700–1740).[38] Both authors write,

> It is a commandment upon the father to serve a meal on the day on which his son becomes bar mitzvah—i.e., on the day that he enters the fourteenth year—just as [he will later do] on the day that he is married. . . . [Luria] writes that if the youth gives a sermon there should be a meal, even if it is not the same day.

Both authors are referring to Solomon Luria, a sixteenth-century jurist, who describes the meal as an Ashkenazic practice, designed to "give praise and thanksgiving to God in that the youth has merited becoming and matured to the doing of the commandments, and that the father has merited raising his son to the point where he can admit him to the covenant of the Torah."[39] Luria explicitly notes that the festive meal is occasioned by the boy's giving a speech.

The history of bar mitzvah is not linear: there is no discernable chain of development from Mishnaic times, when certain religious and social responsibilities fell upon a thirteen-year-old without ceremony, to the fourteenth century, when we begin seeing references to an actual public ceremony, complete with celebration. The presence of a blessing associated in the midrash with a boy's thirteenth birthday indicates, however, that already in early rabbinic times this birthday was marked as a significant transition point. The fourteenth century's attribution of this blessing to an eighth-century rabbi, upon the occasion of his thirteen-year-old son reading Torah publicly, indicates that, in the fourteenth century, linking the blessing with the Torah reading was regarded as a meritorious custom of some antiquity, at least by one authority. But prior to the fourteenth century, we have no way to measure how widely the blessing was employed in a public Torah-reading setting.

With the passage of time, more and more of the ritual actions were seen as privileges to be enjoyed only by those of majority age. Thus *tefillin* and *tallit,* the receiving of the *aliyah,* and the public reading from scripture (both Torah and Haftarah) became rituals marking a boy's coming of age. While the latter two are still technically permitted for a person of minority age,[40] in practice all are reserved for the age of majority.[41]

Confirmation

Jewish worship began to be fundamentally altered in the nineteenth century by religious reforms. While these innovations originated and proliferated primarily in Germany, they also affected Jews in that century who lived as far away as Russia and North America. Confirmation was one of the items on the list of reforms.[42]

Reformers, scrutinizing the rite of bar mitzvah, expressed a preference for a confirmation ceremony at which the thirteen-year-old would answer rehearsed questions about the tenets of Jewish faith. The bar mitzvah boy could at best display ability to read from the Torah and give a discourse; the confirmand could show he knew the religious principles of his faith.

Different justifications have been advanced for confirmation. According to one view, for instance, the bar mitzvah ceremony had simply lost its prominence among some Jews. According to another, people wished to increase the participation of Jewish women in the community; as girls were educated more and more like boys in the secular world, people felt the need for comparable Jewish education. Whatever the reason, the process of confirmation was based on the model of Christian catechism, whereby after a period of study, the confirmand would answer questions that displayed a comprehension of Jewish religious principles. The culmination of the course of study indicated that the adolescent was now sufficiently responsible to graduate to adult status. The content of the ceremony and preparation for it varied (and still do vary) widely, but it was (and in some places, still remains) characterized by some formal confession of faith or statement of principles, following a period of study.

Criticism of the ceremony of confirmation focused, of course, on its Christian roots; the critics argued that practice, not profession of doctrine, distinguished a Jew. Supporters of confirmation pointed out that unlike bar mitzvah, this ceremony included girls. However, there is no evidence of girls being confirmed until 1814 in Berlin,[43] whereas the earliest evidence for confirmation dates from 1803 in Dessau. Soon thereafter girls seem to have been included in the ceremony without exception, not only in Germany, but in Denmark, Russia, and England. The leading American Reform rabbi of the nineteenth century, Isaac Mayer Wise, introduced confirmation to the United States in 1846 while serving in Albany, New York. By the latter 1800s, confirmation had thus become a common practice among the Jews of North America and Europe.

Initially the ceremony was conducted apart from the synagogue, and was linked to the school and home, but, like many other life-cycle rites, it moved from the home to the public arena. By 1831 it was observed in a Berlin synagogue. From an early point the rite was held on Shavuot, the holiday which celebrates the giving of the Torah. The profession of faith by the young generation lends a moving dimension to a holiday otherwise lacking in physical symbols and folk customs. No doubt Shavuot has remained the preferred time for this rite because of its convenience as well: the occurrence of Shavuot in late spring coincides with the end of the school year. Thus confirmation marks the completion of supplementary Hebrew school along with secular studies.

It was rare that confirmation actually replaced, at least *de jure,* the ceremony of bar mitzvah, though *de facto* the latter clearly waned in popularity. In its initial stage, confirmation was conceived simply as a repackaging of bar mitzvah, with a change in the educational focus from practice to doctrinal declaration. To this end, its proponents were always careful to argue that the newer ceremony served a separate educational function. This claim led to a gradual increase in the age of the confirmand to sixteen or seventeen in order that the child's education would be prolonged, as well as to emphasize the independence of the confirmation from the traditional bar mitzvah. By the nineteenth and early twentieth centuries in North America, confirmation generally eclipsed bar mitzvah among North American Jews, most of whom had arrived from Germany, bringing Reform Judaism with them.

But bar mitzvah has enjoyed a rebirth of popularity and significance among the descendants of those liberal Jews who once dispensed with it. A check in the indices of the volumes of contemporary responsa by Rabbi Solomon Freehof (1892–1990), the chief Reform respondent after World War II, yields not even one entry for confirmation, yet there are many entries for bar/bat mitzvah (see below). Freehof even notes explicitly in his 1977 volume that the increasing practice of bar mitzvah among Reform Jews has led to the decreasing significance of confirmation; after bar mitzvah, it is often felt that there is no need for further Jewish education. Now, he cautions, an even greater threat to continuing Jewish education has appeared: bat mitzvah.[44] Indeed, by the 1970s, bat mitzvah had become the norm for many Jewish girls just as bar mitzvah was typical for boys.

Bat Mitzvah

Rabbinic literature is explicit that girls, just as boys, reach the age of majority with attending benefits and responsibilities: moral, legal, social, and religious. So, for example, upon reaching the age of twelve a girl is obligated to participate in public religious fasts.[45] Likewise the vows of a girl who has reached the age of twelve and one day are regarded as valid. Physical maturation marks the transition in the girl's status, just as in the boy's: "If a girl has grown two [pubic] hairs she is subject to all the commandments of the Torah."[46] Maimonides clarifies that, as with boys, the age of majority befalls girls only when the age of twelve and one day is reached, even if physical maturation has already occurred. And the appreciation for the gradual entry into adulthood pertains to girls as well: their vows also were accepted upon examination even from the age of eleven and one day.[47]

Traditionally, access to Torah in any form (e.g., an *aliyah*) has never been given to girls, who were denied equal access to Jewish ritual in general. This lack of access affected their educational preparation, for education was intended specifically to prepare boys—but not girls—for ritual participation. One early rabbinic figure even understood "Teach these [commandments] to your children" (Deut. 11:19) to refer literally to "sons, not daughters."[48] However, we know that at least some girls were educated, albeit with different expectations.[49]

There is no evidence of any rite marking a girl's maturation until the confirmation ceremonies of nineteenth-century Europe, specifically those first recorded in 1814 in Berlin.[50] But since in that period the confirmation ceremony was a repackaging of bar mitzvah, functionally speaking, the confirmed girl was actually becoming bat mitzvah, whether it was recognized as such or not. This seems especially obvious when we recall that one of the rationales for the confirmation ceremony was that girls could participate as confirmands.

In the 1930s something known as a "consecration service" for girls began to be used by a number of congregations in

North America. Based on a model used in England and approved by the British (and strictly Orthodox) Chief Rabbi Joseph Hertz, it was a prototype readily available to rabbis who described themselves adamantly as not being reformers in any way, and who therefore distinguished their service from the Reform confirmation rite. Actual differences were not readily discernable, however. The girls participated as a group, it was held on Shavuot, it was conducted largely in English, and it was independent of the Torah reading. The rationale for such ceremonies was the need to educate girls in the tenets of Judaism and to instill in them loyalty to the tradition.[51]

The first recorded bat mitzvah ceremony in North America occurred only in 1922, when Rabbi Mordecai Kaplan oversaw such a ritual for his daughter, Judith. She received an *aliyah* and recited the requisite blessings over the Torah. This event is the "first bat mitzvah," however, only by virtue of her *aliyah* and recitation of the blessings. It was not the first Jewish public initiation ceremony of a girl, for (as we saw) that had already happened in nineteenth-century Germany, as well as in the United States, with the confirmation ceremony.

The practice of bat mitzvah did not gain widespread currency until later, and then primarily in the Conservative Movement (in 1948 roughly one-third of Conservative synagogues were having bat mitzvah ceremonies).[52] Because of the popular practice of confirmation in place of bar mitzvah among Reform Jews, a separate bat mitzvah for girls was moot and would catch on in Reform temples only when Reform Jews rediscovered bar mitzvah as well. Still, the first Reform bat mitzvah occurred already in 1931, in Chicago; and by 1953, 35 percent of Reform congregations practiced it.[53] Bat mitzvah has only recently been picked up by Orthodox Jews, albeit with modifications which do not involve a woman receiving an *aliyah,* leading the prayers, or reading from the scriptures in the company of men.[54]

As with confirmation, the justification for bat mitzvah has been that it raises the educational standards for girls, thereby benefiting the community at large. The increasing popularity of the bat mitzvah ceremony has led inevitably to individual and organizational considerations of the larger role of women in Jewish ritual. Once a girl's maturation to ethical responsibility is marked and linked to the Torah, the ramifications for her ritual role are obvious. Why can she not be called to the Torah with regularity; or read from it; or preach from it? Why can she not also wear the *tallit* and *tefillin*? Why can she not be counted among the ten adults (traditionally only men) necessary for a prayer quorum? For Reform and Conservative Jews these barriers have been completely broken down, in no small part because of the bat mitzvah ceremony. The ways of marking maturation for boys have been transposed onto girls—the transmission of Torah, which traditionally defined the life-line of the male Jew, now defines the life of the female Jew also.

Conclusion

In Jewish initiation ceremonies,[55] some common themes emerge: the importance of Torah education in the preparation for ritual induction into roles traditionally reserved for adults, and the extent to which education becomes the justification for innovations in the ceremony; the tendency to celebrate initiation on Shavuot and Simchat Torah, holidays which are Torah-centered and are themselves educative; the role which Jewish acculturation has played in the development of the initiation ceremonies; and the increasing involvement of girls in these ceremonies.

Torah emerges as the central theme in these rites of adolescence: children are initiated into the cult of Torah, preparation for Torah centers on the study of Torah, and the holidays on which initiation occurs are themselves Torah-centered. Girls' initiation likewise adopts this focus on the Torah.

Jewish education, which emphasizes ritual behaviors obligatory on adults, focuses on scripture; scripture teaches the ritual behaviors, and study of scripture itself is ritualized. Thus children are enticed into an educational culture, thereby guaranteeing their eventual adoption of its ritual behaviors.

In every rite reviewed here, education is either the stated purpose for the rite or the process through which the child undergoes whatever transformation that the rite offers. The purpose of the children's *aliyah* on Simchat Torah is to begin developing the child's appreciation for the Torah and a respect for the pageantry associated with its reading. The German ceremony of the Middle Ages is entirely an educational one, wherein first the child is taught the Hebrew alphabet and then texts employing that alphabet. The ceremonies of bar/bat mitzvah and confirmation occur after an established period of study, and are designed specifically so that the young adult can display the fruits of his or her education. Education, by virtue of the talk given by the boy, is the sixteenth-century justification for the celebratory meal of bar mitzvah. The Reformers championed educational integrity when justifying confirmation. Likewise the importance of education was invoked by those insisting upon the involvement of girls, whether in consecration and confirmation, or in bat mitzvah. Consistently then, a popular folk life-cycle ceremony marking adolescence and approaching adulthood has been linked with the communal value of education.[56]

Because Jewish religious education focuses on Torah as sacred scriptural text, the holidays on which initiation ceremonies are held tend to be those which celebrate that text. The bar and bat mitzvah celebrations are defined by the child's birthday so they, of course, resist the holiday framework. But we see the honeycakes rite and later confirmation rites celebrated on Shavuot and the joyful occasion of the children's *aliyah* happening on Simchat Torah. Of the two, Shavuot has special significance in these rites, because traditionally the holiday of Shavuot has been regarded as a particularly ripe time for Torah study. The mystics of the early rabbinic period believed that on each Shavuot there was the possibility of God's descending again, so that a reapprehension of God could be achieved through study, which paralleled Moses' ascent of Sinai. Medieval mystics inherited this belief.[57] The modern tendency has been to overlook ancient mystical traditions, and argue simply that ceremonies which focus on Torah education are rightly celebrated on the day which recalls when the Torah was given, and that is partly correct. No doubt too, a holiday which lacks any tangible ritual celebration takes on importance when linked with a communal celebration of the children, so that the practical consideration of raising the popularity of the holidays in question was also at work. But in theory at least, this ancient mystical understanding of the holiday is present in the medieval children's induction into Torah study on Shavuot and even in the modern selection of the holiday for confirmation and induction into Torah study.

The biblical Shavuot marked the end of the trek of the Israelites into freedom from Egyptian bondage, their journey into freedom via Sinai where they received voluntarily a new yoke, that of the laws of the Torah. The Torah-study induction ceremony of thirteenth-century Germany portrayed the child as making the same journey to the place of revelation that the ancient Israelites had made on the very same day. The choice of Shavuot for the confirmation ceremony of the nineteenth and twentieth centuries is a statement that these young adults also, in confirming their faith in Judaism, have made that journey.

The giving of Torah at Sinai resulted in numerous responsibilities for the Israelites in their maturation as a people, just as the coming-of-age rites result in new responsibilities for the adolescent. The responsibilities in both cases are the very same ones of the Torah. Up until this point it has been the responsibility of the father to see to it that the child behaves in accordance with the Torah; now the child takes on that responsibility.

Judaism's perceptions of childhood and maturity, as well as its celebration of maturation, have varied throughout the centuries, demonstrating that Jewish definitions of maturation are more culturally or socially determined than biologically or physically. We know little about the outside influence that accompanied the transition from twenty as the age of majority in the Bible to thirteen in rabbinic times. The Torah-study induction of the five-, six-, or seven-year-old in thirteenth-century Germany, however, corresponded to the age of monastic oblation. As the age for the latter increased to the early teens, the honeycakes rite seems to have died out, only to be replaced by increasing Jewish ceremony around the age of thirteen. Privileges heretofore granted the educated boy were correspondingly denied him until the ceremony of bar mitzvah, reflecting the general society's increasing appreciation for childhood as a status preceding and separate from adulthood. The confirmation rite was an obvious borrowing from Christianity. Like the bat mitzvah, it reflected general society's appreciation for girls and the fact that their secular education increasingly resembled that of boys.

But one thing does not change. In every case of Jewish acculturation, the focus remained Torah and the importance of children's education in Torah. Perhaps outside cultural influences have been absorbed, but they are interpreted through the ancient Jewish values.

Finally, we have seen how the markers of the male's life as defined by Torah have been imposed upon the female. While at present it seems that many Jewish women have embraced this life-line and defined their own lives accordingly, only time will tell whether Jewish women as a whole will continue to choose to define their lives according to this Torah life-line, and whether communities will continue to view women as living according to it.

NOTES

1. For my use of the word "rite," see Ronald Grimes, *Ritual Criticism* (Columbia, SC, 1990), esp. p. 9f. For objections to the use of such terminology, see Jacob Neusner, *The Enchantments of Judaism* (New York, 1987), pp. 139–45, where he emphasizes that the occasion of becoming bar or bat mitzvah is not a "rite." Stuart Schoenfeld, "Ritual and Role Transition: Adult Bat Mitzvah as a Successful Rite of Passage," in *The Uses of Tradition,* ed. Jack Wertheimer (New

York, 1992), p. 353 n. 13, discusses why becoming bar or bat mitzvah is more correctly a *ritual* of identification than initiation; he cites
the relevant literature. Cherie Koller-Fox, "Women and Jewish Education: A New Look At Bat Mitzvah," in *The Jewish Woman: New
Perspectives,* ed. Elizabeth Koltun (New York, 1976), argues (pp.
34–35) that bar mitzvah is an initiation *rite* with reference to the anthropological literature. I think that, depending upon the circumstances, rites of adolescence can be described as initiation without
resorting to Eliade's understanding of the concept. See Mircea Eliade, *Rites and Symbols of Initiation* (New York, 1975). Certainly
reaching the age of majority and being potentially an equal participant within the community can be described as a rebirth of sorts.

2. General historical overviews, complete with textual citations,
for bar and bat mitzvah as well as confirmation, can be found in
Hayyim Schauss, *The Lifetime of a Jew* (Cincinnati, 1950), pp.
112–21; in *Encyclopaedia Judaica,* vol. 4, s.v. "bar mitzvah." The best
historical studies of bar mitzvah remain Leopold Löw, *Die Lebens-
alter in der Jüdischen Literatur* (Szegendin, 1875), pp. 210–17; and
Isaac Rivkind, *Bar Mitzvah: A Study in Jewish Cultural History* [He-
brew] (New York, 1942).

3. By "cult" I mean a system of religious worship or ritual. No
negative judgments are intended, nor any allusions to sacrifice. Jewish religion is text–centered; the worship service and rites are derived
from the Torah and reflect back onto the Torah. As such it is a "cult of
Torah." And full access to this cult is reserved for adults, traditionally
male.

4. The Hebrew word *bat,* meaning daughter, is pronounced
"baht." The phrase means, literally, "daughter of the commandment";
it describes a female with full adult status as well as the rite which
celebrates this coming-of-age.

5. Arnold van Gennep, *The Rites of Passage,* trans. Monika B.
Vizedom and Gabrielle L. Caffee (Chicago, 1960), esp. pp. 10–11.

6. See Lawrence A. Hoffman, "How Ritual Means: Ritual Circumcision in Rabbinic Culture and Today," in *Studia Liturgica* 23,
no. 1 (1993), esp. p. 87, for this interpretation of the "life-line" of the
male Jew.

7. Avot 5:2. All translations are my own.

8. For a detailed history and description of the customs of Simchat
Torah, see Avraham Ya'ari, *Toldot Chag Simchat Torah* (Jerusalem,
1964), esp. pp. 160–65.

9. This verse, clearly used as an incantation meant to call protection upon the children who are gathered in one spot and therefore vulnerable, is sometimes recited after the blessing of the children on Friday evening, at the beginning of the Sabbath, along with the passage "May the Lord make you like Ephraim and Manasseh" (Gen. 48:20, for boys), or "May the Lord make you like Sarah, Rebecca, Rachel and Leah" (adapted from Ruth 4:11, for girls), followed immediately by "The Lord bless you and protect you. The Lord deal kindly and graciously with you. The Lord bestow his favor upon you and grant you peace" (Num. 6:24–26). This latter is known as the Priestly Blessing. See for example, J. D. Eisenstein, *Otsar Dinim Uminhagim* (Tel-Aviv, 1975), p. 56.

The recitation (or reading, in some rites) of Genesis 48:16 ("The angel . . .") is explained by numerous commentators after the sixteenth century as being required by the fact that all the children are gathered together in one place and hence vulnerable to the evil eye. But scholarly speculation links its appropriate use to the fact that the verse itself has the words "*kol ha-na'arim,*" all the children, by which this *aliyah* is known.

But I would also argue that since there is eighteenth century evidence of the Priestly Blessing also being said after this *aliyah,* perhaps it was the verse's popular association with the Priestly Blessing that lent its natural use in this context for magical reasons: perhaps the name of the *aliyah* came from the verse's language.

10. *Siddur Rashi,* ed. Solomon Buber and Jacob Freimann (Berlin, 1911), p. 148 n. 308.

11. Ya'ari, pp. 243–50.

12. The rite is described in two thirteenth-century German sources, *Sefer Haroke'ach,* a collection of laws and customs by Eleazer ben Judah of Worms (ca. 1160–1230), and *Sefer Ha'asufot,* an anonymous compilation of laws and customs, published in Simchah Assaf, *Mekorot Letoldot Hachinukh Beyisra'el* (Tel Aviv, 1925–1947), vol. 1, pp. 11–12. See Ivan G. Marcus, *Rituals of Childhood: Jewish Acculturation in Medieval Europe* (New Haven, 1996). The rite is also recorded in the eleventh-century French source, *Machzor Vitry,* but Marcus identifies that report as a later, probably thirteenth-century, addition to the text. The variants among the different records of the rite are analyzed by Shmuel Eliezer Stern, "Seder Chinukh Hayeladim Latorah . . . ", *Tzfunot* 1, no. 1 (1989): 15–21.

13. Marcus' study illustrates how this rite is an example of ritual-izing metaphor.

14. Ya'ari, pp. 248–49, cites sources which describe an Ashke-nazic practice of Simchat Torah whereby, e.g., a teacher will lead a parade of the children throughout the town, calling out to them, "*Tson kodashim!*" (i.e., sacrificial lambs; the term is one of affection and alludes to Ezekiel 36:38). Just as the sacrificial lambs were un-blemished and ritually pure, so too the children, as sacrifices to the Torah cult. The children would bleat in response.

15. Likening Jewish adult life for men to monastic commitment, Marcus (*Rituals of Childhood,* chap. 6) locates the postponement of the age of responsibility in the parallel preference for monastic obla-tion within the surrounding Christian community. As the age for in-duction of children into Christian monastaries was delayed to the early teens, so Jews postponed the age for induction into the Torah cult to thirteen. Both ceremonies of Torah study and child oblation occurred at school age; in both there is a religious authority, either the bishop or a teacher likened to Moses; both rites occurred on the Spring holiday of Pentecost (Shavuot in Judaism); both required the ingestion of symbolic foods in which a cake with special writing on it figures prominently; both reenacted historical events—the Last Sup-per of Christ and the receiving of the Torah.

16. The only mention of age thirteen in biblical literature is Gen-esis 17:25, Ishma'el's circumcision. But that age is circumstantial, for Abraham was also circumcised at the same time, and at the age of ninety-nine (v. 24). Moreover this episode follows the commandment to circumcise all boys at age eight (v. 12).

17. Solomon Schechter, "The Child in Jewish Literature," in *Studies in Judaism* 1 (Philadelphia, 1915), p. 307, attributes the change to "Roman influence . . . in juristic matters." Schauss, *Life-time of a Jew,* pp. 113 and 313, n. 124, observes that thirteen was a significant number in ancient cultures, including the Jews. In *Ency-clopedia of the Social Sciences,* he cites "age of majority." He there-fore surmises that the biblical age of twenty was a relatively modern change from the more primitive thirteen. Presumably, then, rabbinic attention to thirteen represents a reversion to a more ancient marker, although Schauss does not expressly say this.

18. Ket. 15a. Cf. Yoma 82a.

19. M. Nid. 5:6.

20. M. Nid. 6:11.

21. Maimonides, Mishneh Torah, Ishut, 2:10; see also, Nid. 46a, wherein the discussion reflects the appreciation of the grey area represented by the physical transition, and the continued adherence to the age of thirteen as the absolute marker of maturation. Isserles, S. A., O. H. 199:10 writes that a thirteen-year-old "is regarded as an adult who has grown two hairs."

22. See also Gen. Rab. 34:10; in Pesikta deRabbi Eliezer 26, Abraham is described as being thirteen when he rejects idolatry. In P. T. Ber. 6d, we read that a person's inclination and thoughts are evil from the very point that one enters the world.

23. Maimonides, Mishneh Torah, Laws of Testimony 9:8.

24. M. Nid. 5:6.

25. Sifre to Deuteronomy, #46.

26. Suk. 42a; cf. Tur/S. A., O. H. 37:3.

27. M. Meg. 4:5–6.

28. S. A., O. H. 282:3; cf. Mishneh Berurah, the nineteenth-century commentator, ad loc., who notes that "It is the custom today that we do not call up the minor at all for an *aliyah* . . . except for the Haftarah."

29. Cf. Ber. 47b and Tos. ad loc. d. h. *katan*; S. A., O. H. 55:4 and Isserles' comment to the contrary.

30. Yitzhak D. Gilat, *Studies in the Development of the Halakhah* [Hebrew] (Bar-Ilan, 1992), pp. 19–31, esp. pp. 28–29, argues that in the Mishnaic period all of the commandments of the Torah were regarded as incumbent upon all males, even young children, excepting those commandments which required a certain physical ability or physical and intellectual maturity. In those cases, people would become obligated only once they were able. This individual determination of obligation resulted in the same commandment becoming required at different times for different individuals. Gilat argues that it was the very nature of the legal system to prefer a more standardized set of rules. Hence the preference for the age thirteen began to develop in the Amoraic period.

31. B. M. 96a.

32. Gen. Rab. 63:10, commenting on Genesis 25:25.

33. O. H., Hilkhot Berakhot 58.

34. Magen Avraham to S. A., O. H. 225:2.

35. Gumbiner (Magen Avraham) cites an alternative explanation considered by Mordecai Jaffe (c. 1535–1612), "But the *Levush* [=Jaffe] explains the opposite: that up until now the son is punished

for the sin of the father." The Hebrew, literally, "who has exempted me from the punishment of this one," is ambiguous. The *Levush* understands the boy to be reciting the blessing with reference to the father. This understanding also reflects the responsibility of the father to educate the child—any punishments suffered by the child are ultimately a result of the father's shortcomings. Until adulthood, the child suffers for the sins (irresponsibilities) of his father. But now as an independent adult, the child can begin to take responsibility for himself. This interpretation of the blessing is not generally held to be correct; see Isaac Nissim, *Yayn Hatov* (Jerusalem, 1979), no. 6, p. 241.

36. S. A., O. H. 225:2.

37. See, e.g., Nissim, p. 239.

38. O. H. 225:2.

39. Yam shel Shlomo, B. K. 7:37.

40. See Joel Roth, "May a Minor Read from the Torah?", *Proceedings of the Committee on Jewish Law and Standards of the Conservative Movement,* 1980–1985 (New York: Rabbinical Assembly, 1988), pp. 45–50, wherein all of the relevant halakhic literature is discussed.

41. This correspondence between the loss of certain privileges by the minor and the growing popularity of the ceremony of bar mitzvah is first noted by Schauss, pp. 114–16. Marcus (chap. 6) enlarges on this and ties it to his observation that it is at this time as well that the surrounding culture developed a prolonged perception of childhood. Jews now denied minors certain privileges no longer deemed appropriate for their status, and focused on the age of majority as the appropriate time for induction into Torah.

Birkat Habanim, the Blessing of the Children, is the practice whereby parents bless children immediately following the evening prayers on Shabbat (Friday night), either while still at the synagogue or after returning home therefrom. I know of no literary evidence for this ceremony until the seventeenth century. This would seem to further shore up Marcus' theory of an increasing appreciation for childhood and might be evidence of a ceremony which developed to underscore this appreciation.

42. Information on the ceremony of confirmation can be found in *Jewish Encyclopedia,* vol. 4, pp. 219–20. See also the myriad sources cited by Michael A. Meyer, *Response to Modernity* (New York, 1988), s.v. "confirmation," "bar mitzvah," "bat mitzvah"; Meyer dis-

cusses confirmation as a phenomenon of religious reform, first in Europe and later in North America.

43. Mordecai Eliav, *Jewish Education in Germany in the period of Enlightenment and Emancipation* [Hebrew] (Jerusalem, 1960), p. 268.

44. Solomon Freehof, *Reform Responsa for Our Time* (Cincinnati: Hebrew Union College, 1977), pp. 23–24.

45. Ket. 50a and Yoma 82a.

46. Nid. 6:11.

47. Nid. 5:6.

48. Sifre to Deuteronomy, #46.

49. The eighteenth-century commentary Peri Megadim (Eshel Avraham, O. H. 225:5) says that while a father is obligated to teach his daughter the commandments, he does not recite the blessing for her because she has fewer commandments to observe.

50. There is no comprehensive historical treatment of bat mitzvah, but see Paula Hyman's "The Introduction of Bat Mitzvah in Conservative Judaism in Postwar America," *YIVO Annual* 19 (1990), pp. 133–46, an excellent introduction to its history, the corollary issues, and available literature. See also the application of the classical anthropological approach to the contemporary phenomenon of adult bat mitzvah in Schoenfeld, pp. 349–76.

51. For a description of a consecration service, see Deborah Dash Moore, "A Synagogue Center Grows in Brooklyn," in *The American Synagogue,* ed. Jack Wertheimer (New York, 1987), pp. 313–14. She also points out the value of education which this ceremony's supporters stressed.

52. Hyman, "Introduction of Bat Mitzvah in Conservative Judasim," p. 135.

53. Meyer, *Response to Modernity,* p. 472, n. 73.

54. Evidence of its inroads into the Orthodox community is to be found in the Rabbinic dicta which rail against it: Moses Feinstein, a leading Orthodox authority in the United States, identifies the bat mitzvah celebration as a custom of the Conservative and Reform Jews. He opposes it in synagogues and allows that, if it must take place, one's home is the better location (*Igrot Moshe,* O. H. vol. 1, #104). Another Rabbinic authority, Moses Stern, forbids attending this ceremony. He argues that the father has different educational responsibilities toward a daughter because the blessing was not ordained for a girl (*She'elot Uteshuvot Be'er Moshe* 1:10). On the other

hand, Obadiah Joseph, a former Chief Rabbi of Israel, approves of
bat mitzvah and suggests that the girl's father say the same blessing
as he would for a son; the meal is to be regarded as a legitimate religious meal, assuming words of Torah are taught (*Yekhabed Da'at*
vol. 2, #29). Isaac Nissim, also a former Chief Rabbi, permits the ceremony and the recitation of the blessing, albeit without the mention
of God's name (p. 241). These last two examples indicate not only
the inroads but the growing acceptance within the Orthodox world of
the bat mitzvah ceremony.

55. I believe that *Birkat Habanim* represents a perpetual initiation
of one's children into the people Israel.

56. See Stuart Schoenfeld, "Folk Judaism, Elite Judaism and the
Role of Bar Mitzvah in the Development of the Synagogue and Jewish School in America," *Contemporary Jewry* 9, no. 1 (fall–winter
1987–88), pp. 67–85, for an analysis of how educational standards
have been tied to this folk ceremony in the United States.

57. See Yehuda Liebes, *Studies in the Zohar*, trans. Arnold
Schwartz, et al. (Albany, 1993), pp. 160–61. Liebes points out that
Pentecost "was already of an indubitable mystical character in the
New Testament (Acts 2), since the Holy Spirit came down to Jesus's
disciples on this occasion (although it is certain that it was the mystical nature of the Jewish holiday that was continued in the New Testament interpretation)." Marcus (chap. 3) also treats the mystical
understanding of Shavuot and the importance of study on that day.

Christian Marriage Rituals

PAUL F. BRADSHAW

Of all Christian liturgical rites, marriage ceremonies[1] are perhaps the ones that evidence the greatest diversity, not only between different ecclesiastical traditions but also between different geographical regions. The primary reason for this variety is that the ritual of marriage was neither invented by the church nor intended primarily to embody uniquely Christian values. It belonged rather to the local culture in which the church found itself. It was only with some reluctance that the ecclesiastical authorities became involved in the process at all, and that involvement was chiefly in order to prevent abuses and to bring some order to often chaotic and corrupt situations. There was no intention to devise a peculiarly Christian rite to give expression to a distinctive Christian doctrine of marriage, and hence the church was always willing to permit the continuation of whatever customs and ceremonies were traditional in any particular local culture, provided that they were not in direct conflict with any fundamental Christian beliefs.

Indeed, it appears that ecclesiastical authorities have generally been powerless to prevent traditional pagan customs from continuing, even when they have protested against them or tried to ban them, since Christians seem to be more strongly motivated by a deeply conservative tendency in the area of wedding practice than in any other aspect of life-cycle ritual. What is striking, therefore, amid all the variation of practice that can be observed in Christian history, is the tenacious endurance within particular traditions of many customs and ceremonies throughout long centuries and often down to the present day, even

111

though almost everything else in the culture around has changed. It seems that brides, their mothers, or other women in the community, who have generally been the ones most responsible for the detailed arrangement of weddings, have usually been desirous to do things in the same way that their own mothers did them.

It also needs to be noted that the ecclesiastical rite, when it did evolve, was not the sole element in the wedding ritual of Christian cultures. It was only one part of a sequence of ceremonies, and was not always viewed as the constitutive or paramount element. In some places, for example, the public wedding procession, derived from pagan practice and symbolizing the social as well as physical transfer of the bride from one household to another, was regarded as far more important.[2] What the church had to offer was principally a blessing of the marriage. Thus the church ceremony was often no more than a confirmation and seal of approval of a union already legally contracted and physically consummated. Indeed, in late medieval Germany, for example, it was common to seek the solemn blessing only on the day after the wedding.[3]

Origins

Although evidence for the practices of the earliest Christians is very limited, it appears that they continued to participate in the marriage rites of the cultures from which they came. The first sign that we have of any ecclesiastical involvement in the marriage of church members comes from Ignatius of Antioch early in the second century, who observes that "it is right for men and women who marry to contract their union with the advice of their bishop, so that their marriage is made in the Lord, and not for the sake of passion."[4] Although this *may* mean that the bishop was to conduct the marriage ceremony himself, it is more likely that all that was intended was that the couple were to consult the bishop and obtain his approval before proceeding to the customary rites of the local culture. The reasons for this pastoral involvement were very likely a strong concern felt by Christians about attitudes towards marriage in the contemporary culture, and a desire to maintain Christian standards. From the observations about marriage made by St. Paul in the New Testament, it is clear that the decision whether or not to marry at all was understood to be a matter of God's calling and not just of personal desire; there was also a strong aversion to marriages between Christians and non-Christians, as well as a disinclination towards second marriages following the death of one partner (see 1 Cor. 7). Other early Christian writers tend to follow St. Paul's views, and also reveal that the Christian understanding of the primary purpose of marriage was that it was for the procreation of children,[5] an idea apparently derived from Stoicism.

The earliest evidence for a specifically Christian liturgy of marriage is found in the writings of Tertullian in North Africa at the end of the second century. He condemns clandestine marriages, which were common in pagan antiquity, and urges that the wedding ceremony should take place in church in the presence of Christian ministers.[6] The basic procedure described is that of contemporary Roman (and Jewish) culture,[7] and is in two parts: first a betrothal, and at a later date the wedding ceremony itself. The betrothal ceremony included a kiss between the couple, the joining of their hands, and the giving of a ring and possibly other gifts to the bride—all these customs apparently derived from contemporary pagan practice. However, Tertullian does not happily accept all pagan traditions: he rejects the wearing of floral garlands by the bride, but in its place strongly supports another custom also derived from paganism—her wearing of a veil from the time of the betrothal until the marriage itself. He regarded the former as a sign of wantonness, but the latter as a symbol of modesty. The marriage ceremony seems to have included a blessing of the couple, and probably also the celebration of the eucharist in place of the animal sacrifice which usually formed a part of the pagan religious rite.[8]

Fourth-century authors provide further details, although it is hard to decide whether these are simply traditional customs not

mentioned by earlier writers, or are instead new additions to
the rites made in the changed environment of the Constantinian
age, when Christians were no longer a small, often persecuted
sect, but now part of the mainstream of society. Sources from
the eastern Mediterranean area speak of the crowning of bride
and groom by close members of the family at the marriage ceremony.[9] This crowning seems to have been done at first with
garlands—the pagan practice earlier criticized by Tertullian—
but later with crowns of precious metal. The practice was defended by the great fourth-century theologian and bishop John
Chrysostom on the grounds that the crown symbolized victory
over concupiscence.[10] It must have been regarded as a very important feature of the occasion, since later eastern rites use the
term "crowning" (*stephanoma*) as the designation of the wedding ceremony as a whole.

Great stress is also laid in the early eastern sources on the
nuptial blessing pronounced by the bishop or priest at the marriage ceremony, which is seen as being the means by which the
"yoke" of the marriage is effected.[11] There is also mention of a
"pledge" given before the marriage, which seems to be a ring
placed on the bride's finger,[12] and of the bridal bed, decorated
with flowers, around which prayers were apparently said[13]—a
Christian adaptation of a common pagan fertility rite which
will remain a persistent feature of later eastern and western
marriage ceremonies. But there are also some signs of disquiet
at the Christian adoption of certain pagan marriage customs.
Chrysostom, for example, criticizes excesses of dress and
feasting, and insists that the bride's real adornment should be
her virtues.[14]

Early sources from the western Mediterranean area reveal
both points of conformity and points of difference from the
eastern picture. On the one hand, there is a similar emphasis on
the important part played by the nuptial blessing in the marriage rite; on the other hand, the crowning of the couple appears to be unknown, and in its place there is reference to the
veiling of the bride.

Later Eastern Practice

The oldest extant text of an eastern Christian marriage ritual, the eighth-century Byzantine rite, reveals that the two-stage process of betrothal and marriage was retained from earlier times. For the betrothal, the document merely contains two prayers of blessing for the couple. The absence of any other formularies or rubrics suggests that the priest was not yet involved in supervising or directing the expression of consent itself and other betrothal ceremonies, but that his role was limited to offering a benediction at an otherwise "secular" event. For the actual marriage rite, there are further prayers: first, a litany with three special petitions for the couple; then, a prayer of blessing, after which they are crowned and their hands are joined; and finally, two more prayers of blessing.

From the tenth century onwards the two stages of the rite were usually celebrated on the same day and often in a single ceremony, and they become more elaborate—or at least the directions in the text become more detailed: some of what the texts prescribe may in fact be customs that had long been traditional, but were only gradually coming under ecclesiastical control. First, more prayers were added, and a direction about the giving of a ring was included in the betrothal. Then, from the eleventh century onwards, two rings (gold for the bride, silver for the groom) became usual. In the twelfth century the couple began to be asked to express their willingness to marry one another at the very beginning of the rite. Finally, in the fifteenth century, there emerged the custom of the priest leading the couple by the hand in a circular walk, which is said to symbolize the eternity of the love in which they now share; and a ceremonial removal of the crowns was added to the rite: previously they would have been removed in the bedchamber and hung over the bed.[15]

In spite of these developments, however, the central emphasis of the whole ritual still remained on the prayers of blessing for the couple, which expressed a very positive attitude towards

marriage as created by God and a very clear articulation of the
mutuality of the marriage-act, something which was also brought
out by the crowning of both bride and groom and the exchange of
rings between them. As we shall see later, western Christian attitudes towards the nature of marriage were often significantly different from this.

The Orthodox Church allows second or third (but not
fourth) marriages, whether after divorce or the death of one
partner, but in both cases a special rite is used which contains
penitential prayers, since it is seen as a departure from the
ideal of one marriage unbroken even in death.

The Medieval West

It is important to recognize that there was a marked contrast
between the rites originating from the Christian church at
Rome and those from other parts of western Christendom, both
in their ceremonial details and in their understanding of the
character of marriage.

The earliest Roman liturgical texts provide readings,
psalms, and prayers for use at a celebration of the eucharist in
connection with a marriage, and include a special blessing before the newly married couple receive communion.[16] The material reveals a tendency to focus on blessing the woman alone
rather than both bride and groom, which suggests that marriage was thought of as being concerned primarily with the
change in state of the woman—her transfer from her own family to that of her husband, an idea that entered Christianity
from pagan Roman tradition. Hence, the notion still often
found today in popular culture, that the wedding is "the bride's
day," obviously has its roots in ancient times.

Equally interesting is the choice of readings, which tend
to convey a much less positive and joyful note than those of
the East. Ephesians 5:22–33, with its image of Christ as the
model for the bridegroom, is almost universally used in eastern
rites, but is entirely absent from early western usage. Instead,

1 Corinthians 6:15–20, with its warning to avoid fornication, is frequently found there. Similarly, John 2:1–11, which contains the account of Jesus' presence and first miracle at a wedding in Cana, is not as commonly used in the West as it is in the East, and its place tends to be taken by Matthew 19:1–6, which begins with a question to Jesus about the possibility of divorce and speaks of the couple becoming one flesh.

Other Roman sources indicate that the traditional custom of a betrothal ceremony some time before the wedding continued to be practiced, though at first apparently in a domestic rather than an ecclesiastical setting. It involved an expression of consent, sealed by the giving to the bride of a ring and other gifts as tokens or pledges. It also appears that the bride wore a veil, but it is not clear whether this was put on at the betrothal, at the wedding, or at some other time. It was generally interpreted as a symbol of modesty.

The non-Roman western traditions, on the other hand, are significantly different. The early texts frequently make no mention of nuptial mass at all, but the whole ceremony appears to take place in a domestic setting and generally includes a blessing of the bedchamber and/or marriage bed, and often also of the ring—apparently here a *wedding* ring rather than an engagement ring.[17] These rites also contain a greater element of mutuality than their Roman counterparts. They tend to extend the nuptial blessing to the couple rather than restrict it to the bride alone, and later sources include the spreading of a veil (or pall, as it was known) both over the head of the bride and at least over the shoulders—if not always the head—of the groom during this blessing. Moreover, in Spain there is an exchange of rings between the couple, as in the East, rather than just the giving of a ring to the bride practiced elsewhere in the West. It is also in the Spanish tradition that we first encounter directions for the ceremony of the "giving away" of the bride—her being handed over to the priest by her family— followed by the priest himself joining the couple together by handing the bride over to the groom. This usually takes place towards the end of the wedding rite.[18]

Later, as the Roman church achieved a position of dominance over the other churches of the West, what emerged in liturgical practice was a fusion of Roman material with whatever had been the earlier local tradition. As a result, the rites tend to become more elaborate in nature. Thus they now include prayers and blessings for the bride alone as well as for the couple, and as reasons for marriage they stress such things as a remedy for human frailty and the means for avoiding fornication. As in the East, the liturgical material for both betrothal and marriage eventually became united in a single service on one day (although the act of betrothal itself continued to have a separate existence in a non-liturgical legal form down to recent times, and is of course the precursor of the less formal modern "engagement").

In the rites of northern Europe from the twelfth century onwards, all the ceremonial acts associated with both parts, betrothal and marriage, were usually grouped together at the beginning of the service, before the celebration of the eucharist, which included special prayers and blessings. This first part of the service often took place at the church door rather than inside the building—a sign of its secular origin—and its order tended to be: the expression of consent to marry by groom and bride; the giving away of the bride by her father to the priest, who handed her over to the groom; the joining of hands by the bride and groom; and the giving of the ring and other tokens (generally gold and silver) to the bride by the groom, followed by prayers. The blessing of the ring might take place either at the very beginning or in connection with its giving.[19]

Although most of the service was in Latin, the expression of consent was generally in the vernacular, and its form varied greatly from one region to another, with the gradual emergence in England and other places of some positive form of marriage vow said by the couple themselves in addition to their response to an interrogative formula of consent. These vows usually accompanied the joining of hands, and the bride's version of both the consent-question and the vow often (but not always) began to include some expression of wifely obedience. Thus, for example, the form used in the diocese of Salisbury in southern England (the Sarum rite) in the fourteenth century was as follows:

> N., wilt thou have this man to thy husband, and to be buxom to him, love him, obey to him, and worship him, serve him and keep him in sickness and in health, and in all other degrees be unto him as a wife should be to her husband, and all other to forsake for him, and hold thee only to him to thy life's end?

> I, N., take thee, N. to my wedded husband, to have and to hold (from this day forward), for better for worse, for richer for poorer, in sickness and in health, to be bonny and buxom,[20] in bed and at board, till death us depart (if holy Church will it ordain) and thereto I plight thee my troth.[21]

There was a similar regional variation in the vernacular formula said by the groom at the giving of the ring, but it frequently involved an elaboration in the placing of the ring on the bride's finger, the ring being placed first on the thumb of the left hand, then on the next finger, on the third, and finally on the fourth, where it was left. It was popularly believed that a vein from this finger went directly to the heart: both this idea and the choice of this particular finger for the ring seemingly went back to classical Roman times.

In order that clandestine marriages might be prevented and possible impediments to marriage (such as consanguinity) could be revealed and investigated, the Fourth Lateran Council in 1215 required that "banns of marriage" (announcement of the names of those intending to marry) should be read aloud on three Sundays before the wedding.[22] Licenses in lieu of banns could be obtained from a bishop. Thereafter, a final calling of the banns (in the vernacular) tended also to be incorporated into the beginning of the service itself.

Other features of medieval rites reveal the Christian ambivalence towards human sexuality. While second marriages for those whose original partners had died were always permitted within the Christian tradition, they were strongly discouraged because they were thought to display a lack of the virtue of continence. As a result, the use of the veil and the nuptial blessing were generally forbidden to widows who were marrying again, or, as a concession in less rigorous dioceses, an alternative form of the latter was prescribed; and a widow would usually keep her hands covered by gloves throughout the wedding ceremony. Similarly, some authorities expected couples at their first marriage to abstain from sexual intercourse on the night after receiving the nuptial blessing "out of respect for the blessing itself,"[23] and a custom of abstaining for three nights after the wedding (termed "the nights of Tobias": see Tobit 8:5), although never enforced, was well known throughout Europe.[24] Other authorities did not permit couples to attend church for a certain period after the marriage was consummated and/or provided a rite for the ritual purification of the bride (but not the groom!) when they did return.[25]

In spite of all this, however, it needs to be noted that throughout the Middle Ages very many couples did not contract their marriages in church at all, but continued the ancient custom of exchanging vows privately. Since this practice allowed clandestine and corrupt marriages to take place, it was vigorously opposed by the ecclesiastical authorities; but at the same time, provided that the words spoken included an expression of consent in the present tense, such unions were still accepted as being equally valid and equally binding as those contracted in a church ceremony. It was not until the sixteenth century that a real attempt was made to solve the problem, when the Council of Trent in 1563 declared that only marriages contracted in the presence of a priest and two or three witnesses would thereafter be deemed valid in the eyes of the Roman Catholic Church. The Council also required the inclusion within the rite of the formula "I join you together in matrimony" (or some local equivalent), said by the priest. This had already been the practice in some local rites, but the insistence on its universal usage reinforced the impression that it was the ministry of the priest which effected the marriage, rather than the mutual consent of the couple, as had been traditionally held in western Christianity. This notion was further strengthened in later centuries when priests began to wrap their stoles around the couple's joined hands as they recited the formula. A remnant of the "nights of Tobias" can also be seen in the Council's exhortation that couples should confess their sins and receive holy communion three days before the wedding, or at least three days before they consummated their marriage.[26]

The Reformation

Marriage had been defined as being one of the sacraments of the church since the twelfth century. However, the sixteenth-century Protestant Reformers rejected its sacramental nature on the grounds that it was not a rite instituted by Christ (as were baptism and the eucharist), but instead a state of life ordained by God in creation. For that reason, they were not in principle opposed to marriages being regulated by civil rather than ecclesiastical authorities. At the same time, they recognized the value of involving the church in the process, and thereby communicating something about Christian expectations of marital conduct to those who sought a divine blessing on their union.

Not surprisingly, the marriage rite drawn up by Martin Luther was simple and straightforward. At the church door the minister put a brief question to the couple asking whether they consented to marry. They then gave each other a ring, without any blessing or other formula, and the minister joined their right hands, saying words from Matthew 19:6, "What God has joined together, let not man put asunder"—a formula which had already been used in this way in some European marriage rites from the end of the fifteenth century onwards. The minister then recited a formula declaring them to be married, and the whole party processed into the church to the altar, where a selection of biblical passages was read, beginning with Genesis 2:18, 21–24, the account of the creation of woman. After this, the minister spread out his hands over the couple for a final prayer of blessing. There was no celebration of the eucharist: in this respect, as in some other features of the rite, Luther was simply adopting customs already current in sixteenth-century Germany.[27] Later Lutheran rites tended to follow this same pattern, merely adding further prayers to the service and an address to be read at the beginning.

John Calvin directed that weddings were to take place before the sermon during the regular public worship of the church, but not on days when the eucharist was to be celebrated. His order of service, which became the model for many later Protestant rites, began with the reading of a substantial address explaining the origin and purpose of marriage, and after this the minister asked if there was any impediment to the union. He then said a prayer for the couple, and put to each of them a lengthy question asking whether they consented to be married and would pledge themselves to one another. He then said another prayer for the gift of the Holy Spirit to the couple, read Matthew 19:3–6, and declared that God had joined them together. A long prayer and a short blessing concluded the rite.[28] In accordance with Calvin's regular policy of eliminating all liturgical ceremonies that could be interpreted by people in a superstitious manner, there was no joining of hands or exchange of rings, although these customs were restored by most Protestants in later centuries.[29]

By contrast, the marriage rite of the Church of England retained many of the features of its medieval predecessor, including the celebration of a nuptial eucharist, although this element largely fell into disuse in later centuries.[30] Just as they had in the Middle Ages, clandestine marriages continued to flourish in European countries dominated by the Reformation churches, and were generally recognized as valid by civil law. In an effort to eliminate them in England, the canon law of 1604 required weddings to take place only between the hours of 8 a.m. and noon, and in a church located in the parish of residence of one of the partners. This restriction not only tried to abolish weddings performed at night, in secular establishments, and in locations far away from a place where the couple was known, but it also sought to reduce the likelihood that the participants would be intoxicated at the ceremony, a common problem of the period. Unfortunately, the willingness of ecclesiastical authorities to issue licenses to marry in place of banns in return for a fee, and without asking too many questions, and the willingness of some clergy to ignore the law, rendered this reform largely ineffectual; and it was not until 1753 that a Marriage Act was passed to enforce church rules by civil law. Couples thereafter frequently crossed into Scotland to circumvent it; and Gretna Green, just over the Scottish border, became the regular site for hasty, secret, but legal marriages. The 1753 Act was superseded by another in 1837, which legitimized civil marriages before a state Registrar and so put an end to the requirement of the earlier Act that all citizens except Quakers, Jews, and members of the Royal family must be married in an Anglican church.[31]

The rites and customs of the Reformation churches were brought to the United States by early settlers, and survived with little modification. However, there was one major difference in the American situation compared to that in European countries: families now often lived at very great distances from churches, and so it was permitted for marriages to be celebrated in domestic settings and not just in ecclesiastical buildings. This practice has continued to be a distinctive feature of many American weddings down to the present day.[32]

Recent Developments

Although marriage customs remain very conservative, and hence Christian marriage rites tend to retain a large number of traditional formularies and ceremonies, yet there have been a number of relatively small but significant changes within most Christian denominations in the western traditions in recent years. Churches have both responded to changing attitudes in society and also succeeded in viewing the Christian doctrine of marriage through something other than the rather pessimistic lenses originally supplied by the medieval Roman rites.[33] Many have not only adopted a more contemporary linguistic style for their texts, but have tried to introduce a more optimistic tone. The gloomy vision of marriage primarily as "a remedy against fornication," for example, has generally given way to a stronger expression of its nature as a gift of God for the mutual joy and companionship of the couple. Some rites have reduced the prominence given to the proceation of children in many earlier texts, and some have even introduced a discreet reference to the positive character of human sexuality. The 1980 *Alternative Service Book* of the Church of England, for example, speaks of marriage being given by God so that "with delight and tenderness they may know each other in love, and, through the joy of their bodily union, may strengthen the union of their hearts and lives."

One of the principal areas of attention in the process of revision has been the status of women implied by the ritual, and so most modern rites try to stress the equality of the partners both in the language of the prayers and other texts and in the ceremonial actions (although not always with complete success).[34] They have usually eliminated the bride's promise to obey her husband, which had been retained from medieval times in almost every western ecclesiastical tradition, and now make the words said by both bride and groom identical in form. Moreover, many make provision for an exchange of rings between the couple rather than just the giving of a ring to the bride, and some allow the couple to enter the church together, if they wish, rather than the bride alone being escorted into church by her father or other relative and "given away" to the groom.[35]

Another feature that can be observed in several traditions is provision for some active involvement in the liturgy by the wedding guests. This is often in the form of a response to a question put to the immediate families of the couple and/or to the congregation in general, as to whether they will uphold the couple in their marriage.

In line with the flexibility and potential for adaptation that is characteristic of liturgical revision in general in most Christian traditions today, many rites allow the bride and groom to select what they consider to be appropriate passages of scripture and prayers for their wedding from a wide range of alternatives. A few have gone further still and permitted the inclusion of non-traditional ceremonies, or allowed the couple to write their own prayers or even the vows themselves—a trend begun in the era of "do it yourself" liturgy in the 1960s. However, there have been signs in recent years of a movement away from such highly individualistic creations, and towards a recovered appreciation of the value of shared symbols and rituals which express the character of marriage as a social institution persisting through time and space.

In spite of the emergence of common trends in the marriage liturgy of different Christian churches, a number of important points of contention still remain. A problem arises for some when one of the marriage partners has previously been divorced. While many denominations are now willing to sanction a wedding in church in such a situation, albeit subject to certain conditions and restrictions in some instances, others—in particular the Roman Catholic Church and some Anglican provinces—will not do so, on the grounds that marriage is intended to be permanent or, according to Roman Catholic theology, is by nature indissoluble. However, Anglicans will usually be prepared to offer the compromise of a simple "service of blessing" after a civil marriage ceremony in such cases, and Roman Catholics will allow the wedding to take place in church if an annulment of the first marriage can be obtained from the ecclesiastical authorities.

Problems also arise when one partner is a Christian and the other is not. Can a Christian wedding ceremony be held in such a case? And what should be done if the other partner professes another religious faith? Can there be a wedding ceremony which includes elements of both traditions, or would that be regarded as a denial of the claims of Christianity to be the uniquely perfect revelation of God? Over these issues,

different churches have taken different positions; and Roman
Catholics also face a similar dilemma when one of the partners, though a Christian, does not belong to the Catholic
Church, since they understand the sacraments to be for the
members of that church alone. In light of the theological difficulties encountered in this respect, therefore, it is scarcely
surprising that virtually no Christian group has yet wanted to
face the question of whether a single-sex union may legiti-
mately be blessed, let alone to provide a liturgical rite for that
purpose.

NOTES

1. I am indebted for much of the information contained in this
chapter to Kenneth Stevenson, *Nuptial Blessing* (London/New York,
1982), which those interested in the history of Christian marriage
rites are encouraged to consult. Texts of various marriage rites (in
English) are reproduced in Mark Searle and Kenneth Stevenson,
Documents of the Marriage Liturgy (Collegeville, MN, 1992), hereafter cited simply as *DML*.
2. See further Nicole Belmont, "The Symbolic Function of the
Wedding Procession in the Popular Rituals of Marriage," in Robert
Forster and Orest Ranum, eds., *Ritual, Religion, and the Sacred* (Baltimore, 1982), pp. 1–7.
3. See Hanns Bächtold-Stäubli, ed., *Handwörterbuch des deut-
schen Aberglaubens* 4 (Berlin, 1932), pp. 155–65.
4. Ignatius, *Ad Polycarpum* 5.2 (SC 10:150).
5. See, for example, Athenagoras, *Legatio* 33 (PG 6:966);
Clement of Alexandria, *Stromata* 2.23 (PG 8:1085).
6. Tertullian, *De pudicitia* 4.4 (CCSL 2:1287); *De monogamia* 11
(CCSL 2:1245–47); *Ad uxorem* 2.8 (CCSL 1: 392–94).
7. For a description of Roman weddings in the classical period,
see Mary Johnston, *Roman Life* (Chicago, 1957), pp. 126–39; and for
the later period, Brent D. Shaw, "The Family in Late Antiquity: The
Experience of Augustine," *Past and Present* 115 (1987): 33–36. For
weddings in ancient Greece, see Robert Garland, *The Greek Way of
Life* (Ithaca, NY, 1990), pp. 217–25.

8. Tertullian, *De corona* 13.14–14.2 (CCSL 2:1062–64); *De virginibus velandis* 8.3; 11.3 (CCSL 2:1218, 1220–21).

9. Evagrius Scholasticus, *Historiae ecclesiasticae* 6.1 (PG 86:2844–45); Gregory of Nazianzus, *Oratio* 40.18 (PG 36:381–84); *Epistola* 231 (PG 37:373); Gregory of Nyssa, *De oratione* 1 (PG 44:1119–36).

10. Chrysostom, *Homiliae in 1 Timotheum* 9 (PG 62:543–48).

11. See Basil, *Hexaemeron* 7.5 (PG 29:157–60); Gregory of Nazianzus, *Epistola* 230 (PG 37:372–73).

12. See Chrysostom, *Homiliae de Capto Eutropio et de divitiarum vanitate* 13 (PG 52:408).

13. Gregory of Nazianzus, *Epistola* 231 (PG 37:373).

14. Chrysostom, *Homiliae in Colossenses* 12.4 (PG 62:385–87); *Homiliae in Ephesios* 5.20 (PG 62:135–50).

15. Text of the rite in *DML,* pp. 55–78. See also John Meyendorff, *Marriage: An Orthodox Perspective* (Crestwood, NY, 1975).

16. *DML,* pp. 40–54.

17. See *DML,* pp. 100–106, 113–16.

18. See *DML,* pp. 120–47.

19. See *DML,* pp. 107–12, 148–62.

20. A very late manuscript comments that this phrase means "meek and obedient," a sign that it had by then become an archaism.

21. *DML,* pp. 165–66 (spelling modernized).

22. See James B. Roberts, *The Banns of Marriage: An Historical Synopsis and Commentary* (Washington, DC, 1931).

23. First attested in the fifth-century *Statuta ecclesiae antiqua* from Gaul. See further Pierre J. Payer, "Early Medieval Regulations Concerning Marital Sexual Relations," *Journal of Medieval History* 6 (1980): 364–65.

24. See P. Saintyves, "Les trois nuits de Tobie ou la continence durant les premières nuits du mariage," *Revue Anthropologique* 44 (1934): 266–96. Caesarius of Arles in the sixth century attempted to overcome the obvious problems which this expectation presented by giving the blessing three days before the wedding itself! See H. G. J. Beck, *The Pastoral Care of Souls in South-East France During the Sixth Century* (Rome, 1950), pp. 232–33.

25. See Stevenson, *Nuptial Blessing,* pp. 89–91, for examples of such rites "introducing" or "enthroning" the bride from fifteenth- and sixteenth-century Germany.

26. For the text of the post-Tridentine Roman Catholic marriage rite, see *DML,* pp. 179–88.

27. See *DML,* pp. 210–14; and also Bryan Spinks, "Luther's Other Major Liturgical Reforms: 3. The *Traubuchlein," Liturgical Review* 10 (1980): 33–38.

28. See Bryan Spinks, "The Liturgical Origins and Theology of Calvin's Genevan Marriage Rite," *Ecclesia Orans* 3 (1986): 195–210; and for the version drawn up by John Knox for use by Scots Presbyterians, see *DML,* pp. 227–33.

29. Superstitions concerning the ring certainly abounded in popular culture. In sixteenth-century England, for example, it was thought to be endowed with magical and curative power, and women would carefully avoid ever removing the ring or even washing the ring finger: see John R. Gillis, *For Better, For Worse: British Marriages, 1600 to the Present* (New York, 1985), p. 62.

30. Text of the 1559 version in *DML,* pp. 215–26.

31. See Gillis, *For Better, For Worse,* pp. 90–98, 140–42, 195–96.

32. For the early history of marriage legislation in the United States, see G. E. Howard, *A History of Matrimonial Institutions* (Chicago, 1904), 2:121ff.

33. There is no single collection of texts of modern marriage rites available, nor a comprehensive study of them, but for a study of the 1969 Roman Catholic rite, see Kenneth Stevenson, *To Join Together: The Rite of Marriage* (New York, 1987), pp. 127ff.; for the text of an ecumenical marriage rite drawn up in 1985 by the Consultation on Common Texts, see *DML,* pp. 239–51.

34. For some infelicitous examples from the revised Roman Catholic rite, see Stevenson, *To Join Together,* pp. 138, 146.

35. See further below, pp. 241–42.

The Jewish Wedding Ceremony

LAWRENCE A. HOFFMAN

Early Ritual and Terms

The classical rabbinic ceremony of marriage, followed more or less to this day by all branches of Judaism, consists of two discrete parts: *erusin* (known also as *kiddushin*) and *nissuin* (called also *chuppah*). While generally translated as "betrothal" and "marriage" proper, the two stages of marriage really have little correspondence to the connotation associated with these English terms. *Erusin* derives from the root *'.r.s*, meaning "to be bound or joined,"[1] and implying here the ceremony by which a woman is joined to her husband, the key liturgical act of which was called *kiddushin,* from the root *k.d.sh. Kiddushin* probably entails the notion that she was set aside as his in the same way that sacred property, or *hekdesh* (from the same root), belonged exclusively to the Temple. As the terms imply, the Rabbis assumed as their paradigm the dominant biblical metaphor of wife-purchase (though, as we shall see, they actually replaced this paradigm even as their terminology implied that they retained it). Still, from the moment of *kiddushin,* a woman was known technically as *eshet ish* ("a [given] man's wife,") while her husband was her *ba'al* (literally, her "master" or "owner"). While she retained her own property rights in many ways, her husband was responsible for any vows she might make, and with certain exceptions, he took possession of any income she produced either from her own labor or by virtue of such chance events as her finding lost property.[2] He was held in fact to have "purchased" his wife, in

129

the sense that she moved legally into his domain—the classical Mishnaic account thus juxtaposes the ways in which "a woman is acquired" with instructions for "acquiring" servants, cattle and property in general.[3] Should she engage in sexual relations with another man after *kiddushin,* she would be guilty of adultery; like marriage proper, betrothal could be terminated only by legal divorce.

But *kiddushin* was not yet marriage proper, in that a woman did not yet take up residence with her husband. She remained instead a ward of her father, postponing sexual relations with her husband until the final act of marriage, designated as *nissuin* (literally, his "carrying" her to his abode) or *chuppah* (nowadays the term applied to the canopy under which the ceremony occurs, but originally, just the process by which a woman transferred legal domain by going to live in her husband's home).[4] In the course of time, *chuppah* became associated with a variety of things: the room where the couple went alone after the ceremony, and where, presumably the marriage was consummated; a marriage canopy; a pillow on which the couple sat; a bridal veil; or even a covered chair (known in English as a palanquin) in which the bride sat while she was carried to the groom's home.[5] All are correct in that the original meaning was simply the rite of transfer from domain to domain, whether by carrying in a palanquin, or by common domicile symbolized in various ways. Classical sources thus refer to it as *chuppah*—without the definite article—since it is not a thing, but a state of being, as the English "marriage," but not "the marriage" is.

The parallel term, *nissuin,* probably implied ownership, in that "lifting up" designates a means of taking possession; in rabbinic law, ownership of an item is transferred not when the purchase price changes hands, but at the moment when the buyer takes physical possession of that which is bought, normally by lifting it up. As we shall see, money changes hands at the moment of *kiddushin*; but the bride as sexual partner is forbidden to her husband until *nissuin,* the moment when she enters his domain as his *eshet ish,* the moment when he takes possession as her *ba'al.*

In many of these details, rabbinic marriage mirrored the parallel Roman institution, although it is not always clear how much the former owes to the latter, and how much its development can be explained as a matter of evolution that was internal to Jewish tradition alone. But Roman marriage too depended on the concept of wife-purchase, albeit only as a symbolic legal fiction.[6] Even the classic Mishnaic ruling, "A woman is acquired in three ways . . ." has its Roman parallel in the second-century textbook on Roman law written by the established jurist Gaius, who describes the most common form of marriage, that associated with *manus* (being in one's husband's "hand," or authority); "In the old days," he says, "there were three ways in which women came into it."[7]

For the Rabbis, the meaning of marriage as actual ownership was blunted, so that even as they depended on the biblical prototype of wife-purchase, they simultaneously commuted it into a symbolic liturgical event. Evidence for the change is legal, ceremonial, and linguistic.

From Wife Purchase to Kiddushin

The legal innovation that deserves primary consideration is the marriage document known as a *ketubah,* attributed to Shimon ben Shetach (first century B.C.E.).[8] It constitutes a conditional promissory note by which a husband agrees to pay his wife a stipulated sum of money if he divorces her without cause or mistreats her such that a Jewish court grants her a divorce from the abusive relationship. *Ketubah* was linked to a view of Jewish marriage as having two stages. Roman marriage, too, customarily had two stages separated by as much as a year or even more. Customarily, a common-law marriage known as *usus* gave the wife to the husband, but only after a year of living together successfully did full *manus* take effect. Alternatively, a woman might be promised before she matured physically, in which case she was legally her husband's wife, even though she did not go to live with him until such time as she became physically able to do so. She might also be betrothed for a year or more because, for example, her husband's career took him on long trips abroad, or on account of bad health.[9] In the Jewish case, however, the division of marriage into two stages is generally explained as a consequence of the legal implications of the *ketubah*. In that it is a promissory note, it required that its maker, the husband, own property which a court might seize should his wife successfully argue a claim for divorce against him. While such property might be his at the time of *kiddushin,* he might equally still have to earn it, in which case after the ceremony of "betrothal" he would leave to establish his financial independence while his wife remained domiciled with her father. Technically his wife, she would still not live with him, and would be assumed to retain her "market" value as a "virgin," which she would give up to her husband only after a *ketubah* was in her hand. The Rabbis thus frowned on sexual relations prior to *nissuin,* not for moralistic reasons, but for the practical end of protecting a woman against divorce by her husband prior to his having attained property that she might collect as her rightful damage settlement according to the *ketubah.* Second-century sources polemicize against sexual relations in this interim period,[10] leading us to question the extent to which betrothed couples abided by the rule, a conclusion underscored by other sources which try to explain away exceptions to the rule by confining them to a particular geographical locale.[11] Still, the innovation of a *ketubah* giving women legal recourse in case of unwarranted divorce or mistreatment symptomized a new attitude by which women were no longer purchased at all, despite the biblically derived legal fiction that they were. Similarly, the act of *kiddushin* now required a woman's free consent, before it was valid.

Ceremonially, the transfer of money during *erusin* was commuted from the biblical *mohar,*[12] an actual purchase price paid to the woman's father, to a symbolic transfer of money (or its equivalent) that the bride herself received from her husband as a token of that consent.[13]

If attributions can be trusted, we might reconstruct the legal-ceremonial changes as a steady movement over a course of three centuries. The *ketubah* arises toward the end of the second century B.C.E. By the time of the Hillelite-Shammaite controversies a century later, the amount of the token sum that effects betrothal is an issue, though the fact of its being merely a symbolic payment to the woman herself is already well established. One hundred years later (second century C.E.), the system is in place, supported by the Rabbis against people who circumvent it by engaging in sexual relations despite the fact that no *ketubah* has yet been delivered by the husband.

We find linguistic evidence supportive of the move away from wife-purchase in the change in terminology from *erusin* to *kiddushin*.

> If he [the groom] gave her [the bride] money or something worth money, saying to her, "Behold, you are sanctified to me [*mekudeshet*]," or "Behold, you are joined to me [*me'ureset*]," or "Behold, you are a wife to me," then she is sanctified [*mekudeshet*].[14]

A careful reading of this text demonstrates that the preferred term at the time it was written was *mekudeshet*—"sanctified." The question at issue is whether a woman is "sanctified" to a man if he does not use the right word, and the answer given is that even if he says something else, like, "You are joined to me," or "You are my wife," she is in fact "sanctified" to him. *Me'ureset* must have emerged as an early term for betrothal, but later, been replaced by *mekudeshet*. So *mekudeshet*, from *kiddushin*, and probably implying a similarity to *hekdesh*, becomes the preferred term, such that by 200 C.E., when the Mishnah is promulgated, its tractate detailing marriage regulations is labelled *Kiddushin* (not *Erusin*), and its preferred verb explaining the groom's actions during the ceremony is *mekadesh*—"he sanctifies."[15]

The changeover in wording by the year 200 C.E. indicates novel theological considerations as well. If the parallel with Temple goods (*hekdesh*) is apt, the property paradigm has not been completely relinquished, even though the woman in question is no longer purchased from her father. True, her movement to her husband's domain, geographically and legally, requires her consent, but she is still set aside for her "master" (*ba'al*); she is his woman (*eshet ish*), reserved for his "use," in the same way that temple property may be used only by priests.

But *kiddushin* may carry novel theological significance beyond the *hekdesh* model. As we saw above, the paradigmatic formula by which *kiddushin* is accomplished became the husband's statement, *Harei at mekudeshet li,* "Behold, you are *mekudeshet* ['sanctified'] to me." The *pu'al* verb, *mekudeshet,* is the passive of the active *pi'el* construction, *mekadesh,* which means here as elsewhere, "to *declare* something holy," in the performative sense of making it so by the very saying thereof.[16] We see clearly the significance of a performative declaration in the act by which the rabbinic court declared the new month to be holy. On the one hand, the Rabbis believed that holy time arrived of its own accord; on the other, their view of ritual entailed the conviction that *declaring* something sacred under appropriate conditions brought holiness into being. In the Temple, after all, it was the *declaration* that one's property henceforth belonged to God that transformed it from private property into the state of *hekdesh.*[17] Here too, it was the court and then the people *saying* of the new moon, "It is sanctified; it is sanctified,"[18] that made the occasion a holy day. Knowing that the new moon came and went even without the court's permission, but wishing to retain the theory of sanctity coming into being by verbal fiat, the Rabbis ruled that in the event that the court fails to voice the declaration of sanctity, some other agent does so.

> R. Eleazar b. R. Tzaddok says, "If it did not appear in its expected time . . . heaven has already declared [!] it sanctified. R. Simeon b. R. Eleazar says . . . the prior month has declared [!] it sanctified.[19]

In similar fashion, we must conclude that the groom's saying to his wife, "Behold, you are sanctified unto me," accomplished more than reserving her as his possession. It made a woman *mekudeshet li,* "sanctified to me [the groom]," which meant the bride's covenantal status was transferred from being sanctified by virtue of her father to being sanctified by virtue of her husband. At stake is a woman's standing in the covenant made at Sinai. Prior to marriage, a woman is covenanted by virtue of her father's covenantal status; after marriage, she is covenanted because of her husband. The father and husband become so by virtue of circumcision, the sign of the covenant. Men are thus covenanted directly; women only indirectly through their men.

By 200 C.E., then, the *kiddushin* rite featured above all, the legal formula by which a man pronounced a woman "sanctified" to him, which is to say, covenanted through him rather than through her father. The formula was accompanied by his giving her the token monetary payment called for in the Mishnah, originally (it appears) anything at all that she accepted as a symbol of her willingness to enter into the marriage, including just wine in a cup; but by the Middle Ages, the token became a ring.[20] We have, then, (1) a gift of wine (or something else as well), (2) a blessing over the wine (in keeping with rabbinic rules of benedictions preceding eating or drinking), and (3) a declaration of intent, usually in the form, "Behold, you are sanctified to me."

Finally, we find also (4) a *Birkat Erusin,* a "Betrothal Blessing," which seems to have functioned as a prophylactic against sexual relations in the interim between betrothal and marriage proper.

> Rabin bar Rav Ada and Rabbah bar Rav Ada both said in the name Rav Judah: "Blessed art Thou . . . who has sanctified us by his commandments and commanded us regarding illicit sexual relationships, forbidding to us those who are [only] betrothed and allowing us those who are married [*hanesu'ot*] by means of *chuppah* and *kiddushin.*"
>
> Rav Acha the son of Rava concluded it in the name of Rav Judah, "Blessed art Thou, Lord, who sanctifies Israel by *chuppah* and *kiddushin.*"[21]

This blessing is fraught with problems, not the least of which is the fact that nowhere else is there a benediction

thanking God for what we are forbidden to do![22] We shall see
that many moderns, finding the explicit sexism repugnant,
have excised this blessing from their rite.[23] Even the medievals
found the blessing's conclusion troubling, in that surely the
sanctification of the people Israel is not dependent on whether
or not its members decide to marry.[24] In the context of the second century, however, we can readily understand the blessing
as having been motivated by the desire to postpone sexual consummation until after *chuppah.*

By the geonic age, possibly because economic conditions
no longer necessitated that a prospective husband work for a
period of time so as to establish financial independence prior
to his wife's moving in with him, the two halves of the ancient
rabbinic rite were combined into the single ceremony that is
enjoyed to this day. But in two ways, the two stages of *kiddushin* and *chuppah* are still separated symbolically. First,
wine is consumed independently in each (as if drinking it in
the former does not count for the latter); second, a short break
in time is observed between them, usually with a reading of
the *ketubah,*[25] though in the Middle Ages, other strategies
were common—Rashi, for instance (eleventh-century France),
would dismiss those assembled momentarily after the conclusion of betrothal, and then reassemble them for *chuppah.*[26]
This second half of the combined ceremony features what are
known as the "Seven Benedictions" (*Sheva Berakhot*), a series
of blessings including (1) a blessing over a second cup of wine;
and (2) six more blessings on the themes of creation, the restoration of Zion, and the happiness of the bride and groom. In addition, the same blessings are repeated as part of an extended
Grace after Meals (*Birkat Hamazon*) following the wedding
feast.

The Sheva Berakhot *(Seven Benedictions)*

It is generally assumed that the two-fold recitation of the
Seven Benedictions (at a separate *chuppah* rite and then following that, at the wedding feast) informed ancient rabbinic

practice. But that assumption deserves a second look. The "Seven Benedictions" are found in the Babylonian Talmud, or Babli,[27] but the list there is suspect. It is almost certainly a late editorial compilation of what were once independent blessings. To begin with, the list contains redundancy—three blessings on the theme of creation, for instance, and two blessings on the subject of the bride-and-groom's happiness together. Moreover the list is prefaced by a discussion referring to the blessings as *Birkat Erusin,* the "Groom's Blessing" (singular!), which is said in the groom's house. Our list is therefore a late collection of alternative "Groom's Blessings," which came to be said together only during the geonic period, when talmudic precedent from the written page replaced oral memory of actual tannaitic and amoraic practice.[28] That happened only in Babylonia, for only there was the Babli regnant, though a similar bunching of blessings may have occurred in Palestine also, since a late geonic source informs us that "Easterners [Babylonians] bless the groom with seven blessings; Palestinians say three."[29]

So there had been a single Groom's Blessing, and it was said not twice (once in a marriage rite and again at the wedding banquet), but solely at the feast, for that was all they had! Unlike today, where the bride and groom stand under a canopy within the synagogue sanctuary and have the blessings recited as the second part of a combined religious ceremony, after which they repair to a wedding banquet and have the blessings said yet again as part of the grace after meals, the practice in talmudic times was simply to celebrate the bride's arrival at the groom's home with a feast, accompanied by a "Groom's Blessing." The marriage was consummated that night, and the party was apt to continue for several days.

We can isolate two distinct stages by which the ancient custom was altered. Prior to the Talmud's canonization, no concept of "Seven Blessings" even existed. But after canonization in Babylonia, geonic authorities (c. 757–1038)[30] unanimously read their text as mandating such a liturgical staple. Still, they retained it only for the feast, where in ancient times the single blessings (out of which the composite seven are constructed)

had been said. Western European authorities, however, introduced the novel custom of a liturgical recitation of the Seven
Blessings separately from the feast, so that the old reading at
the wedding dinner occurred afterward. The wedding meal,
once primary, now became secondary; the newly devised ritual
performance of the blessings prior to the meal now became
central, and was itself called by the old word *chuppah*. Eventually (by the sixteenth century), this new liturgical event was
outfitted with a permanent canopy under which a couple stood,
and which itself became known as *the*(!) *chuppah*.[31]

The medieval world thus inherited a rite of *kiddushin* plus a
mistaken idea of a putative collection of seven benedictions
that became a rite of *nissuin* (or *chuppah*) in its own right.
Both rites were continued virtually intact until our time. These
two rites were elaborated, while simultaneously, the feast at
which the original "Groom's Blessing" had been said, and
where the combined Seven Benedictions had found their
geonic home, was virtually abandoned from a liturgical point
of view. Before taking up the theme of the elaborations, let us
look more closely at the wedding feast.

The Wedding Feast

As we have seen, in antiquity, the wedding proper was identical with the wedding feast. Instead of our Seven Benedictions, moreover, there was only a single blessing which was
addressed to the groom as an extension of the Grace after
Meals.[32] The wording for that blessing would have varied,
since it would have been composed spontaneously by the individual guests, but judging from the extant benedictions which
have survived in the Babli's list of seven, it would have had
something to do with creation, Zion's restoration, or the happiness of the bride and groom. The feast was therefore implicitly
eschatological, emphasizing the symbolic role of the couple as
embodying paradise past and future.

The Groom's Blessing was not the only extension to the
Grace after Meals. Already in Mishnaic times, Jews had

elaborated upon the invitation to say Grace so as to match the number of people present.[33] But the Grace attracted other embellishments too, no doubt because rather than the feast serving a secondary purpose to a separate liturgical event (such as is our custom today), it was originally the feast that bore the whole weight of the liturgical celebration, it being all that there was. But this accent on a feast was in keeping with liturgical ritual in general during tannaitic and amoraic times. The Groom's Blessing at the wedding, for instance, was likened to the Mourner's Blessing (*Birkat Avelim*) said by people making calls to a house of mourning, seven days of a wedding feast and seven days of mourning being paired as a joint edict said to have been promulgated by Moses himself.[34] Both blessings were thus said all seven days.[35]

We can summarize by observing that custom differed in Palestine from what the Babylonian Talmud would suggest. Only in Babylonia did "Seven Benedictions" ever emerge, because the Palestinian Talmud never collected blessing options in one place. In Palestine, both funerals and weddings lasted seven days, however, and both were marked by daily feasting at which time a blessing was said either for mourners or for the groom. Once seven blessings did become normative (in geonic Babylonia only), they were said where the single Groom's Blessing had once been—as an addendum to the Grace after Meals. The Grace was similarly outfitted with other allusions to the wedding, including a reference to God "in whose dwelling there is joy."[36] As time went on, other poetic additions were added to the feast, including a short poem in the introduction to the Grace that is still said, and is generally attributed (probably incorrectly) to the tenth-century Spanish poet, Dunash ibn Labrat.[37] Throughout the medieval period, the feast thus served as the locus for ceremonial rejoicing, including poems in the vernacular, not all of which were officially recognized as liturgical by the authorities. The expanding revelry attracted issues of propriety, including the extent to which music was appropriate, and even whether professional entertainers might be invited.[38]

Other longtime customs associated with the feast were end-ing just as the poetry and singing was increasing. The most notorious such instance is *Birkat Betulin,* the "Blessing of vir-ginity."

The Blessing of Virginity (Birkat Betulin)

The texts for the blessing of virginity are found in several geonic responsa, but not in either Talmud, even though the blessing probably goes back to that period of time. The Talmud rarely gives us texts of rites that are not halakhically required, and this was a folk custom that the Rabbis never officially rec-ognized. We noted above the institution of the *ketubah* as a conditional promissory note to compensate a maltreated or wrongfully divorced wife. In keeping with social mores of the time, the sum promised varied with the status of the bride. Among other things, virgins received more than women who had already been married. The Mishnah thus provides for the possibility of a virginity suit the day after the wedding, should a husband wish to charge his wife with lying about her vir-ginity.[39] Variously attributed geonic responsa, from the eighth century on, detail a ceremony connected with ascertaining whether a wife has been a virgin.

> When he takes out the sheet, he must say this blessing, and if he has a cup and spices, he says blessings over them, namely, "Blessed . . . who creates the fruit of the vine," and " . . . spice trees." Then he says, "Blessed art Thou . . . who planted a nut in the Garden of Eden, 'a lily of the valleys' [Song of Songs 2:1], that no stranger might rule over the sealed wellspring (or foun-tain). Therefore, 'a lovely hind and a graceful doe' [Pr. 5:19] [other texts complete the verse: 'a lovely hind and a graceful doe, let her breasts satisfy you always, be ravished by her love.' She] has watched over the apple [other texts: has kept watch in purity] without fail. Blessed art Thou who choose the seed of Abraham. [Other texts: In purity and in joy, give her the seed of the holy ones. Blessed art Thou who has chosen Abraham, our father and his progeny after him.]"[40]

The idea of saying such a blessing can be traced exegetically to Psalm 68:27, "Bless God . . . you who are of Israel's fountain."[41] The Hebrew for fountain, *makor*, can mean source, and hence by extension, womb, so the biblical text is generally taken by rabbinic tradition to mean that even embryos in the womb should bless God.[42] But a variant interpretation attributed to Yehudai Gaon (eighth century) held it to be "a blessing that is said over the womb on account of conception."[43] Just what blessing he means and when it is to be said or by whom remains unclear, but for some, it was interpreted as the Blessing of Virginity, thanking God for the purity of the womb whence the new husband's progeny would come.

The means by which the ritual unfolded was drawn from Deuteronomy 22:17, "They shall spread out the sheet before the elders of the town," a biblical verse that some Rabbis interpreted literally, while others did not. But even the latter held, "This is one of the things that R. Ishmael interpreted from the Torah as symbolic (*kemashal*). Let the witnesses for the bride and witnesses for the groom come and report the way things were to the elders of the city."[44] A fourteenth-century Karaite in Constantinople, Aaron b. Elijah, urges his own community to follow the rival rabbinites and take up this symbolic reading of the verse, thus allowing friendly witnesses to report the facts, rather than to make the bride and groom submit to a public testimony before strangers; and he calls the witnesses *shushvinim,* the standard rabbinic term for the groomsmen.[45] In the rabbinite community, these *shushvinim* (who were friends of both the bride and the groom) checked the sheet for blood, and reported results, rather than summoning the town elders to do so, thus sparing the bride and groom that ignominy.[46] The Karaites, on the other hand, who tended toward biblical literalism, kept the custom of holding court with town elders directly, and they too had a blessing like the rabbinic one cited above.[47]

But officially, many rabbis railed against the benediction. Chief among its opponents was Maimonides, who called it "a disgusting custom," urging "God-fearing men not to be seen in such a crowd under any circumstances."[48] It is still listed, however, in Jacob ben Asher's influential thirteenth-century

code, the *Tur,* and as late as the sixteenth century, Joshua Falk
(1555–1614) felt the need to assemble the many arguments
against it.[49] One gets the impression that *Birkat Betulin* largely
dies out in the Middle Ages, but that it was retained in some circles, and in fact, it is still found in some prayer manuals as late
as the nineteenth century![50]

Birkat Betulin, then, is an ancient folk custom that slowly
disappears. On the other hand, the medievals expanded the
classical core of their liturgy in other ways, particularly in the
conclusion of the *nissuin* rite, which now featured the smashing of a glass, as a symbol of mourning for the Temple.

Smashing a Glass and Veiling the Bride (Bedecken)

To explain the custom of smashing a glass, most sources
cite a talmudic tale, according to which "Rav Ashi made a
wedding feast for his son. When he saw the Rabbis becoming
unruly, he summoned a white crystal glass and smashed it
in front of them, and it sobered them up."[51] The Tosafot
(twelfth–thirteenth century, France) gloss the tale by remark-
ing, "It is therefore customary to break a glass at weddings."[52]
That a glass was broken as part of the wedding ceremony by
the high Middle Ages is therefore assured, all the more so as it
is mentioned elsewhere: the twelfth-century German classic
Roke'ach, for instance.[53]

But whether the custom may accurately be traced back to
the talmudic account is doubtful. More likely, we might postu-
late that there arose a series of customs, not necessarily Jewish
in origin, which Jews adopted only in medieval times, but then
read back to antiquity and usually explained as ways to remember the Temple. Among these were a variety of practices
performed at weddings, including the breaking of a glass and
"putting ashes on the bridegroom's forehead," and "putting a
crown of olive branches on the bridegroom's head, because
olives are bitter." The ashes were a German practice and the
olive crown was customary in Mediterranean lands.[54] In sixteenth-century Poland, both were in vogue.[55] But how each

custom arose in the first place is unrecorded in our sources, which take as their topic only what they came to mean after the fact, and the details of how the custom should be carried out.

Another example is the Ashkenazic ritual of veiling the bride, known to this day by the Yiddish term, *Bedecken*. Veiling was common in antiquity, but Jews eventually reinterpreted it as coming from the Hebrew root *b.d.k* (= "to check, investigate"), and as symbolizing the groom's checking to see that his bride was in fact the woman he intended to marry, rather than a stranger—lest he be deceived as Jacob had been when he married Leah. That the latter interpretation is incorrect, we may glean from the fact that it would require the groom to lift the bride's veil so that he might see her face, whereas in fact, the opposite is the case—he covers her up.

Similarly, there is no reason to believe that the breaking of a glass by the groom meant from its outset the recollection of the Temple's destruction. In fact, Jacob Moelin (known as the Maharil, Germany, 1365–1427) knew of the custom of remembering the Temple at a wedding, but he associated it with the cowled cloak that the groom wore, not with the breaking of a glass (which the groom smashed against the wall rather than breaking it under foot, as is the case today).[56]

In sum, current Jewish practices like the marriage canopy, the veiling of the bride, marriage at a communal religious center and the breaking of a glass were actually common to Jewish and Christian society in medieval Europe.[57] Since the twelfth century, both cultures had increasingly outfitted weddings with timing, props, and acts that conferred symbolic sacrality upon them,[58] and they shared certain common symbols of sacred propriety. Jewish exegesis related these common customs as they emerged in Jewish practice to specifically Jewish interpretive schemes, so that the veiling of the bride (as a symbol of the groom's certainty that he was about to betroth the right woman) and the smashing of a glass (as a sign of mourning for the Temple) were retained as if they had been uniquely Jewish customs associated with equally particularistic Jewish themes. As such, they are still commonplace today.

The Ceremony Today

As an outcome of the historical processes traced above, the contemporary ceremony in traditional circles features the following sequence of events:

1. *Bedecken* (veiling the bride) and signing the *ketubah,* just prior to the marriage ceremony.
2. *Kiddushin* (= *erusin*): (a) the presider welcomes the bridal party and guests;[59] (b) *Birkat Erusin* (the Betrothal Blessing) is recited; (c) the bride and groom sip wine, prefaced by the proper blessing; (d) the groom hands a ring to the bride, saying the legal formula that declares her betrothed to him ("Behold, with this ring, you are sanctified to me, according to the laws of Moses and Israel").[60]
3. Interlude: the *ketubah* is read.
4. *Nissuin*: (a) the Seven Benedictions are recited, including a blessing over wine which is drunk for a second time, and from a second cup, to symbolize the separation of *nissuin* from *erusin*; (b) the glass is smashed underfoot.

Liberal Jews nowadays have introduced a variety of changes into this received tradition, largely to correct the theological presumption, explicit in the Bible and implicit since rabbinical times despite ritual/legal innovations such as the *ketubah,* that marriage is essentially the act by which a groom purchases a bride. Instead, the rite is reconceived as a covenant between two equal parties. In the *kiddushin* part of the ceremony, the Betrothal Blessing, which warns against sexual relations prior to the delivery of the necessary promissory note (the traditional *ketubah*), is often omitted, with the exception of its final line which affirms the sanctity of Israel by virtue of marriage. Two rings are usually exchanged, and both bride and groom profess their "vows" to each other; central to these vows is the traditional statement that effects betrothal, but it is recited by both groom and bride to each other; or, in some places, the groom alone recites the traditional legal formula, and the bride says a similarly appropriate line, perhaps from the Bible (especially Song of Songs). To this skeletal affirmation, the couple may add their own words expressing their understanding of what their relationship means to each other.

The *ketubah* has been redefined as a document having nothing to do with conditional monetary penalties that might be levied upon a morally repugnant groom; instead, it has become a wedding certificate (sometimes composed by the bride and groom themselves) recording the terms of a modern marriage, usually in accordance with contemporary norms of mutual support, respect, love, and so forth. It may or may not be read at the ceremony, but either alongside of it or instead of it, a personal charge to bride and groom is common.

The Seven Benedictions of *nissuin* are still recited, though not necessarily in their totality, sometimes deliberately in translation so as to emphasize the image of the bride and groom as Adam and Eve in Paradise, on one hand, and the messianic vision of the end of days, on the other. As the ceremony concludes, the groom stamps upon a glass wrapped in a napkin, after which those assembled shout "*Mazal tov*" ("Congratulations")—a response attested since the fifteenth century, and well known now as an anticipated climax marking the ceremony's end.[61]

The whole ceremony takes place under a *chuppah,* which may be embroidered or decorated by friends and family. In material, it ranges from a traditional prayer shawl (*tallit*) tied to four poles and held up by four friends in the wedding party, to a free-standing floral canopy established for the occasion. A procession and a recession are normative, but only to satisfy the customs of the surrounding society, not for any Jewish reason. Similarly in keeping with expectations borrowed from the social milieu, but having no Jewish rationale, the officiant may proclaim the couple married according to the laws of Judaism and the state.

A festive meal is still the norm, but the Seven Benedictions are rarely repeated there. If they are, they may be augmented by freshly composed wishes (perhaps in the form of benedictions) created and recited by friends and family members. In general, however, the sacred nature of the celebratory meal has entirely been lost.

Perhaps the most striking feature of the history of the wedding ceremony is the gradual separation of life into sacred and profane. The Jews of antiquity knew that division—indeed, they emphasized it.[62] But sacred was not necessarily religiously solemn, and even the profane could be expected to yield here and there to a moment of sacrality—as in blessings that introduced meals and the Grace that concluded them; or, for that matter, even a benediction that accompanied relieving oneself in the bathroom.[63] Ingestion and defecation are bodily functions to be sure, but not on that account seen as altogether alien to God. Marriage was thus a religious rite, but it was at the same time a festive event entailing a banquet, the celebration of sex, good wishes for groom and bride, hopes for fertility, drinking to the point where even the Rabbis had occasionally to be sobered up: it was fun. This entire scenario was the focus of the sacred without its being excerpted from life.

By the Middle Ages, however, a distinctly sacred (and serious) ambience had been added to the event, so that the liturgy that mattered (so to speak) was now the newly devised *chuppah* ritual which followed immediately upon the ancient rite of *kiddushin.* A private family ceremony had become public; it moved to the synagogue or other public domain; the rabbi was expected to officiate there.[64] The feast, however, was not yet removed from the realm of the sacred; it was still a religious event, even though its joyous side sometimes exceeded the bounds of what religious sensibilities allowed—hence the rules governing propriety regarding music and entertainment. At the very turn of the modern era, for instance, David ben Samuel Halevi (the Taz, 1586–1667) noted, "In many wedding feasts, it is customary to sing the *Kaddish* [associated with mourning], and that is certainly a great sin, for it is permitted only as a recollection of God's compassionate works. All the more so, it is very sinful when people hire an entertainer who makes fun of biblical verses or sacred texts."[65]

In some circles today, religious sensitivity still intertwines easily with the pleasures of life; the wedding feast is both lavish in joy and intrinsically inseparable from the Seven Benedictions, the Grace after Meals, and the like. But for most, the sacred has become a specialized domain that is held to exclude "ordinary" pursuits like meals, let alone banqueting and hilarity. The marriage feast is still the locus of life itself, complete with singing, dancing, eating and drinking. But contrary to the situation in antiquity, these affairs of the flesh have been separated from the domain of the spirit, which survives only in the liturgical rite. Only the rite is seen as sacred; the meal that ensues has been relegated to the role of profane, a time for fun as it always was, but now, for fun alone. It generally proceeds without benefit of marriage ceremonial, and the rabbi who officiated under the *chuppah* has long gone home. Fun has been severed from religion.

On Divorce

This detailed treatment of the evolution of marriage has prevented due attention to divorce, which deserves at least passing treatment. Though by no means taking divorce lightly, Jewish tradition has sanctioned it as a legitimate way to end an unhappy marriage, or, for that matter (in theory, though not necessarily in practice), a step that is actually mandated in some instances—the case of proven adultery, for example. Technically, however, since marriage is theoretically a case of wife-purchase, only the husband can sue for divorce. But without the religious divorce, a woman would remain technically married to her husband and would be unable to contract a second marriage. To describe such a woman, Jewish law coins the phrase *agunah,* meaning literally, someone "tied down" by her old relationship. By contrast, her husband could more easily remarry, since polygamy, though banned rabbinically, was obviously the norm in biblical days; a second marriage by a man still married to another woman was therefore held to be less serious an offense than the same situation entered into by a woman.

In practice, as long as a Jewish legal system held sway, a husband could be forced by a Jewish court to issue a writ of divorce under threat of punishment. The tragedy of an *agunah* is exacerbated today, however, in that modern Jewish society lacks the power of autonomous legal sanction. Women who deserve a divorce are often unable to get it from recalcitrant husbands who withhold compliance for punitive reasons. This inequity in practice leads many Jews to alter or even to abandon the Jewish divorce procedure. Conservative Judaism tends to build into the *ketubah* itself a conditional divorce agreement that is considered to take effect automatically under the conditions specified, thus dispensing in advance with any need later on to convince a stubborn husband to do anything at all under adverse conditions. Reform Jews generally accept civil divorce alone as binding, and offer the option of a religious divorce in addition, should both parties prove willing to cooperate.

The actual drawing up of a divorce document (known as a *get*) and the ritual means by which it is delivered to a wife are exceedingly complex.[66] A specially trained scribe writes it according to elaborate rules, using indelible ink on parchment. Meticulous care is taken to fill twelve lines of print exactly, and to spell out the details of the case (names, date, place) such that no later misconstruing of what happened can occur. Duly witnessed, the *get* is ceremoniously handed over from husband to wife with verbal assurance of intent to divorce. Symbolic of the break with the past is the process of tearing the *get,* ostensibly to prevent its ever being used again by others. Modern ceremonies may also include statements by husband and wife asserting the freedom of each other to go their separate ways in peace and blessing, with the fractured marriage behind them and the promise of new and healthier relationships ahead.

NOTES

1. Marcus Jastrow, *A Dictionary of the Targumim, the Talmud Babli and Yerushalmi, and the Midrashic Literature* (1903; reprint, New York, 1971), p. 124.

2. See summary of property rights in marriage, in George Horowitz, *The Spirit of Jewish Law* (New York, 1963), pp. 295–316.

3. M. Kid. 1:1–5.

4. For details, see Lawrence A. Hoffman, "Life-Cycle Liturgy as Status Transformation," in E. Carr et al., eds., *Eulogema: Studies in Honor of Robert Taft, S.J.* (Rome, 1993), pp. 161–77.

5. Cf. *Arukh,* s.v. *"iparyon,"* B. Sot. 12a; S.A., E.H. 55:1. For summaries, see Solomon B. Freehof, "The Chuppah," in Daniel Jeremy Silver, ed., *In the Time of Harvest* (New York, 1963), p. 187; Jacob ben Rabbi Yisra'el Chanokh Wirdiger, *Sefer Edut Leyisra'el* (Tel Aviv: Am Olam, 1977), provides a traditional collection of medieval opinions.

6. See Susan Treggiari, *Roman Marriage* (New York, 1991), p. 25.

7. Cf. M. Kid. 1:1, Treggiari, *Roman Marriage,* p. 17.

8. Shab. 14b.

9. Treggiari, *Roman Marriage,* pp. 21, 42.

10. Ket. 44b.

11. Cf. Ket. 7b, 12a.

12. Cf. Genesis 34:12, Exodus 22:16, 1 Samuel 18:25.

13. M. Kid. 1:1.

14. T. Kid. 1:1.

15. Kid. 2:1, 5–10; 3:5; etc.

16. On performativity in Jewish ritual, see Hoffman, "Liturgy as Status Transformation."

17. See summary of Jewish law in this regard in *Entziklopediah Talmudit,* s.v. *"Hekdesh,"* vol. 10 (Israel, 1971), col. 353.

18. M. R.H. 2:7: "The head of the court says, 'It is sanctified.' Then the whole crowd answers him, 'It is sanctified; it is sanctified.'"

19. T. R.H. 2:9.

20. One would suspect that Jews in the Roman empire already used a ring, since Roman custom called for rings. On the other hand, Paulinus of Nola (c. 353–401) mentions no rings, though the early Byzantine rite featured it (Mark Searle and Kenneth W. Stevenson, eds., *Documents of the Marriage Liturgy* [Collegeville, MN, 1992], pp. 30, 61). Only in the ninth and tenth centuries do we hear of it in Jewish sources, first with Saadiah, who interprets Nehemiah 7:46 (The Taba'ot Family) as the family of ring[makers], opining that people once celebrated betrothal with rings, but ceased because it implied permission for sexual relations prior to marriage proper (*The Commentary to Ezra and Nehemiah*

Attributed to Saadiah, cited in Wirdiger, *Sefer Edut Leyisra'el,* p. 38). But Saadiah's *siddur* mentions no ring; instead (echoing M. Kid. 2:2, where *kiddushin* is effected merely by wine or some other drink that the groom offers the bride), Saadiah calls for "this cup and what is in it." But he further stipulates, "it contains something silver" (I. Davidson, S. Assaf, B.I. Joel, eds., *Siddur Saadiah* (Jerusalem: Mekitsei Nirdamim, 1963), p. 97). So Saadiah knew of rings either prior to his time or elsewhere, but did not himself use them. A century later, however, Sherira or Hai Gaon tells us explicitly that Jews in Khurasan (northeast Persia, including Afghanistan and Turkestan) "have betrothed with rings for more than 100 years" (B. M. Lewin, *Otsar Hageonim,* vol. 8 [Jerusalem: Mosad Rav Kook, 1939], #60, p. 18). Hai himself, however, followed Saadiah's example, performing the rite "with the wine that is in this cup and with the silver that is in it" (*Siddur Saadiah,* n. to line 5, p. 97). Khurasan's proximity to areas where the Byzantine rite was in force may explain the origin of a ring in Jewish custom. It was borrowed from Christian ceremonial there. In the west, *Machzor Vitry* (eleventh-century France) still has only a cup of wine (pp. 589, 592). The groom expressly "gives the bride something to drink, since he performs *kiddushin* upon her by means of what is in the cup" (p. 589), that is, "by the wine in the cup . . . so he gives it to the bride, and pours the rest out" (p. 592). But twelfth-century Norman custom featured a ring (see the marriage rite at Bury St. Edmunds, 1125–1135, in Kenneth W. Stevenson, *To Join Together: the Rite of Marriage* (New York, 1987), p. 40.

21. B. Ket. 7b.

22. As recognized by traditional commentators—see, e.g., Rosh, ad loc.

23. Cf. wedding services in Reform Movement's *Rabbi's Manual* (New York, 1961; rev. ed., New York: CCAR, 1988).

24. See responsum by Hai Gaon, discussed in Lawrence A. Hoffman, *Canonization of the Synagogue Service* (Notre Dame, IN, 1979), pp. 141–44.

25. A practice going back at least to the twelfth century, and known to the Tosafot and Asher ben Yehiel; cf. Tos. Pes. 102b and Rosh ad. loc. #8 (both of which also link the two independent cups of wine to the two ceremonies). The latter knows only that *yesh mekomot shenahagu*—"There are places where it is customary" to read

the *ketubah,* indicating that other customs occurred also. On the identification of the Tosafot as Rabbenu Tam, see Wirdiger, *Sefer Edut Leyisra'el,* p. 16.

26. From *Sefer Hayashar Lerabbenu Tam,* cited in Wirdiger, *Sefer Edut Leyisra'el,* p. 16.

27. Ket. 7b–8a.

28. Difference of opinion on the blessings was rampant even then; *Siddur Saadiah* (tenth century) e.g., varies from *Seder Rav Amram* (ninth century). See also the question put to Sherira Gaon, in Lewin, *Otsar Hageonim,* vol. 8, #87.

29. *Chillufei Minhagim sheben Anshei Mizrach uvenei Erets Yisrael,* Mordicai Margoliot, ed., #25, p. 143. We have no idea what these three blessings were.

30. For geonic dates, see Hoffman, *Canonization of the Synagogue Service,* p. 187.

31. Known as a novel institution by the sixteenth-century Polish authority, Moses Isserles. See S.A., E.H. 55:1.

32. P.T. Ket. 1:1 and P.T. Meg. 4:4 carry the earliest descriptions, though the locus of a meal is not expressly given. All later authorities assume the meal context, however, and the parallelism between *Birkat Chatanim* and *Birkat Avelim* (which seems more certainly to have been part of the meal of condolence) makes the identification more probable.

33. M. Ber. 7:3.

34. P.T. Ket. 1:1.

35. P.T. Meg. 4:4 = P.T Ket. 1:1. Geonic tradition is ambivalent; on the one hand, it recollects that "the Mourners' Blessing is the blessing that was said in the town square," to which various European authorities note that the meal of condolence occurred there, and add even the exact wording for the blessing in question. Other responsa identify all of this as a custom that has come to the Babylonian geonic attention, but that has no basis in their own personal recollection. See Lewin, *Otsar Hageonim,* vol. 4, *Mashkin,* pp. 43–44.

36. Ket. 8a. For its placement in today's rite, see Hyman E. Goldin, *Hamadrikh* (New York, 1939, 1956), p. 23.

37. The poem is still extant—see Goldin, *Hamadrikh,* p. 23. On its history, see literature cited by Davidson, *Otsar Hashirah Vehapiyyut,* vol. 2 (1929; reprint, New York: Ktav, 1970), p. 106.

38. Cf. literature cited by Hayyim Schauss, *The Lifetime of a Jew* (New York: Union of American Hebrew Congregations, 1950),

p. 317, n. 199; and primary sources (esp. Tos. to Git. 7a, s.v., *Zimrah mena lan.* . . ., discussed in *Tur*/S.A., O.H. 560, and commentaries thereto.

39. M. Ket. 1:1.

40. Lewin, *Otsar Hageonim,* vol. 8, pp. 14–16. See Ruth Langer, "The Birkat Betulim: A Study of the Jewish Celebration of Bridal Virginity," *Proceedings of the American Academy of Jewish Research* 61 (1995): 53–94, which appeared after this chapter was written.

41. NRSV translation.

42. Cf. Targum Onkeles and Rashi to Psalm 68:27.

43. Carried in Tos. Ri'd to Ket. 7b.

44. Sifre to Deuteronomy 22:17, #237.

45. Jacob Mann, *Texts and Studies,* vol. 2 (Philadelphia, 1935), p. 162.

46. Ibid., p. 1127.

47. Ibid., p. 181.

48. Lewin, *Otsar Hageonim,* vol. 8, #50, p. 16.

49. *Tur,* E.H. 63, and *Derishah,* 63:2.

50. *Sefer Kehillat Shelomo,* Shelomo Zalman London, ed. (Duhrenfürth, 1818), p. 100, under the heading, "A groom who sees the blood of virginity, says. . . ."

51. Ber. 30b–31a.

52. Tos. to Ber. 31a, s.v. "They brought. . . ."

53. *Roke'ach,* #343.

54. Cf. *Tur* #560, *Bet Yosef,* s.v., "*Mah sheperesh rabbeinu.* . . ."

55. *Darkhei Moshe* to *Bet Yosef* of *Tur* #560, n. 2.

56. Maharil, *Minhagim, Hilkhot Nissuin.*

57. See Joseph Gutmann, "Jewish Medieval Marriage Customs in Art: Creativity and Adaptation," in David Kraemer, ed., *The Jewish Family: Metaphor and Memory* (New York, 1989), pp. 46–62.

58. See Esther Cohen and Elliott Horowitz, "In Search of the Sacred: Jews, Christians and Rituals of Marriage in the Later Middle Ages," *Journal of Medieval and Renaissance Studies* 20, no. 2 (1990): 225–49.

59. Omitted from discussion above, but added in the late Middle Ages, largely in response to Kabbalistic custom.

60. "According to the laws of Moses and Israel" is identified nowadays as the rules under which licit Jewish marriage is contracted. Originally, however, it meant the rules of the ritual itself, either its legal statutes ("laws of Moses") or its social mores ("laws of

Israel"); cf. M. Ket. 7:6 (where *dat yisra'el* occurs as *dat yehudit*); T. Ket. 7:6/7; As late as the *Tur* (as in the Mishnah), the ritual featured any number of phrases, not just this one. The *Shulchan Arukh* too does not know *dat moshe veyisra'el,* but Isserles (E.H. 27:1) says, "Some people say that he should say to her, *kedat moshe veyisra'el,* and that is the custom a priori, and similarly, the custom is to betroth with a ring, and they have reason from *tikkunei zohar."*

61. Responsum 101 of Germany's Moses Minz, cited by Gutmann, "Medieval Marriage Customs," p. 50.

62. See *"Havdalah,"* in Lawrence A. Hoffman, *Beyond the Text* (Bloomington, IN, 1987), pp. 20–45.

63. Ber. 11a.

64. See Cohen and Horowitz, "In Search of the Sacred."

65. Taz to O.H. 560, n. 5.

66. See Isaac Klein, *A Guide to Religious Practice* (New York, 1979), pp. 476–91.

Christian Rituals Surrounding Sickness

Karen B. Westerfield Tucker

From the days of the early church, Christians have provided ritual care for the sick and dying in imitation of the ministry exercised by Jesus and the apostles towards the infirm and the possessed. According to the New Testament writings, the healing miracles of Jesus witness to his identity as Messiah and proclaim, as effective signs, the advent of the new age (e.g., Matt. 9:35; 11:4–5; Luke 11:20; John 20:31). His disciples (and the church) were commissioned to continue the ministry of healing in Jesus' name in conjunction with preaching the gospel (Mark 6:7–13; Matt. 10:1; Luke 9:1–6; 10:1–11). The work of the church in caring for the sick is summarily expressed in James 5:14–16, a passage often read in later ritual texts as a warrant for healing ministry:

> Are any among you sick? They should call for the elders of the church and have them pray over them, anointing them with oil in the name of the Lord. The prayer of faith will save the sick, and the Lord will raise them up; and anyone who has committed sins will be forgiven. Therefore confess your sins to one another, and pray for one another, so that you may be healed. The prayer of the righteous is powerful and effective. (NRSV)

Although all Christians share this text in common, various interpretations of it have resulted in different ritual practices within the church.

Because of the centrality of James 5:14–16 for justifying Christian ministry to the sick, the structure of that text will form the thematic framework for this present chapter. Discussion of how the understanding and practice of rituals surrounding sickness developed, declined, and were renewed will be subsumed under the thematic headings, as will an accounting of the historical, geographical, and cultural variations of the rites.

Sickness: A Christian Perspective

The classical Christian tradition views sickness,[1] in a general way, as a symptom of the fallen condition of humankind (resulting from the disobedience of Adam), which is marked by decay and death. The connection, early on, between sickness and sin (either inherited "original" sin or actual personal sin) and between physical and spiritual healing is indicated by the repeated usage of two Greek verbs throughout the New Testament: *asthenein* ("to be sick," "to be weak in faith"); and *sozein* ("to heal," "to save").

The association of sin and sickness does not necessarily imply a direct correlation between any particular case of illness and the iniquity of the individual: when Jesus healed the man born blind, he declared that neither the man nor his parents had sinned, but that his plight would allow the works of God to be made manifest in him, in that it called forth the healing action of Jesus (John 9:1–7). On the other hand, when the paralytic was brought to Jesus by his friends, Jesus declared, "Your sins are forgiven," and the man picked up his bed and walked (Mark 2:1–12); this latter case establishes the possibility of a more particular connection between sickness and sin, such as the linkage in James 5:15 implies.

Christians of later generations have relied upon the testimony of the New Testament as proof and warrant of the connection between sin and sickness for the content both of theological and pastoral treatises (e.g., Gregory the Great's *Regula pastoralis* III.12, late sixth century) and of liturgical texts for the care of the sick (particularly prayers and exhortatory statements). The 1543 order for the communion of the sick produced by Cologne reformer Hermann von Wied contains a lengthy exhortation outlining the cause, purpose, and

possible outcome of sickness.[2] In this text (and other comparable sixteenth-century Protestant texts), sickness is interpreted
as the product of sin and defined as a divine instrument for encouraging spiritual discipline. Health may be restored, and reconciliation with God is, in any case, assured for those who
confess their sin, believe, and have faith.

Healing by the divine physician—or recognition of such a
possibility—occasions thanks and praise for both physical and
spiritual restoration. This is exemplified in the response of the
Samaritan leper (Luke 17:11–19) and echoed in a Byzantine
prayer for the sick:

> Holy Father, physician of our souls and bodies, . . . [deliver] him
> by the grace of your Christ from the bodily sickness which besets
> him, and give him life according to your good pleasure, so that he
> may, through good works, offer you due thanksgiving.[3]

The Ministers of Healing

Care for the sick and infirm has, from apostolic times, been
included as one of the corporal works of mercy expected of
all Christians (Matt. 25:31–46). In some areas of the ancient
world, as is attested in the so-called *Apostolic Tradition* of
Hippolytus, dating perhaps from the third century, and deriva-
tive church orders, the church specifically inquired of candidates (catechumens) prior to admission to baptism whether
they had been faithful in the visitation of the sick.[4] The ability
to heal was regarded as one of the gifts of the Holy Spirit that
could be possessed by any member of the church,[5] but by the
third century some Christians began to regard such ability as a
recommendation for ordination to an ecclesiastical office.[6]

Although ministry to the sick by the general laity has continued in various forms within the church, those who had been set
apart for leadership within the Christian community were given
particular responsibilities for oversight of the infirm. Such specialized ministry is clear from the recommendation in James
5:14 that the "elders of the church" are to be sought in cases of

sickness. Historically, and in practice, the term "elder" (in Greek, *presbyter*) here has been interpreted in one of two different ways: either as referring to ordained bishops and priests (especially within the Catholic and Orthodox traditions); or as denoting certain experienced and spiritually mature, but not necessarily ordained, representatives of a community (particularly among Protestants).[7]

Among the recognized ministries in the early church were the offices of widow (1 Tim. 5:9–10) and deaconess (Rom. 16:1–2; 1 Tim. 3:11), which developed differently in East and West but which were instituted, in part, as a response to the need to provide disciplined prayer for the ailing and to visit and nurse sick women (social and cultural restraints deemed male visitation improper).[8] Although these two offices declined in the West by the Middle Ages, ministry to the sick by women continued at the hands of pious women and women in religious orders (nuns). A brief revival of the office of deaconess for ministry to the sick occurred in parts of Protestantism during the sixteenth century; the office was eventually restored to many churches in the nineteenth century, and continues even to the present day.

Deacons, priests, and bishops each were entrusted with responsibilities at times of sickness, as was the minor office of exorcist in the West.[9] These responsibilities are mentioned in many of the respective ordination rites, particularly those of the East, in which priests and bishops are instructed and empowered to lay hands upon and heal the afflicted,[10] and deacons are directed to visit the sick and to assist their superiors in service.[11]

In the early church, the bishop, as the chief minister of healing by virtue of his ordination, tended to the infirm along with his priests. If the sick were unable to come to the church, the bishop or his appointees visited them at their residences; and as the church increased in size, ministrations for the ill were in fact more often performed by the priests and other ministers rather than by the bishop.[12] Visitation by the clergy was accompanied by prayer and anointing. By the late

Middle Ages, clerical rituals for the sick had expanded in number and in length, and comprised complex anointings, special prayers and orders of service for the infirm, the daily services celebrated in the church or at the bedside,[13] and holy communion. In the churches of the Reformation, the pastor assumed primary responsibility for a simplified ritual ministry to the sick.

The Anointing of the Sick

In the New Testament writings, testimony to the apostolic anointing of the sick with oil is limited to two places: Mark 6:13 and James 5:14, where it is applied "in the name of the Lord." Yet the abundance both of texts for blessing the oil and of formularies for administering the unction indicate, from the third century onwards, the widespread use of the practice of anointing for purposes of healing in both East and West.[14] Olive oil, historically, has been the type preferred, and it is often administered from a vial or an oil stock, though several Christian traditions from the East (e.g., the Copts and Armenians) anoint with oil from the sanctuary lamps or from lamps standing before icons in a rite called the "Ritual of the Lamp."

The earliest known text for the blessing of oil occurs in the ancient church order known as the *Apostolic Tradition*. It is located immediately after the eucharistic prayer[15] and indicates that the oil could be used internally or externally for the benefits of strength and health; it may, however, be questioned whether the purpose of the oil there is specifically for the anointing of the sick.[16] Comparable prayers, which do indicate usage for the sick, are found in two collections dating from the fourth or fifth centuries, the *Apostolic Constitutions* (8.29, with affinities to *Apostolic Tradition*) and the Egyptian prayer-book attributed to Sarapion; in these prayers, water (and in the case of Sarapion, also bread) along with the oil is regarded as possessing therapeutic value.[17] Thus the prayer of Sarapion:

> We call upon you who have all authority and power, the Saviour of all people, Father of our Lord and Saviour Jesus Christ. And we

pray that you send forth a healing power of the Only-Begotten upon this oil, that it may become for those who are anointed with it, or partake of these your created elements, for a throwing off of every disease and every sickness, for a remedy against every demon, for a banishment of every unclean spirit, for a casting out of every evil spirit, for a driving out of every fever and shivering fit and every illness, for good grace and forgiveness of sins, for a medicine of life and salvation, for health and wholeness of soul, body and spirit and for complete bodily health and strength.[18]

Hints of a relationship between anointing the sick and penance are evident in this prayer ("forgiveness of sins"), a connection which increases in importance both in the East and in the West as the texts and accompanying rituals evolve.

From the beginning, the bishop in the West reserved to himself the right to bless the oil used for anointing, though some texts from the first millenium indicate that his priests could take part with him in the service of consecration.[19] Priests in the East, from an early date, were permitted to bless the healing oils as part of their ministerial duties (e.g., *Apostolic Constitutions* 8.29); by the eleventh century, some Byzantine texts instruct that seven priests are to participate together in the blessing of oils for healing and in the liturgical rites (e.g., eucharist, matins, or vespers) surrounding the care of the sick.

The clerical blessing of the oil, using prayers that invoked the agency and power of Jesus (himself, literally, the "Christ" or "anointed one") or the Holy Spirit,[20] increasingly came to be regarded as imbuing the oil with a sacramental efficacy (though its identification as one of the seven sacraments in the West did not come officially until the thirteenth century). Although the preparation of the oil was made by the clergy, evidence within prayers and other documents indicates that in early days application of the oil could be made not only by clerics, but also by lay people—and indeed by the infirm themselves.[21] Recipients of unction were always baptized Christians, though Christians guilty of serious sins and under penance were denied it until they had been restored to the church.

Apart from prayers for blessing the oil, no full ritual texts for the actual administration of the unction survive from before the late seventh/early eighth century, and so no information exists concerning the mode or modes of application. By the time such texts are available (and possibly as early as the fifth century in some regions), the privilege of anointing had been reserved to the clergy and was reinforced by conciliar legislation.[22] These texts indicate that anointing was often accompanied by one or more other clerical liturgical actions, such as laying on of hands, sprinkling with water or salt, and holy communion.

Ninth-century manuscripts from the West indicate diversity of practice and regional variety in the placement of healing oil on the body and in the presence (or absence) of specific formulas accompanying application. Gallican formularies show that sanctified oil could be applied in the sign of the cross to the nape of the neck, the throat, the breast, the back, and places most stricken with pain or injury.[23] On the basis of the anointing formulas, Antoine Chavasse has identified three ritual types: rituals where one or two formulations of a simple "In the name of the Trinity" kind cover all the placements; rituals in which each anointing is accompanied by an indicative formula appropriate to the part of the body being anointed (e.g., "I anoint your eyes with sanctified oil, that whatever offense you have committed by your sight may be expiated by the unction of this oil"); and rituals limiting the anointing to the five senses with an accompanying deprecative formula ("May the Lord remit . . .").[24] Having appeared respectively in the middle of the ninth century and towards the end of the tenth, these last two types became more frequent as the anointing came to be taken less as medicine for healing and recovery from illness and more as a purging of the entire body from sin in preparation for death. In addition to the five senses (ritually defined in some areas as the eyelids, the inside or outside of the nose, the ears, the lips, and the hands), oil was occasionally placed on other body parts believed to be a locus for sin (e.g., the feet, the loins for men, the navel for women).[25]

The shift from anointing the sick to anointing for penance and in anticipation of death came gradually, as is evident in the construction of the ritual texts and in theological writings, beginning as early as the eighth century.[26] Contributing to this change (or illustrating this shift) are several factors: the proximity, in liturgical books, of prayers for anointing the sick and rites provided for the dying and the dead; the association of anointing with deathbed penitence (*paenitentia ad mortem*); the developing view that sacramental anointing was unrepeatable; the elaboration of monastic rituals of penance utilizing anointing at the time of death; and the placement in some areas, by the twelfth century, of anointing as the last ritual action prior to death. From the fifteenth century onwards, ritual texts (like many theological documents dating from as early as three centuries before) no longer prescribed anointing for the sick, but described anointing as extreme unction (*extrema unctio* or *unctio exeuntium,* a term apparently used first by the twelfth-century theologian Peter Lombard). Anointing, which originally anticipated restoration to life, now foretold impending death.[27]

Many of the Protestant Reformers, who based their arguments upon their own exegesis of James 5, refuted the Roman restriction of anointing to the dying and the definition of the rite as a sacrament (since Christ himself had not ordained it). The German reformer Martin Luther saw in anointing a means of encouraging faith for those bearing their illness with impatience.[28] John Calvin, and others of the Reformed tradition, rejected both extreme unction and sacramental anointing, concluding that "that gift of healing, like the rest of the miracles, which the Lord willed to be brought forth for a time, has vanished away in order to make the new preaching of the gospel marvelous forever."[29] An exception to the negative critique was the Church of England's 1549 *Book of Common Prayer,* where Thomas Cranmer formulated on the basis of the English medieval rite (the Sarum Use) an "Order for the Visitation of the Sick," which retained an optional anointing (if desired by the infirm themselves, upon the forehead or breast) and included penitential elements and themes related to impending death. However, Martin Bucer, in his published criticism of the 1549 *Book of Common Prayer,* advocated the removal of the order for visitation because of the inclusion of anointing (a practice not instituted by "divine law").[30] In response, the 1552 revision of the *Book of Common Prayer* retained the order of visitation but omitted the anointing; this pattern was repeated in the 1662 revision.

With the exception of the Church of the Brethren and some Seventh-Day Adventists who anointed their infirm, and the presence of movements within Protestantism that sought recovery of the ancient practice (e.g., the eighteenth-century Non-Jurors of the Church of England), Protestant denominations generally did not recover the anointing of the sick until the twentieth century. The same is true for Roman Catholics where the sickness was not life-threatening, though the seeds for change were sown as early as the fourteenth session of the Council of Trent in 1551 and its resulting canons, where it was decreed that the anointing was to be applied to the sick, but especially to those who were in danger of death.[31] The statements of the Second Vatican Council (*Sacrosanctum Concilium,* 73–75; *Lumen Gentium,* 11) reinforce that unction is for all the sick, and that by the grace of the Holy Spirit forgiveness, healing, and strength may be bestowed. Many new provisions were made in the ritual text (*Ordo unctionis infirmorum eorumque pastoralis curae*) that was promulgated in 1972 along with the papal constitution *Sacram unctionem infirmorum:* in cases of "true" necessity, priests (rather than the bishop) may bless the oil; a minimum of two anointings are to be made (hands and forehead); vegetable oils other than olive oil may be used if cultural circumstances warrant it; and a congregational setting for the rite is encouraged.[32]

The Prayer of Faith

According to the text from James 5, the anointing of the sick is set within the framework of persistent prayer: the "prayer of faith" by the righteous of the community and the confession of sins by those in need of healing. Christian ritual texts have included both of these types of prayer, with and without the accompaniment of ritual anointing, for use in simple domestic rituals or within the context of larger, more elaborate communal and public rites.

Because of the absence of full ritual texts from the first centuries of the church, it is difficult to place in ritual context the isolated prayers that were included in various collections of liturgical material that date from or before the ninth century (e.g., Sarapion, and the Gelasian and Gregorian families of sacramentary manuscripts). These prayers, as they reappear (sometimes edited) in later and fuller collections, may provide clues as to the early practice, though caution must be exercised in reading more recent developments back into the past. The collections assign these prayers to the clergy, though this does not preclude the possibility that extempore prayers or established formularies were available for use by the laity, particularly those with gifts of healing, in the centuries before ritual care for the sick was restricted to the clergy.

Liturgical books produced after the ninth century record rites (*ordines*) that were established for the sick to be celebrated either in church or at the bedside, and that vary in the matter of their content and in the degree of elaboration and complexity; the rites for the infirm produced by monastic communities were quite detailed and lengthy, sometimes requiring the leadership of several priests. Multiple prayers within a particular rite might focus upon confession of sin, absolution, petition of divine aid for healing, and blessing. Accompanying the prayers were other ritual components which could include the sprinkling of sanctified water, the use of incense, the recitation of psalms and antiphons (particularly the seven penitential psalms), the declamation of lessons from scripture (especially healing stories from the Gospels), the singing of hymns (e.g., the Old Spanish or Mozarabic *Christe, caelestis medicina Patris*), the imposition of hands, or, as in the Byzantine rite after the eleventh century, the placement of the gospel book upon the head of the sick person.

The complexity of the ritual action often obscured the power and centrality of the "prayer of faith," a frequent complaint lodged by sixteenth-century Protestants. Prayer (extempore and formulated) and readings from the Bible constituted the core of the rites for visitation of the sick for many of the continental reformers.[33] Often, no ritual texts—but only rubrics—were included in their liturgical books, with the indication that the content of ritual care for the sick was to be determined by the pastor's own judgment (this was Calvin's preference and the practice, until recently, among Christians of the Reformed tradition). Extempore prayer was encouraged by some groups. Pastoral exhortations were expected; the 1549 and 1552 *Book of Common Prayer* included statements in print, whereas the Presbyterian *Westminster Directory* of 1644 outlined in detail suggested contents of the exhortation.

The centrality of prayer and scripture for Protestant ritual care of the sick has continued in the generations following the Protestant Reformation, as evident in the publication of prayer collections designed to guide the minister of care as well as to sustain the sick individual. Such compilations can be found in the breadth of Protestantism, from the *Manual for the Sick* published in the seventeenth century by Anglican Lancelot Andrewes, through the *Getreue Anleitung zur wahren Seelencur bey Krancken und Sterbenden* of the Lutheran pietist Bernhard Walter Marperger (Nuremburg, 1717), to the anthologies of prayers available today to pastors and constituents of the Free Churches.

Since the days of the early church, the imposition of hands upon the sick often accompanies prayer, and sometimes appears as a ritual action distinct and separate from anointing.[34] The New Testament Gospels attest that Jesus laid hands upon the infirm, and an alternate ending of the Gospel of Mark (found in numerous manuscripts) has Jesus instructing his disciples that "they will lay their hands on the sick, and they will recover" (Mark 16:18). The phrase in James 5:14, "let them pray *over him*" (in Greek, *'ep[i] auton*) has often been interpreted as a basis for the liturgical action of laying hands upon or over the sick.[35] This may be the assumption in the *Canons of Hippolytus* (canon 24), but is more likely the case in a prayer for the sick in Sarapion's prayer-book in which the "Lord God of mercies" is invoked to "stretch out [a] hand and grant that all the sick be healed."[36] For many Protestant traditions, laying on of hands has been an acceptable action to accompany prayer for healing (in lieu of anointing), as it has association with general liturgical gestures for blessing and peace, and has precedent in the action of Jesus himself.

Prayer thus far described has been that offered by the clergy and/or the community on behalf of the sick. In addition, ritual texts and customs often have the expectation that the sick individual will make his or her own prayer, usually in the form of ritual confession, with resulting absolution or words of forgiveness from the clergy, following the model provided in James 5:15. The medieval English rites, and the Church of England rites based upon them, accompany confession with the charge to the sick person to give generously to the poor. Some rites for the sick from the sixteenth century onward juxtapose personal confession of sin with a reaffirmation of the Christian faith using the form of an historic creed (occasionally in the interrogatory form, as at baptism in some traditions). In some services, it is unclear whether confession is linked directly with the rite for healing per se, or with the service of holy communion that often accompanies it.

The Communion of the Sick

Although ailing Christians were enjoined, with the rest of the Christian community, to partake of communion in the corporate celebration of the liturgy, there is documentation from Justin Martyr in the second century (*I Apology,* 65, 67) and onward that provisions were made to take the sacrament to those unable to attend. As was the case in the anointing of the sick, evidence from the first seven centuries attests that the laity along with the clergy could bring the consecrated eucharist to the infirm, but by the Carolingian period, distribution had

become the sole prerogative of the clergy. The normative practice until the Protestant Reformation was to "reserve" for distribution to the sick the bread and the wine (though often only
the bread) that had been saved from a previous liturgy celebrated in a consecrated building; there is only rare testimony to
the celebration of the full eucharistic liturgy in the home of the
ailing person. The custom was to rehearse in the presence of
the sick some parts of the eucharistic rite (e.g., a scripture
reading, a profession of faith, the Lord's Prayer, and the
Peace), but not the consecratory eucharistic prayer itself, since
communion was taken from the reserved sacrament (a *missa
sicca* or "dry Mass").[37] As with anointing, the sick could, in
principle, receive communion daily.

Sixteenth-century Protestant liturgies demonstrate the variety of Protestant opinion regarding the practice and the method
of giving communion to the sick.[38] For some, the communion
of the sick was restricted to the corporate eucharist of the community at the church. A few Lutheran church orders permitted
private services (the sick person and the pastor or priest alone)
at the church at a time other than regular service hours. On the
other hand, rites from the Reformed tradition, in general, instructed that members of the congregation (albeit a small number) be present at any celebration of the eucharist, either in the
home or in the church building, since to do otherwise would
obscure the sense of the fellowship of the church inherent in
the rite of eucharist. Communion of the sick from the reserved
sacrament was allowed in some rites; both Luther and, very re-
luctantly, Calvin gave sanction to the reservation of the sacrament as an option if such practices as solemn procession and
display of the sacrament were avoided. The definition of reservation could vary, and could refer to the eucharist reserved
from any previous service ("perpetual" reservation), or that retained from the same day's service. Celebration of the entire
communion liturgy in the dwelling of the sick was provided for
in some of the rites. Many texts included the requirement that
confession and absolution of sins be made prior to the reception of communion.

Occasions when the communion service was celebrated at the home of the infirm became opportunities for friends and family to receive the sacrament as well. Bedside communion was an important factor in satisfying the need for frequent communion desired by the Methodists in eighteenth-century England, who were often refused the sacrament at the hands of Anglican priests.

Communion of the sick, either by reserved sacrament or by the celebration of special rites, remains a vital component in pastoral care shared by all Christian traditions. Those churches that historically practiced communion of the sick and the visitation of the sick as two separate rites have, in the late twentieth century, often produced inclusive rites (with scripture readings, prayers, laying on of hands, anointing, and eucharist) that constitute an extensive liturgical ministry to the sick.[39] The ritual texts for both Roman Catholics and many Protestants demonstrate flexibility in locating the rites (church, home, or hospital) and in identifying the recipients of particular versions of the rite (e.g., for individuals, groups, children, and the terminally ill).

Rites for the Dying

The comprehensive rites for the sick—anointing, prayers for healing, prayers of confession, imposition of hands, and communion of the sick—were used also, throughout the centuries, for those near death. As has been seen, by the late Middle Ages, anointing of the sick came indeed to be termed extreme unction and was regarded as a penitential rite in preparation for death. Some texts refer to other penitential actions complementing the anointing, such as sackcloth (which the invalid wore or reclined upon) or hair shirts, and the imposition or sprinkling of ashes.

Medieval rites for the dying also included the reading of scripture, particularly portions of the Gospels dealing with the suffering of Christ before his death, the saying or singing of psalms, and prayers—all practices that have continued in the twentieth century within the Roman Catholic and other rites.[40] Monastic communities, such as that at Cluny, attended the dying with music, a practice that has been recently revived in some places.[41] Prayers for the commendation of the soul of the dying (*commendatio animae*) were used, texts for which are found in numerous medieval manuscripts. The prayer *Proficiscere anima* ("Go forth, O Christian soul, out of this world . . ."), which is first attested in the eighth century (in the sacramentaries of Gellone and Rheinau) and later spread widely throughout the Christian West, remains in use among Roman Catholics and is found in the rites for the dying of other Christians (e.g., twentieth-century revisions of the American Episcopal *Book of Common Prayer*). This prayer, in its various recensions, connects the dying person with God's people of every time and place, and reflects the Christian belief that death marks the transition to life in the nearer presence of God.

Preparation for the new life (or the judgment) anticipated at death was—and is—made through the administration of communion to the dying faithful. The practice of *viaticum* (literally, provision for the [last] journey) has its roots in the New Testament saying of Jesus that those who eat the flesh of Christ and drink his blood will be raised up at the last day (John 6:54). Since Christ instituted the eucharist immediately before his suffering and death, dying Christians were to partake of the holy meal in imitation of Christ's own actions and in the hope that they too would pass from death to life. Understood as the "medicine of immortality,"[42] communion was, at least from the fourth century on, deemed a duty for the dying Christian; canon 13 of the Council of Nicea (325 C.E.) legislated that penitents were not to be deprived of the eucharist at the hour of their death. Christian hagiography is rich with accounts of the saints receiving communion with their last breath, thereby providing encouragement for reception of the final communion by others and for the trials and pains of death.

NOTES

1. For more specific information on views of sickness by various Christian denominations, see the series published by the Crossroad Publishing Company, "Health/Medicine and the Faith Traditions," which includes separate volumes for Catholics, Anglicans, Lutherans, Methodists, and the Reformed.

2. Hermann von Wied, "Von der Kommunion der Pilger und Kranken," in *Einfältiges Bedenken* (Düsseldorf, 1972), pp. 164–65.

3. This prayer, from one of the earliest known eastern prayer books, is recorded in Aleksej Dmitrievskij, *Opisanie Liturgitseskich Rukopisej* (Kiev, 1901; reprint, Hildesheim, 1965), 2:5. In other texts, Jesus Christ is the one described as the "physician" or as the "medicine of souls." See, for example, Ignatius of Antioch, *Ad Ephesios* 7 (SC 10:62–65).

4. *Apostolic Tradition* 20; Geoffrey J. Cuming, *Hippolytus: A Text for Students,* Grove Liturgical Study 8 (Nottingham, 1976), p. 17. Cf. *Canons of Hippolytus* 19 and *Testamentum Domini* 2.6.

5. 1 Corinthians 12:9–10; cf. Justin Martyr, *Dialogus cum Tryphone* 39 (PG 6:559–62); Irenaeus, *Contra haereses* 2.31.2; 2.32.4–5 (SC 294:328–30, 340–43).

6. See *Apostolic Tradition* 14; cf. *Canons of Hippolytus* 8.

7. Exegesis of James 5:14 by the sixteenth-century reformer Martin Luther led him to suggest that the "elders" were not necessarily the clergy, but possibly senior lay people. See "The Babylonian Captivity of the Church," in the Weimar edition, *Luthers Werke* 6:569, lines 26–36, or the American edition, *Luther's Works* 36 (Philadelphia, 1959), p. 120.

8. The rather complex evolution of these two offices is delineated in Aimé Georges Martimort, *Deaconesses: An Historical Study* (San Francisco, 1986), and Bonnie Bowman Thurston, *The Widows: A Women's Ministry in the Early Church* (Minneapolis, 1989).

9. The duties of exorcism also belonged to deacons, priests and, supremely, to bishops. Churches of the East generally did not appoint exorcists as a distinct order. Evidence for a separate order of exorcists is found in the West (Rome) by the middle of the third century: see Eusebius, *Historia ecclesiastica* 6.43.11 (PG 20:621). Rubrics and liturgical rites for appointing or ordaining exorcists appear in, for example, the Gallican *Statuta Ecclesiae Antiqua* (c. 490); the *Missale*

Francorum (early eighth century); the Sacramentary of Angoulême, a late eighth-century composite of ancient Roman and Gallican forms; and the eleventh-century Leofric Missal. For these texts, see Paul F. Bradshaw, *Ordination Rites of the Ancient Churches of East and West* (New York, 1990), pp. 222, 224, 237–38; and F. E. Warren, *The Leofric Missal* (Oxford, 1883), p. 212.

10. See, for example, *Canons of Hippolytus* 3 and 4, and the texts for the East Syrian (post-fifteenth century), Georgian (tenth or eleventh century), and Jacobite (twelfth and thirteenth century) traditions in Bradshaw, *Ordination Rites,* pp. 161, 164, 171–72, 181, 184. Early western rites speak more generally of the episcopal authority to "bind and loose" (Matt. 16:19) and to remit sins (John 20:23).

11. E.g., *Canons of Hippolytus* 5 (cf. 24) and the fourteenth-century Coptic rite, cited in Bradshaw, *Ordination Rites,* p. 144.

12. Polycarp, *Epistola ad Philippenses* 6.1 (SC 10:184); *Apostolic Tradition* 34; *Canons of Hippolytus* 24 and 25.

13. E.g., "Ordo ad visitandum et unguendum infirmum," in Warren, *The Leofric Missal,* p. 241, where vespers and matins are mentioned.

14. A helpful study of eastern and western rites of anointing can be found in Elie Mélia, "The Sacrament of the Anointing of the Sick: Its Historical Development and Current Practice," in *Temple of the Holy Spirit: Sickness and Death of the Christian in the Liturgy* (New York, 1983), pp. 127–60.

15. The Roman Church retained the practice of blessing the oil at this point in the rite.

16. *Apostolic Tradition* 5. Evidence for the internal and external application of oil, specifically for the sick, continues in ninth-century manuscripts such as the Gelasian Sacramentary and the Bobbio Missal.

17. Blessings for a sick person's bread and water are also found in the early ninth-century St. Gall Sacramentary (Cod. Sangall. no. 350); see nos. 225, "Benedictio panis ad egrotum," and 226, "Benedictio aquae ad egrotum," in Georg Manz, ed., *Ein St. Galler Sakramentar-Fragment,* Liturgiegeschichtliche Quellen und Forschungen 31 (Münster, 1939), p. 30.

18. Prayer 17 in R. J. S. Barrett-Lennard, *The Sacramentary of Sarapion of Thmuis,* Alcuin/GROW Liturgical Study 25 (Nottingham, 1993), pp. 47–49; see also prayer 6. Some scholars speculate

that the second half of this prayer (not quoted here) is a prayer for the application of the oil.

19. In Rome, the blessing of the oil of the sick occurred on Holy Thursday, a practice that later spread throughout the West. Also on Holy Thursday, the bishop granted remission of sins to those who were penitent.

20. Emil Joseph Lengeling, "'Per istam sanctam unctionem . . . adiuvet te Dominus gratia Spiritus Sancti': Der heilige Geist und die Krankensalbung," in *Lex orandi, lex credendi. Miscellanea in onore di Cipriano Vagaggini,* Studia Anselmiana 79 (Rome, 1980), pp. 235–94.

21. E.g., *Epistula 25 ad Decentium* 11 (PL 20:560); and Gregorian Sacramentary, no. 334, in Jean Deshusses, ed., *Le sacramentaire grégorien: ses principales formes d'après les plus anciens manuscrits* (Fribourg, 1979), 1:172–73.

22. E.g., Councils of Chalon (813), Aix-la-Chapelle (836), and Mainz (847).

23. E.g., the ninth-century Sacramentary of Corbie/Rodradus and the Sacramentary of Tours, cited in Deshusses, *Le sacramentaire grégorien* (Fribourg, 1982), 3:146, 152.

24. Antoine Chavasse, "Prières pour les malades et onction sacramentelle," in *L'Église en prière,* ed. A. G. Martimort (Tournai, 1961), pp. 584–87. For a complete study, see Antoine Chavasse, *Étude sur l'onction des infirmes dans l'église latine du IIe au XIe siècle,* vol. 1, *Du IIIe siècle à la réforme carolingienne* (Lyons, 1942).

25. See the rubrics in the Sacramentary of Corbie and the Sacramentary of Tours, cited in Deshusses, *Le sacramentaire grégorien* 3:146, 153.

26. Differing opinions about anointing as a rite for the dying are evident in the writings of the early scholastic period. Compare, for example, Hugh of St. Victor, *De sacramentis* 2.15.2–3 (PL 176:577–80) and the *Epitome theologiae christianae* 30 (PL 178:1744–45).

27. This position was reinforced by the Decree for the Armenians from the Council of Florence (1439).

28. "The Babylonian Captivity of the Church," Weimar edition *Luthers Werke* 6:570, lines 7–10, and American edition *Luther's Works* 36:121.

29. John Calvin, *Institutes of the Christian Religion* 4.19.18, ed. John T. McNeill (Philadelphia, 1960), 2:1467. See also 4.19.19–21.

30. Bucer's *Censura,* in E. C. Whitaker, *Martin Bucer and the Book of Common Prayer,* Alcuin Club Collections 55 (Great Wakering, 1974), pp. 124–27.

31. See André Duval, "L'extrême-onction au Concile de Trente, sacrement des mourants ou sacrement des malades?" *La Maison-Dieu* 101 (1970): 127–72.

32. Helpful studies on the evolution and practice of the revised Roman Catholic rite include Pierre Marie Gy, "Le nouveau rituel romain de malades," *La Maison-Dieu* 113 (1973): 29–49; Charles W. Gusmer, *And You Visited Me: Sacramental Ministry to the Sick and the Dying* (New York, 1984), pp. 33–37, 51–98; and Annibale Bugnini, *The Reform of the Liturgy, 1948–1975* (Collegeville, MN, 1990), pp. 684–93.

33. E.g., the 1537 rite produced by the Strasburg reformers (including Bucer), outlined in G. J. van de Poll, *Martin Bucer's Liturgical Ideas* (Assen, 1954), pp. 53–54.

34. The connection between laying on of hands and anointing is clear in the Ambrosian liturgy of Milan where unction is called *impositio manuum.*

35. E.g., Origen, *Homiliae in Leviticum* 2.4 (SC 286:110).

36. Prayer 30, in Barrett-Lennard, *The Sacramentary of Sarapion,* p. 19.

37. See, for example, the *missae de infirmis* from the Irish Books of Dimma and Mulling in F. E. Warren, *The Liturgy and Ritual of the Celtic Church* (Oxford, 1881), pp. 167–73.

38. One of the best sources discussing historic Protestant perspectives on communion of the sick is still the now somewhat-dated essay by Charles Harris in W. K. Lowther Clarke, ed., *Liturgy and Worship* (New York, 1932), pp. 541–615. The material included here is summarized from Harris.

39. See, for example, the rites produced in the United States by the Episcopal Church (1979), the United Methodist Church (1992), and the Presbyterian Church, U.S.A (1993).

40. Discussion of early medieval rituals for the dying are included in Frederick S. Paxton, *Christianizing Death: The Creation of a Ritual Process in Early Medieval Europe* (Ithaca, NY, 1990).

41. See the work of Therese Schroeder-Sheker and the Chalice of Repose Project.

42. Ignatius of Antioch, *Ad Ephesios* 20 (SC 10:76).

"Visiting the Sick" and the Deathbed Confession in Judaism

Stacy Laveson

Introduction: Bikkur Cholim *("Visiting the Sick") as Ritual*

In Jewish tradition, *bikkur cholim*—literally, "visiting the sick"—is more than a voluntary act of kindness. Raised to the level of *mitzvah,* it becomes a personal religious duty, on a par with daily prayer or the various practices associated with observing sacred time. It has therefore become a fully liturgical accompaniment to the course of human progress from birth to death.

To be sure, it is not normally associated with our modern conception of "life cycle," probably for two reasons. To begin with, life-cycle events in Judaism are conceived as things people do for themselves (they marry, for instance), or things that get done to them by others (they are inducted into a covenant at the time of birth, or are buried when they die). But *bikkur cholim* is in neither category: others initiate the visit and pray for the patient, but most moderns, at least, do not readily grant any immediate effect upon the subject in the same way that we do in the case of circumcising a boy or depositing a body in the earth.

More than that, however, is the second factor: life-cycle ritual is intensely marker-related. That is, we have been taught to see a human life as falling into discrete stages going from birth to death, each initiated by ritual markers; and it is these markers that normally are said to constitute the cycle of a life. Even when traditional rites do not easily or automatically fall at particular biological points of reference, we like to think that they

173

do, and if need be, we erect a fiction that says so. Circumcision (in Judaism) and baptism (for Christians), for instance, are not necessarily birth rites, but we conceive of them as such. People marry at any age, but we decide it marks young adulthood—in fact, people celebrating second or third marriages, or even a first marriage in old age, often tell the rabbi not to make too much of the event; it seems ill-timed, wrongly placed in the life-cycle list of expectations.

Sickness is, of course, associated most easily (albeit painfully) with death. Jewish law codes know this; they invariably juxtapose the chapter regulating sick care with a following one that details the ritualizing of funerals. But sickness, we know, comes many times in life; we balk, therefore, at attaching it to the single event with which it has the most in common, preferring to believe that more often than not we will get better when we feel a cold coming on; and indeed, we usually do. Nonetheless, if a religious rite is a set of actions that are ritualized around religious values, visiting the sick in Judaism is such a rite. The term "visiting" falls short of "anointing" or "praying over"—other actions that come to mind in other traditions; even secularists "visit." But "visiting" is here used technically: the English equivalent of *bikkur* from *bikkur cholim,* the normal term used by Jewish law codes to describe "visiting the sick." We shall see in what follows just how ritualized the religious *mitzvah* of visiting the sick is in Jewish tradition; and how it eventuates in extreme instances in prescribed actions designed to prepare the terminally ill patient for death. At that point, it begins to look like religious ritual, and a life-cycle one at that, since it is outfitted with prayer and confession, and seen as a preparation for death. We will turn to it in due time, but first, we need to survey the less than critical situation in which visiting alone is sufficient.

After a brief description, therefore, of the religious quality invested in visiting the sick generally, we will survey the ritual called for at the bed of the dying. At that point, we will emphasize the historical development of the rites in question, seeing especially how the confession that is so widely taken for granted today is actually an innovation of the Middle Ages (albeit with earlier precedent). And we will consider the use of that rite today, particularly among more secularized Jews for whom preparation for death is distinctly secondary to its prevention, even when prevention is no longer a feasible option. I turn first, however, to visiting in general, where a historical perspective is not required, since the attitudes in question were all in place by the time the amoraic age came to its close.

Visiting the Sick and Praying for Recovery

The Rabbis enjoined all Jews to comfort the sick, to be present at their bedside, and to pray for mercy on their behalf, finding a variety of biblical proof texts for the practice, but particularly Genesis 18:1, God's visit to Abraham following his circumcision. Implicitly, however, the Rabbis linked *our* visits with parallel visits designed for the dead as well, whether to comfort mourners or to bury the deceased. They thus juxtaposed Genesis 18:1 with Genesis 25:2 and Deuteronomy 34:6, which are taken to denote God's comforting Isaac after Abraham dies, and God's burying Moses, respectively.

"The Holy One visits the sick, as it is written, 'God appeared to him [Abraham] at Elohei Mamre.' So should you visit the sick. . . . The Holy One also comforts mourners, for it is written, 'After the death of Abraham God blessed Isaac his son.' So should you comfort mourners. The Holy One buries the dead, for it is written, 'God buried him in the valley.' So should you bury the dead."[1]

Hence, visiting the sick, like burying the dead and comforting the bereaved, are related instances of *imitatio dei,* instances of human striving to be God-like. The sick are to be visited regardless of religion, age, or class.[2] Visiting is a *mitzvah* of such overriding significance that it is one of only six deeds whose reward is enjoyed in this lifetime and the next, for on earth it conveys honor from others while meriting protection from the evil inclination and suffering, and in the world to come its practitioners are saved from hell itself.[3] And as for those visited, visiting in and of itself was held to relieve their pain, to the point where not to visit was equivalent to actually bringing on the patient's death, which the visit might have delayed or even prevented.[4]

Rabbinic ritual directing visitors in the proper performance of this commandment advocates arranging one's visit so as to protect the patient from as much suffering as possible, and to avoid leading the patient incorrectly to conclude that the visitor has arrived only because death is imminent. With the exception of relatives and close friends, visits are to be delayed three days, in the hope that the illness will abate of its own accord.[5] Visitors should not arrive early in the morning as attendants are usually occupied with the patient then, so that the suffering of the illness lightens and visitors may not be sufficiently moved to pray for the illness to lift. But it is disadvantageous also to visit in the evening when the patient is so tired that the visit may prove onerous, and in any case, visitors should not sit on a plane higher than the patient's gaze, lest again, the patient be unusually troubled rather than helped by the mechanics of the visit.[6] It may also be that the patient is to be protected from looking heavenward whence those forces who bring the end may appear.

Whatever their logic, these and similar rabbinic regulations governing *bikkur cholim* are not just points of etiquette or even good judgement recommended by the hospital staff; they are religious dictates that shape mere voluntary visits into predictable ritualized sequences of behavior. Though not yet formalized religious rites that constitute Judaism's ritual, those rites are only a short step away, visible, for instance, in the medieval practice of formally changing a sick person's name (*Shinui Hashem*) and in the *Mi Sheberakh,* the prayer from the same period uttered in the synagogue for the recovery of a sick relative or community member. The latter, fully recognizable as liturgical "ritual" in a western context, is still the most widely practiced rite connected with sickness, and in fact, is undergoing a sort of renaissance among liberal Jews who abandoned it as superstitious only a few generations ago.[7] The former, still common in some Orthodox circles especially, derives from the talmudic notion that changing a name can cancel the doom of the dying.[8] It is mentioned specifically by the twelfth-century German authority, Judah Hechasid.[9]

Given the high value that Jewish tradition accords to life—saving a life (*pikuach nefesh*) supersedes every positive religious duty, and even cancels out most prohibitions that stand in its way[10]—and given also the rabbinic assumption that God can be moved by prayer to heal the sick, it is no surprise to find that prayer becomes the basic element of *bikkur cholim*. It is a powerful tool in the hand of the visitor, the whole point, in fact of the visit:

> Rav Dimi said, "One who visits the sick causes them to live, while one who does not, causes them to die."
>
> Shall we interpret his reasoning as being that one who visits the sick prays that they should live, while one who does not prays that they should die?
>
> 'That they should die?' It is not believable that someone would pray so! He must therefore have meant to say that one who does not visit the sick prays neither that they may live nor that they may die.[11]

It is the visitor's act of prayer or its absence, then, that matters, and visiting is above all an occasion to pray.

To be sure, medieval authorities influenced by Islamic medicine modified the dependence on prayer that the Talmud seemed to imply. Thus, for instance, the thirteenth-century Spanish rabbi-physician, Moses Nachmanides (whose treatise on sickness and death, *Torat Ha'adam,* will recur in these pages), cautioned that visitors must first endeavor to bring all available medical care, and only afterward, resort to prayer. But he advocated also the traditional belief that a visit without prayer, even by a physician, falls short of fulfilling one's requisite religious obligation. Prayer, therefore, is the basic ritual response to illness, and (as we shall see, when we later arrive at the rite of confession) even the deathbed confession is a last resort that comes about only after prayer seems to have failed to effect a cure.

Until the medieval period, however, little is written about the exact nature of the prayers to be recited by or for the ill. Prior records contain only a few liturgical formulas, no doubt as suggestions rather than as mandatory or exclusive wording. The Talmud, for instance, prescribes, "May God have mercy upon you among the sick of Israel."[12] Typical of others that we will encounter later, this short prayer invokes the divine attribute of mercy. Psalms are also to be recited during illness, either by the sick themselves, or by those standing by them at their bedside—in particular, Psalm 119, which consists of twenty–two stanzas corresponding to the letters of the Hebrew alphabet; Psalm 23, which replaces a patient's fear with resolute faith in God; and Psalm 103, which affirms God's pardoning and redemptive power.

Deathbed Confession: Tannaitic, Amoraic, and Geonic Precedent

When prayer seems to fail and illness becomes so critical as to suggest that death is imminent, however, a deathbed confession is prescribed. Our earliest reference to deathbed confession (*Vidui al Hamitah*), is found in the specific and very limited case of a criminal whom the Mishnah advises to confess his sin before being executed.[13] As proof text, we find the case of Achan whose theft at Jericho brought about the Israelites' defeat at Ai. When the culprit, Achan, was located, Joshua entreated him, "Pay respect to the Eternal, the God of Israel, and make confession to God; tell me what you have done; hide nothing from me" (Josh. 7:19). This passage recurs as precedent in later literature on the deathbed confession, even when the subject has been extended beyond criminals to include everyone for whom death is imminent.

According to the Mishnah, confessing at the time of death earns the confessor a share in the world to come. It is apparent, then, that for the Tannaim, confession was the way for people guilty of a crime serious enough to warrant execution to atone and to achieve redemption. While no specific confessional formula is given, the Mishnah does state that if one does not know how to confess, it is acceptable to say, "May my death be an atonement for my sins." This brief formula is later incorporated into the liturgy of the confession on the deathbed as we know it still today.

It is the Talmud which extends the circumstances calling for confession to include terminal illness in general:

> Whoever becomes ill and is about to die, is told, "Make confession, for all who are about to die must confess." If you go into the street, you should imagine that you are being placed in police custody; if you get a headache, think of it as being handcuffed; if you are bedridden, see yourself as if you were ascending the scaffold for punishment; for anyone who ascends the scaffold but who has powerful advocates, gets saved. . . . And these are a person's advocates: repentance and good deeds.[14]

Illustrated in this talmudic passage is the great redemptive power of confession and of good deeds. Those on their deathbed are presumably unable to effect any of the latter, but they can still take advantage of the former. The parallelism between Achan's sentence and ordinary sickness is expressed here in the extended metaphoric description of life's ordinary vicissitudes as divine retribution for sin. It is sin, therefore, which causes sickness, and confession that brings about healing, possibly even rescuing a person from the very grip of death.

The midrash extends our picture somewhat for the early period, but not by much. We do however find a proof text (Num. 5:6–7) that takes us beyond analogy to the case of Achan: "When a man or woman wrongs another, breaking faith with the Eternal, that person incurs guilt and shall confess the sin that was committed." As the midrash interprets it, "This passage is the foundation for the principle that all who are about to die must confess their sins."[15]

The tannaitic and amoraic periods thus provide the fundamental mandate that one must confess before one's death, but as with liturgy in general in that early period of time, the deathbed ritual remains largely undeveloped with only a brief confessional formula prescribed. Between 500 and 1000, only passing mention of the deathbed confession can be found. Of major importance, however, is the prayer for recovery composed by Saadiah Gaon (892–942). It begins with a first-person singular adaptation of the standard petition for healing from the daily *Tefillah* ("Heal me, God, and I shall be healed"), and continues with praise of God and the recitation of God's saving attributes.[16] The prayer thus includes not only petition, but affirmation of faith in God who can and will save us. It later is adopted as the kernel whence the standard deathbed liturgy evolves.

But apart from Saadiah Gaon's prayer, geonic literature and even the early material from authorities in North Africa and western Europe display only minor contributions to the liturgy for the ill and dying. We find, for instance, Rabbenu Nissim (990–1062) noting an opinion to the effect that people should constantly request mercy so that they will not fall ill.[17] Praying as a prophylactic against getting sick must have been commonplace. And Rashi (1040–1105), of northern France, adds that when the Talmud obliges those who are ill and about to die to confess, the responsibility to see that they do so rests upon those who are standing by the patient's bedside.[18] Thus, while Rashi does not develop the actual confession, he does indicate obliquely that one should not die alone, that others must be present at the time of death, and that the rite of confession is in some way bound up with a further obligation that the bystanders implicitly accept by being there.

Influence of Mysticism; Innovations of Nachmanides

Only in the post-Crusade environment of the twelfth and thirteenth centuries does a specific confessional formula begin to take shape. Contributing to the proliferation of confession as an important part of Jewish life-cycle ritual are the German Pietists, or Chasidei Ashkenaz, for whom direct confession becomes a central component of religious life.[19] But even more influential than these northern mystics is a representative of

Spanish Kabbalah, Moses ben Nachman (1194–1270, also known as Nachmanides), whom we have already met. It is he who actually records the deathbed confession that is still central to what people say today. Thus, roughly 1,000 years passed from the first mention of confession in the Mishnah, until a confessional formula finally appears in all its fullness in our textual tradition.

One must ask, therefore, why the confessional formula is written specifically during this period, and why is it Nachmanides who records it. The answer is to be found in the doctrines of the Kabbalah. Nachmanides anticipated the composition of the *Zohar,* which came into being between 1280 and 1286, by Moses Shem Tov de Leon of Spain. But like the *Zohar*'s author, Nachmanides was a central figure among Spanish Kabbalists, and in addition, a legalist and thinker of incomparably greater stature, who actually "prepared the way for reception of the Kabbalah in Spain."[20] The Kabbalistic emphasis upon the soul, redemption, and yearning for the Divine fueled interest in prayer and confession on the deathbed.

The *Zohar,* for instance, reflects upon the fate of the soul following its departure from the body, understanding the last day of one's life to be the ultimate and final Day of Judgment. A serious illness, therefore, is seen as a dangerous crisis, which the *Zohar* presents in stark imagery, beginning with patients on the verge of death being forced to record every act that they have done:

> They give an account of it all, and [heavenly appointees] write it all down in their presence. This is the meaning of, "Behold, the One who formed the mountains and creates the wind tells human beings what their thoughts are" [Amos 4:13]. They [the sick] confess them. Why? Because every deed that they perform ascends the stand to testify about them. These deeds complete their testimony, and then descend from the stand in order to be listed in the presence of those who did them. They are recorded in the doers' presence, and then they stand in front of them, refusing to depart until the time arrives for them to be judged through their deeds in that other world.[21]

The effect upon the body of the dying patient is evident to all around,

> When the time comes to depart from the world, and the dying person sees what there is to see, the spirit moves through every part of the body, following all its convolutions, like someone who sets out to sea without oars, going up and down without any peace. It enters and exits every bodily organ, so that no time is more violent than the day when the soul separates from the body.[22]

Informed by such notions as these, Nachmanides acknowledges the crisis of sickness and impinging death, recording his views regarding illness, mourning, and resurrection of the dead in a treatise entitled *Torat Ha'adam.* Illustrative of the potency of confession for Nachmanides is his assertion that "there are many who confess and do not die, and there are many who do not confess and die anyway . . . [but] on the merit of our dying confession, we shall live." As a physician, he knew well that confession and death are not interrelated, so he warns against a simplistic view that posits confession as a simple preparation for imminent demise; and simultaneously, he retains the rabbinic faith in confession to ward off early death, should God respond with merciful healing even at the eleventh hour. But, he claims, even if we die, it remains true nonetheless that we live because of our confession—that is, the ultimate life of the soul depends on confessing before the death of the body occurs. Nachmanides thus provides his own advice on how confession ought to occur: out loud, if possible, and in full grasp of one's senses, so that the gravity of the act is fully in mind at the time; but not in front of simple people who might wrongly conclude that they are watching the death throes of their loved one.

As for the text itself, if one is unable to voice a more extensive confession, one should say at least, "May my death be an atonement for my sins." In addition, borrowing on the Yom Kippur confession recorded in the Talmud (Yoma 36b), one should add, *aviti fashati chatati* ("I have committed iniquity, transgression and sin" [Lev. 34:7]). If possible, however, one should say a somewhat longer text, which Nachmanides claims to have received from *chasidim ve'anshei emunah* ("pietists and men of faith"):

> I acknowledge before You, my God and God of my ancestors, that my recovery and my death are equally in your hands. May it be your will that You heal me with a complete recovery. But if I die, may my death be an atonement for all the mistakes that I have made, the sins I have committed, and the rebellious behavior for which I am responsible. May You grant me a portion in the Garden of Eden, and may You allow me to merit entrance into the world to come which lies in store for the righteous.[23]

Nachmanides' prayer of confession—it is generally attributed directly to him, since his is the first citation of it—quickly became the accepted text for the deathbed, and later, when it was outfitted with other material, it remained the primary prayer of the liturgical service recited by the sick and dying.

The next step was the outfitting of Nachmanides' text with liturgical additions, a process that occurs by the mid-sixteenth century, in a body of literature that comes into being specifically to prepare people for death. Both practical and theological, these books take for granted the validity of the Kabbalistic tradition, usually citing it at great length in a popular format accessible to Jews who could not have mastered the complex tracts that only scholars understood. They effectively transformed elitist Kabbalistic doctrine into popularized everyday belief, altering Jewish ritual enormously in the process. The most important of these works are *Ma'avar Yabok* ("The Ford of the Yabok") and *Gesher Hachayim* ("The Bridge of Life").

Ma'avar Yabok *by Aaron Berechiah ben Moses of Modena*

Ma'avar Yabok is the work of Aaron Berechiah ben Moses of Modena (d. 1639). It quickly gained acceptance as the standard for ritual practice for the sick and dying. First published in 1626, the work was reproduced in an abbreviated form in 1682, and by 1800, at least eighteen editions of the latter had been issued by presses in Bohemia, Germany, and Italy.[24] Two principal factors influenced Aaron's writing of *Ma'avar Yabok*. First and foremost was his passion for Kabbalah, the Lurianic version of which had taken Italy by storm via Israel Sarug, Luria's disciple and a prominent Kabbalist in his own right.[25] *Ma'avar Yabok* thus emphasizes the familiar Kabbalistic themes of the fate of the soul, the need to care for its overall spiritual well-being by purging it of impurity, and the therapeutic power of ritual and prayer during illness and death.

Of equal importance, however, was a sociological phenomenon to which Aaron was drawn: involvement in a mutual aid society known as a Holy Brotherhood (*Chevrat gemilut chasadim*). The brotherhoods had begun in Spain, where they reflected the Kabbalistic concern to provide rest for the soul.[26] As such, their members went from house to house caring for the sick, and provided worship services where there were mourners—where, that is, the souls of the departed required prayers if they were to ascend to heaven as they should. By the sixteenth century, brotherhoods began appearing elsewhere, especially in Germany, prompted in large part by the rash of persecution that typified Jewish life there,[27] but also in Italy, where a brotherhood was formed in Mantua in 1516. Kabbalistic theology and the social phenomenon of the *Chevrat gemilut chasadim* came together in Aaron's handbook for taking care of the sick and preparing the soul for its ultimate journey back to its source.

Ma'avar Yabok thus provides an intricate liturgy for the sick and dying, an actual *Seder Tefillah,* or order of prayer, complete with psalms and readings to guide the patient back to health, if possible, and if not, to facilitate the necessary process of dying. Aaron defines successive stages of the journey: self-examination, standing in judgment, spiritual cleansing, acceptance of death, and finally, an affirmation of God. At each stage, the patient invokes God's attribute of mercy, especially in its unique Kabbalistic overtones which assigned to the merciful side of God's nature the power of healing and of salvation in the afterlife.

Patients who sense that death may come soon are first to wash their hands, as a symbolic gesture of purification. They then take the *tsitsit* (the fringes on the corners of a *tallit,* the ritual prayer shawl) and wrap them around their hand, weaving the fringes through the fingers. The fringes serve to remind the patient of God's commandments—in this instance, the commandment to give *tzedakah* (charity). As a final physical gesture, they actually dispense charity, either "with the hand or the mouth" (physically giving coins to the needy or instructing another to do so on their behalf).[28] This act serves as a reminder to the dying of the transience of life on earth.[29]

If in addition, death seems imminent, the gravely ill follow up their act of charity by confessing—if need be, prompted to do so by those in attendance; if patients are themselves too weak or too sick to recite the confession, a community member recites it for them. The community's presence is all-important here; one gathers the customary quorum of ten (a *minyan*) around the dying person because, says Aaron, "Holiness resides within them and within the ten sparks of their souls which keep away Satan and evil."[30] The point is not just theological, however, but intensely practical: to assure that no one dies alone! It is necessary for the soul to be ushered into the world-to-come only alongside the accompanying prayers of its community. Aaron thus cites as his motivation for composing *Ma'avar Yabok* in the first place, the desire "to make sure that the community can join in song and prayer at the time of the soul's departure."[31]

The title, *Ma'avar Yabok* ("The Ford of the Yabok") is borrowed from Genesis 32:23, Jacob's crossing the Ford of Yabok, but here implying the crossing over of the soul after death, Yabok being a sort of River Styx in Kabbalistic Jewish lore. Like Jacob, the dying are to look back, gather their spiritual resources, confront the person they really are, and then cross to the other side where they will encounter the Presence of God and ultimate reconciliation. As Aaron puts it,

"I present [my book] as an offering and as incense in love and in reverence . . . so that it will prepare a way in the midst of the

shaking worlds. It is a bridge from the world of change and destruction, with its sinful condition . . . to the heavenly pleasures
of unity, blessing and holiness. [The dying] will pass over the ford
of Yabok to wrestle with God . . . until the dawn—that is, immortality—for then our soul and body will no longer be called Jacob,
but Israel, in that we will be a kingdom of priests and we will be
worthy of seeing God face to face."[32]

Confession is the means for traversing the bridge between
worlds, and as such, it is expanded in Aaron's handbook. It is
prefaced, however, with an abundance of prayers for healing,
including Saadiah Gaon's by-now familiar formula, "Heal me
and I shall be healed. Save me and I shall be saved."[33] The
prayers include Psalm 4, in which David pleads for God's
mercy all the while proclaiming his faith in God and urging
others to do so; they culminate in a moving declaration that is
particularly profound when spoken moments before death:
"Safe and sound I lie down and sleep, for You alone, Adonai,
keep me secure."

Aaron's confessional text closely resembles the confession
of sins from the Yom Kippur liturgy, in that it is composed in
an acrostic that guides the patient through an alphabetical list-
ing of sins. In the opening words of the confession, the dying
person appeals to God to heed the words about to be uttered,
imploring (again, from the Yom Kippur service), "Do not be
deaf to my plea, for I am not so arrogant and stiff-necked in my
confession as to say before You, Adonai, God of my ancestors,
I am righteous and have not sinned, but rather, I have sinned, I
have committed iniquity, and I have rebelled."[34]

Of great significance here is Aaron's inclusion of a version
of this text in the feminine. The Jewish class system gave priority to men over women and within the class of men, to
scholars in particular. Aaron himself demonstrates his loyalty
to hierarchy in that he provides for a special prayer if the
dying person is a Torah scholar. (Those in attendance refer to
the scholar's lifelong search for knowledge, after which the
latter pleads, "May I be worthy of hearing the words and se-
crets of the Torah from the head of the Academy on High.")[35]

Generally speaking, this class system prevents our knowing for sure just how much any particular liturgy was used also for women, but here we find certain evidence that Aaron intended his own contribution to serve for men and women equally.

The next prayer integrates the short confession found in the Talmud (San. 43b) originally intended only for criminals, "May my death be an atonement for my sins," with Nachmanides' familiar text (see above). In sacrificial images typical of the Kabbalah, the liturgy then develops its own momentum:

> May my body be an altar and may my soul be a pure sacrifice. Through my death may I be granted forgiveness, and may my illness be an atonement for all of my transgressions, iniquities, and sins that I have committed before You from the first day of my existence until today. May my lot be among the righteous in the Garden of Eden.[36]

The body may perish, but the soul is pictured as rising like smoke from a burnt offering to God on high. Beyond expectation of cure, the dying have cleansed their soul of the dross of mortal sin; what confession has not accomplished, the ultimate sacrifice of death will manage, for "the garment of the body is a kind of imprisonment for the soul; it shackles it and forms a barrier between it and its origin in the upper world."[37] With death over and done with, however, the soul will cross over the Yabok to be joined to the other pure ones who make up Israel. As a final preparation for the journey, Aaron stipulates praise of God as the source of mercy and atonement. But the dying person may also recite: *Oseh Shalom* from the *Kaddish*—an affirmation that God makes peace on high; the *Shema*; the *Yigdal*—a poetic version of Maimonides' thirteen principles of faith, including an affirmation of resurrection; and *Adon Olam*, a medieval prayer of uncertain origin that concludes, "At the time to sleep, I deposit my soul with God; I will awaken, body and soul; God is with me; I do not fear."[38] Death will come with God's name on one's lips. Aaron knows that this way, one may actually rejoice on the day of death, "for the day of death is perfectly complete, for one inherits eternity. . . . The Talmud rightly records, 'To die smiling is a good omen.'"[39]

The deathbed is then moved away from the wall and the window is opened to facilitate the departure of the soul. A candle is lit, since "the life of the dying is like a dripping candle."[40] Those present recite the words that legend ascribes to Moses when he was told he had only one moment to live, "Blessed is God's name; God lives and endures forever."[41]

Ma'avar Yabok thus reflects a two-fold attitude toward death. On the one hand, one attempts to avert it by praying for a complete recovery. On the other hand, one approaches it joyously with the knowledge that soon, the soul will be set free to encounter the Divine Presence in the world-to-come. Prayers move deftly from petitions for healing to requests for forgiveness and the search for atonement. Once our physical condition deteriorates to the point where death seems unavoidable, the liturgy shifts its focus to an acceptance of death, faith in God's goodness, and the joy attendant upon the soul being freed from the fetters of this world.

Sefer Hachayim *by Simon Frankfurter*

Like *Ma'avar Yabok, Sefer Hachayim* presents us with a system of prayers and ritual designed to guide those who are sick through their illness, and those who are mortally ill, through the dying process. In addition, this manual is intended to instruct others how to properly administer to their spiritual needs. The role of caretaker for the sick and dying, says Frankfurter, is vital, for it encompasses the burden of encouraging the deathbed confession, and if need be, even the recitation of the confession and its accompanying liturgy on behalf of patients who may not be able to do so themselves. Published first in Amsterdam in 1703, *Sefer Hachayim* presents practical and accessible guidance for the masses.

The atmosphere of the seventeenth century was especially conducive to the publication of manuals such as this one. Popular piety, which has been characterized as "religion of the heart," swept through Europe in general, provoking heightened interest in religious ritual.[42] Jews in particular had to contend with the traumatic end of the Sabbetai Zevi controversy. Sabbetai's messianic pretensions had raised eschatological hopes from the Ottoman empire, where he lived and preached, all the way to Amsterdam, where the newly Protestantized Netherlands engaged in trade with the Ottoman Turks. Sabbetai's conversion to Islam so as to avoid execution only increased the hopes for a world-to-come, as his followers claimed that their master's apostasy was a final act with a mystical purpose designed only to hasten the end. In addition, Jews were frequently victimized by uncontrolled violence, the most well-known being the 1648 Chmielnicki Massacres in Poland and the Ukraine, wherein entire Jewish communities died. In the wake of all this ideological and physical turmoil, the "religion of the heart" for Jews turned increasingly to concern for the dying.

Frankfurter's main objective was to make daily ritual accessible to all Jews, many of whom lived in isolated, rural communities. Toward that end, he combined practical instruction and prayer in a manual for use during illness and on the deathbed, simplifying or omitting entirely many of the esoteric notions that he found in *Ma'avar Yabok*. Contained in *Sefer Hachayim* are confessions for the gravely ill, prayers to be repeated by sufferers, prayers on behalf of the sick to be recited by a rabbi or others who are present, prayers of thanksgiving upon recovering from an illness, and reflections of thanksgiving upon recovering from an illness.[43] Throughout it all, one hears the voice of Frankfurter assuring us that "through prayer, confession, and repentance, God's judgment may be transformed into mercy, thus averting the evil decree."[44] As Ezekiel has promised on God's behalf, "I take pleasure not in the death of the wicked but in the return of the wicked from evil, that they may live."[45]

While Frankfurter borrows heavily from Aaron Berechiah in the arrangement and contents of *Sefer Hachayim,* he also departs from his predecessor's format in significant ways. One striking example of Frankfurter's own innovation is the inclusion of a general confession of sins to be recited by the sick person even before death seems imminent. Crucial to Frankfurter is that one is able to recite this important confession before the physical and mental condition worsens significantly enough to prevent its proper recitation. Moreover, Frankfurter emphasizes the curative efficacy of prayer and confession. Since life and death depend entirely on the will of God, one must continually pray to avert death, knowing that if, perchance, it is God's will that one should die anyway, prayer and confession are preparations also for death. "Prayer and confession very often cause our days to be prolonged," he explains, so that we "should rely not only on the human physician, and on medical prescriptions, but on God, who causes us to die, and who revives us."[46] Prayer is thus necessary if we are to make peace with death.

Frankfurter also breaks new ground in his contention that confession before God alone is insufficient. If we are to attain complete forgiveness before dying, we also must seek pardon from individuals whom we have wronged, and forgive others who have injured us by word or deed.

Following the final confessions, the dying person recites prayers which testify to faith in God. God's attributes are extolled: "The Eternal is merciful and gracious, slow in anger and abundant in mercy."[47] In the last moments before death, one turns to God humbly and faithfully, resigning oneself to God's decree, and thanking God for being allowed to die undisturbed on one's bed. So that one's soul may depart the body and enter the heavenly realm, the dying are urged to recite Psalm 118:19 (*Pitchu li sha'arei tzedek . . .*), "Open for me the gates of righteousness, and I will enter there to thank the Eternal."[48] Other psalms are recited by those in attendance, until the dying patient is escorted out of this world with the words of the *Shema*.

Like Aaron Berechiah of Modena, Frankfurter too believes that death warrants rejoicing: "When we enter life, a life pregnant with troubles and sorrows, we all ought to be sad, inasmuch as we are not certain whether we will be able to stand up to them; while at our tranquil exit from life, we all ought to rejoice, for we then know that our mundane sufferings are terminated."[49] Death announces the joy of ultimate peace that awaits us in the world-to-come.

Conclusion

With the appearance of *Sefer Hachayim,* liturgy for sickness and dying became commonplace in Jewish life. Frankfurter's work was itself printed many times over, not only in Hebrew but also in Yiddish and English translation. A shortened liturgy dependent upon it, as well as upon *Ma'avar Yabok* and that volume's predecessors from the Talmud to Nachmanides, was included in prayer manuals the world over, for instance, in Hyman E. Goldin's *Hamadrikh,* first published in New York in 1939 as a practical guide to second-generation eastern European immigrants. Goldin devotes short sections of his work to "Laws Concerning Visiting the Sick," "Prayers on Behalf of the Sick," "Service for Adding [i.e., Changing] a Name," and "Laws of and Service for Confession."[50] But his sections are short, and his inclusion of material from Aaron Berechiah and Frankfurter is not extensive. The changeover to modernity is evident here: unlike the Kabbalist writings, where dying is of primary concern, this 258-page American manual restricts the rites connected to death to a mere ten pages.

An American who more than anyone else evoked contemporary interest in the process of dying, Elisabeth Kübler-Ross, once remarked,

> I have always wondered why the Jews as a people have not written more on death and dying. Who better than they could contribute to our understanding of the need to face the reality of our own finiteness? It is the Jewish people who have suffered more than any others over the centuries, who have been faced with more threats and attempts at their annihilation.[51]

Kübler-Ross turns out to be wrong on at least two counts. To begin with, Jews have actually written a great deal on dying, as we have seen. But also, though persecution may have something to do with it, Judaism's fascination with sickness and death has more to do with its theology and religious anthropology, especially in the Kabbalah, without which Judaism might indeed be limited to its pre-Nachmanides proto-liturgy: a mere confession, as in Saadiah, and some elementary speculation from talmudic literature.

Nonetheless, Kübler-Ross is entirely correct for the era of which she spoke, our own time, in which Jewish ritual is remarkably reticent about the process of death. If *Hamadrikh* shortens the Kabbalistic tradition, at least it contains it. In contrast, the Reform Jewish *Rabbi's Manual* of 1961 cuts down rites of dying further to only seven pages of text: five of those are just standard prayers said in the synagogue, not at the bedside, to ask for the health of relatives who are sick; one page more is a prayer to be said at the synagogue by a patient who recovers; only four pages of the seven really deal with deathbed care, and two of those are in Hebrew only and intended for rabbinic recitation over the dying patient whether or not the patient even knows what is happening.[52] In practice, more often than not, no ritual whatever accompanies modern Jews across the threshold between life and death, or, as Aaron Berechiah would have insisted, across the ford called Yabok.

Today, navigating the ford between life and death and charting the path of sickness that may lead up to the ford are usually relegated to the realm of science. Yet with all its sophisticated medical advances, science alone cannot adequately respond to the mystery and awe of death or to the fear and isolation associated with illness. Medicine may promise expert care for the body, but prayer and confession are necessary for the soul. Jews living in this postmodern age are thus turning once again to religious as well as medical tools as they face encroaching illness or death.

As emphasis on ritual healing has expanded, prayers for healing have been incorporated in synagogues around the country, and worship services devoted solely to healing are becoming common.[53] Jewish Healing Centers have opened in San Francisco and New York, and since 1994, there have been a series of healing conferences called *Refa'einu* ("Heal us . . .," from the prayer for health in the daily *Tefillah—Refa'einu . . .,* "Heal us, O Eternal One, and we shall be healed"). Following the precedent of the Middle Ages, *Bikkur Cholim* societies are being reestablished in Jewish communities, and some have even produced manuals which, like *Sefer Hachayim,* present liturgies to guide modern Jews through the dying process.

The traditional ritual for illness and death embodies hundreds of years of insight. Its confessional liturgy promotes self-examination and the acceptance of death, while intensifying the acknowledgement of God's abundant kindness, power, and presence. When accompanied by ritual, death looms less as the feared and final end of life, and more as the next stage in the life-cycle journey itself. When guided by the deathbed ritual, even death may be experienced as sacred.

NOTES

1. Sot. 14a; cf. Rashi to Genesis 18:1.
2. Git. 61a.
3. Cf. Shab. 127a, Ned. 14a.
4. "R. Acha, son of R. Chanina said: 'One who visits an invalid takes away a sixtieth of their pain'" (Ned. 39b). One-sixtieth is not literal; it a standard amount used to symbolize change in status. Elsewhere, e.g., it stands for the least amount of milk that, falling into a meat soup, renders the soup unkosher. Here, it represents the removal of the amount of illness that moves a healthy person into the category of unhealthy and perhaps, fit for death. Hence, when the sages failed to visit R. Chelbo, the latter cited Rabbi Akiba's dictum, "One who fails to visit the sick is considered a murderer" (Ned. 40a).
5. S.A., Y.D. 335:1.
6. Ned. 40a.
7. For text and early reference, see O.H., Y.D. 335:10. On its history, see Ismar Elbogen, *Der jüdische Gottesdienst in seiner*

geschichtlichen Entwicklung (Frankfurt, 1913); Eng. trans. in Raymond Scheindlin, ed., *Jewish Liturgy: a Comprehensive History* (Philadelphia, 1993), p. 162. On practice today, see, e.g., Lawrence A. Hoffman, "From Common Cold to Uncommon Healing," *CCAR Journal* 41, no. 2 (spring, 1994): 21.

8. R.H. 16b.

9. *Sefer Chasidim,* ed. J. Wistinetzki (Berlin, 1891), #365.

10. See, e.g., M. Yoma 8:6 and Yoma 85b, where Sabbath desecration is permitted to save a life.

11. Ned. 40a.

12. Shab. 12b.

13. M. San 6:2. Cf. Tractate Semachot, 44a.

14. Shab. 32a.

15. See Sifre to Numbers 5:6–7.

16. Cited by Chaim Binyamin Goldberg, *Mourning in Halachah* (Brooklyn, 1991), p. 438.

17. Commentary to Shab. 32a.

18. Commentary to Shab. 32a.

19. Cf. *Sefer Chasidim* by Judah Hechasid (1150–1217), and Bachia Ibn Pekudah's *Chovot Halevavot,* written in the early eleventh century.

20. Gershom Scholem, *Kabbalah* (New York, 1974), p. 50.

21. *Zohar* III, 126a–127a, cited by Isaiah Tishby, *Wisdom of the Zohar* (New York, 1989), p. 846.

22. Ibid, p. 832.

23. *Torat Ha'adam,* end of *Inyan Havidui.*

24. Jacob Rader Marcus, *Communal Sick Care in the German Ghetto* (Cincinnati, 1947), p. 230.

25. For a detailed discussion of Kabbalah, and more specifically, Lurianic Kabbalah, which in particular influenced Berechiah, see Gershom Scholem, *Kabbalah* (Jerusalem, 1974.)

26. Marcus, *Communal Sick Care,* p. 216.

27. Ibid., p. 64, where over 300 incidents of massacre are cited.

28. *Ma'avar Yabok* (1626; reprint, B'nai B'rak, 1929; henceforth, MY), p. 86.

29. The amount of money one is instructed to give (26, 91, or 112 *perutot*) corresponds to three configurations of God's name, thus symbolizing attention on God that is appropriate to the final moments of life.

30. MY, p. 86.

31. Ibid., p. 19.

32. Ibid., p. 14.

33. For prayers of healing in *Ma'avar Yabok* and in *Sefer Hachayim,* see Steven A. Moss, "The Attitude Toward Sickness, Dying and Death as Expressed in the Liturgical Works *Ma'avar Yabok* and *Sefer Hachayim*" (unpublished thesis, Hebrew Union College-Jewish Institute of Religion, Klau Library, NY, 1974).

34. MY, p. 87.

35. Ibid.

36. Ibid., p. 88.

37. Tishby, *Wisdom of the Zohar,* p. 835.

38. MY, pp. 89, 93.

39. Ibid., p. 144, citing Ket. 103b.

40. Marcus, *Communal Sick Care,* p.270.

41. MY, p. 104.

42. See Ted A. Campbell, *The Religion of the Heart* (Columbia, SC, 1991).

43. See *Sefer Hachayim: The Book of Life and Expression of the Tongue* (London, 1863).

44. Ibid., p.106.

45. Ezekiel 33:11, cited in *Sefer Hachayim,* p. 44.

46. Ibid., p. 120.

47. Ibid., p. 134.

48. Ibid., p. 169.

49. Ibid., p. 175.

50. Hyman E. Goldin, *Hamadrikh: The Rabbi's Guide* (New York, 1939), pp. 96–106.

51. Elisabeth Kübler-Ross, cited by Jack Riemer, *Jewish Reflections on Death* (New York, 1975).

52. *Rabbi's Manual,* rev. ed. (New York, 1961), pp. 55–62.

53. See analysis by Hoffman, "From Common Cold to Uncommon Healing."

Christian Rituals Surrounding Death

Karen B. Westerfield Tucker

Christianity was born in an environment, Jewish and pagan, which offered established methods for the proper disposal of the dead and for acceptable displays of public and private grief. Ritual activities at the time of death described in the New Testament are clearly grounded in the older cultural practices: preparation of the body by washing and anointing with oils and spices (John 19:39–40; Acts 9:37); the enshrouding of the body (Mark 15:46; John 11:44); the procession of the body to the place of burial (Luke 7:12–14); and wailing and weeping (Acts 8:2; 9:39). Most of these pre-Christian practices were retained as the church developed its own expressions, indicating from the outset that Christians have been willing, in general, to adopt or adapt local cultural observances surrounding death as long as they have not contradicted overtly the church's understanding of the nature and meaning of death, and the manifestation of that theology in sacred word and symbolic action.

A Christian Understanding of Death

The subject of death—and the reversal of death—is discussed throughout the New Testament writings, as it comprises a central component in the witness concerning Jesus Christ, who himself died and yet, it is believed, conquered death by rising from the grave. Christians claim that the death of Christ was necessary as an atonement for the sin of Adam (original sin) and the personal sins of all others, both of which estrange human beings from their Maker in whose image they were created. Since "the wages of sin is death" (Rom. 6:23), human salvation is not possible unless sin and death are overcome. By his resurrection from the dead, Christ, the Son of God, was victorious over the sting of death (1 Cor. 15:55–57), and thereby tasted death for all, restored humanity to God, and freed those who believe for eternal life (Heb. 2:9; 1 Cor. 15: 21–22). Although the faithful must still experience "natural" death, Christ has delivered them from the "second" or spiritual death of alienation from God and subsequent condemnation at the final judgment (cf. Rev. 2:11; 20:6,14–15).

The centrality of the death and resurrection of Christ for Christians, from the earliest period onward, has been attested liturgically by the weekly celebration of the day of the Lord's resurrection (Sunday), and by the annual observance of the Christian Passover or Pascha culminating at Easter. One of the principal understandings of the initiatory sacrament of baptism has been that persons thereby participate symbolically in the paschal mystery—the death, burial, and resurrection of Christ—and anticipate the promise of eternal life (Rom. 6:4). The sacrament of the eucharist, traditionally understood to have been instituted by Jesus on the night before his death, reminds Christians of the paschal mystery and incorporates them by faith into that event. Rites surrounding the death of faithful Christians are placed within this broader liturgical and theological framework.

Christian attitudes toward death have shifted over time as wider theological perspectives and cultural perceptions about death have also changed. The early church was optimistic about death, regarding it as the time for passage from the temptations of mortal existence to the joy and peace of eternal life.[1] For this reason, the day of an individual's death was called the *dies natalis* ("day of birth"), upon which date subsequent anniversary commemorations (particularly of the martyrs and saints) were held. Death for the Christian was regarded as sleep, rest, perpetual light, or refreshment;[2] the term cemetery (*coemeteria*, literally, "sleeping place") was used by Christians to describe the place where their departed rested from their labors in expectation of the future day of resurrection promised to all the faithful.[3] Metaphors of a journey, voyage, or travel are often included in prayers related to death, with the destination of the journey described variously as paradise, the heavenly Jerusalem (or Zion), and Abraham's bosom.[4] A title given in some early medieval liturgical manuscripts for the series of rites surrounding death, *Incipit de migratione animae* ("The beginning [of the rites] of the migration of the soul"),[5] points to the interpretation of death as a journey, as does the practice, used universally by Christians, ancient and modern, of the movement of the body in procession from and to different locations.

The sense of transition at the time of death, rather than finality, also encouraged Christians to believe that a continuing relationship existed between the living and the dead since, in Christ, the barrier of death had been broken. A prayer included in the fourth-century Egyptian prayer-book of Sarapion interweaves several of these metaphors and themes, and includes not only the commendation of the deceased but also petitions for the consolation of the bereaved:

> O God, you have the power of life and death, you are God of the spirits and Master of all flesh, you bring death and give life, you lead down to the gates of Hades and bring back again, you create the human spirit and receive the souls of the saints and give them rest; you change and convert and transform your creatures as is right and expedient, you alone being immortal and unchanging and eternal: We pray to you for the repose and rest of this man, your servant (or this woman, your servant). Make his soul and his spirit rest in green places and in secret places of rest with Abraham and Isaac and Jacob and all your saints, and raise up his body on the day which you have appointed according to your trustworthy promises in order that also you may bestow, as he deserves, the inheritances in your holy pastures. Do not remember his trespasses and sins; make his departure peaceful and blessed. Heal the griefs of his relatives by the Spirit of comfort, and give to us all a good end, through Jesus Christ. . . .[6]

Many of these images and themes have persisted, and are included in liturgical texts of the present day. The rites of eastern Christianity, in particular, have maintained an emphasis on the triumph and joy which should characterize Christian burial in expectation of resurrection at the last day, as have funerals in African-American churches.

A significant shift started to emerge, however, before the second millenium, and by the twelfth and thirteenth centuries came to dominate perceptions of death in the West. No longer was death approached with confidence, but rather with fear, an attitude exemplified by the increasing use, from the early thirteenth century, of the sequence *Dies irae, dies illa* ("Day of wrath, O dreadful day") in the Roman mass for the dead. Stress came to be placed less on heavenly bliss and more on God's wrathful judgment of sinners and the accompanying need for absolution and intercession at the point of death and *post mortem*. Teaching on the doctrine of purgatory, foundations for which are present in Augustine (*The City of God,* 21.13; 21.24), became more explicit. Prayers and rites developed to ensure the welfare and destiny of the departed. The tradition of the *ars moriendi* flourished in the late Middle Ages as a means by which persons could prepare for inevitable judgment at death by learning and practicing the "art" of dying (and living) well.

Attempts were made by the sixteenth-century Protestant reformers to bring again to the fore the confident hope in the resurrection of the faithful dead which had been so prominent in the early church.[7] Concern about abuses and superstition led to the breakdown or demise of many existing rituals, particularly those expressing the continuing connection between the living and the dead, since most Protestants rejected the doctrine of purgatory.[8] Despite the reformers' efforts, deeply ingrained and pre-existing cultural and religious patterns persisted in many areas, perpetuating the attitude of fear at the approach of death. In contrast, the evangelical revivals of the eighteenth century encouraged the faithful to anticipate a "happy death" full of confidence in the promises of God, recognizing that death, though the penalty for sin, was also the cure of sin and the gateway to the resurrection of the body.[9]

In the modern period, the individualist and rationalist emphases of the Enlightenment in the West have contributed to changes in the way Christians (and others) have interpreted the nature of death.[10] The understanding that earthly life was the preparation for eternal life was slowly supplanted by a growing attachment to the material world, and with it, an uncertainty about death and what lay beyond the grave. Whereas in previous generations death was regarded as an unavoidable part of the fabric of life, in the early modern period death became taboo, a forbidden subject. Several Christian traditions in the twentieth century have reacted against this prominent western cultural attitude and have reclaimed the inheritance of the early church by restoring to a central place within the rites paschal images and the eschatological hope of resurrection to eternal life. The United Methodist Church, in its *Book of Worship* (1992), has gone so far as to call its rite "A Service of Death and Resurrection."

Rituals in the Domestic Setting

Interment marks the end of the journey for the physical body of the deceased, but prior to that final action, Christians have engaged in a series of preparatory rituals which have varied in substance and complexity according to time and local custom.[11] The earliest documents which provide texts for rituals at the time of death (generally utilizing the headings *ordo defunctorum* or *agenda mortuorum*) often do not begin with death per se, but with the last moments of life, thereby witnessing to the perceived continuity between life and death. The first actions prescribed in many of these texts were to be done in the company of the dying and included the chanting of psalms and responses, the reading of the Passion account from one of the four Gospels, the imposition of extreme unction, the administration of *viaticum* (final communion), and the commendation of the soul (which can occur before or after the last breath).[12]

The earliest descriptions of Christian funeral rituals report that, after death, the body of the departed was washed, dressed (in white garments or linens, symbolic of victory over death), and in some communities, anointed.[13] Liturgical books dating from the sixth century onward provide an assortment of psalms, antiphons, hymns, readings of scriptural or non-canonical material, and prayers to be said during the washing and laying out of the body and immediately after the washing. Many of these prayers connect the ritual action on earth with a comparable action in heaven, as in the Gelasian prayer *Suscipe domine animam servi tui* ("Receive, O Lord, the soul of your servant"), which petitions that the soul of the departed be clothed in heavenly vestiture and washed in the holy font of eternal life.[14] A simple order was provided for use in the home of ordinary Christians, while more complex prescriptions accompanied comparable actions for the clergy and for persons in monastic orders. Although the practice eventually diminished in the West, yet in some Christian traditions, particularly those of the East, the body is still prepared for burial in the domestic setting to the accompaniment of ritual prayers (nowadays the preparation of the body is often relegated to the professional funeral home). The practice of anointing the dead with oil among eastern Christians, either by application to the body, or by pouring upon the body in the casket (in the home or in the church), or by pouring in the grave, is attested in early eastern documents and in later prayer-books which provide a service called the "Euchelaion for the Deceased." Testimony to the ritual anointing of the dead in the West is extant, though limited.[15]

In general, throughout their respective liturgical histories, Roman Catholic and Orthodox Christians have continued the ancient practice of prayers in the home of the deceased. Prayers comprise part of the brief services, vigils, or wakes that may follow the preparation of the body. The rite for the burial of laypersons in some Orthodox churches includes a *pannychis* (an abridged version of the normal daily morning service), which is repeated until the body is placed into the coffin for transport to the church. The 1969 *Ordo exsequiarum* of the Roman Catholic Church, which provides for three full types of service for the deceased, includes the option of a domestic vigil (with prayers, psalmody, scripture readings, and optional homily) and the possibility that all the Christian rites for death may be celebrated in the home (in accordance with local custom).[16]

The sixteenth-century Protestant reformers reacted against many medieval funeral customs and rites because these embodied superstitious beliefs or doctrines, concerning purgatory and prayer both for and to the dead, that the reformers rejected. Consequently, many did not provide either full liturgical rites for the burial of the dead or formularies for use in the home of the deceased, though extempore prayers for the bereaved (if not for the deceased) undoubtedly were still said. Nevertheless, when Protestants a few generations later published burial rites, they presumed that the rites would begin from the home, as that was still the place where the body was prepared and where, according to cultural custom, the wake could be held. Many of their ecclesiastical descendants today have recognized the benefits of ritual formulations (beyond spontaneous prayer) for use in the domestic setting as a means of pastoral care and a signification of the ongoing intercession of the church. They have therefore restored such formularies to the rites for use at the time of death.[17]

If the body of the departed is lodged in the home (or funeral home), necessity demands that the body be relocated for rites either in the church or at the grave, according to the custom of the particular Christian denomination or local tradition. Likewise, movement of the body from the church to the grave may be required; this type of procession became, in fact, more ritually elaborate and, for many Christians, constituted the more important of the two processions. In the early period, burial processions testified to the distinctive Christian optimism concerning death: they were held in the daytime (unlike their pagan counterparts, which were held at night), and their participants, like the deceased, were clothed in white (not black) garments. Pagan wailings and lamentations were displaced by the joyful singing of psalms, hymns, and alleluias in the procession and at the funeral liturgy proper;[18] candles and incense were used, once their pagan associations had been lost. Over time, however, these jubilant parades were transformed into somber processions reflective of the more fearful attitude toward death characteristic of the Middle Ages in the West. Persons bedecked in black garments and other appurtenances no longer chanted psalms of victory, but rather employed penitential psalms and hymns. Western Christians since the Reformation have, periodically, striven to return the funeral cortege to its primitive shape regardless of whether the body was borne on foot, by wagon, or by carriage. However, with the advent of the automobile and urban development, the prayers and praises that accompanied the processions from the home and to the grave have been all but lost in most areas.

Rituals at the Church

Christian practice and ritual texts, past and present, exhibit wide diversity in the sequence of events that follow the removal of the body of the deceased from the home. Some texts prescribe that rites (of different types and durations) be held in the church before proceeding to the place of burial which may be "within walls" of the church building, in an adjacent cemetery in the churchyard, or in a public cemetery. In other cases, interment and accompanying rites may precede services in the church, or all the rites may occur at the grave.

The types of rites held at the church, or sometimes at the funeral home itself, vary considerably among the various Christian denominations. Sometimes within a particular tradition distinctive forms are utilized for persons of a specific ecclesiastical status, gender, or age group (e.g., children, adults, and—a modern addition—stillborn or newborn infants). The variations in practice can be distilled to two separate yet related patterns: the service of the word and the service of the eucharist.

The service of the word, which is generally composed of readings from scripture, prayers, hymns, psalms, and sermon, can stand independently as a separate office or be linked with the celebration of the eucharist. A separate service of the word for funerals along these lines (with the funeral oration or homily generally delivered on another occasion) is evident from an early time. Liturgical documents from the eighth century indicate that, by that date, the funeral office was shaped to correspond with the more elaborate structure used for the regular daily services of the church, probably under monastic influence. While Orthodox funeral rites generally followed the pattern of regular morning prayer, the medieval western office of the dead (*Officium pro defunctis*) consisted of two parts, an evening service (known as *Placebo* from the first word of the opening antiphon), and a morning service (similarly called *Dirige,* from which comes the word "dirge") on the following day. (Though this somber office was first developed for use in connection with the funeral itself, it later came to be used on a daily basis in conjunction with the regular services of the church, in order to provide continuing supplications for all the departed.) Regional variations of the office of the dead, manifested particularly in the selection of psalms and scripture readings, occasionally shaped or informed the content of local Protestant funeral services as they developed. For example, the funeral office of the Church of England, in its successive revisions, shows the inheritance received from the local medieval rite, as do those liturgical formulations that have then borrowed from the Anglican rite.

While readings from scripture were easily adopted from the medieval office of the dead for Protestant funeral rites, the content of many of the prayers was not, given that the welfare of the deceased was a frequent subject addressed within the prayers. Most Protestant leaders disdained employment of petitions for the departed, since prayer was to provide hope for the bereaved living and not to grant any benefit to the dead. Vestiges of prayers for the departed present in the 1549 Anglican *Book of Common Prayer* were quickly removed in the revision published three years later.[19] Printed funeral prayers were not produced immediately in the Lutheran and Reformed traditions, and hence prayer was silent or extempore, left to the discretion of the presiding pastor. One can only surmise whether in their free prayers local pastors followed their theological mentors or succumbed to the dictates of popular piety, which found it difficult to relinquish prayers for the deceased. By the mid-sixteenth century, some church orders begin obliquely to include prayer for the departed.[20] Some Protestants, at later times, have reintroduced prayer for the departed into the burial liturgy on account of the example of the early church, but making clear that such prayers are *for* the departed and not *to* them.

Funeral sermons or homilies have been a prominent component of Protestant praxis. At first, in the sixteenth century, sermons (or more accurately, exhortations or admonitions) that expounded upon biblical themes related to death and resurrection were preached in the church at a time after the burial; in some parts of the Reformed tradition, the sermon was the *only* element of a funeral "rite," as is clear from the instructions in John Knox's Genevan *Forme of Prayers* (1556).[21] Standardized funeral sermons were occasionally provided as part of a ritual text, as exemplified by the inclusion of three such sermons in the Cologne burial liturgy of Hermann von Wied.[22] While the preaching of sermons grounded in the biblical text continued, another practice later arose, that of lengthy eulogies or sermons that included a generally overstated *curriculum vitae* of the deceased. During the seventeenth and eighteenth centuries, sermons typically intertwined these two approaches, a factor which had contributed to the condemnation of funeral sermons by groups such as the English Puritans, who saw in them a resemblance to prayers for the dead.[23] Fees sometimes were charged for the pastor's homiletical services, a custom often exploited by the clergy and deplored by the laity. Today, sermon fees have been abandoned, but Protestants continue to utilize both sermon and/or eulogy in funeral services.

The association of the eucharist with funeral rites may be traced to the Christian appropriation—and reinterpretation—of the Jewish and Roman customs of funeral feasts. Among

Christians, these meals (termed *silicernia* or *refrigeria*) were celebrated at the time of death and, with the growth of the martyr cult, also on anniversaries of the *dies natalis,* and marked an opportunity for continuing contact between the living and the dead. Evidently the abuses of disruptive behavior and gluttony associated with these graveside meals, as well as the practice of offering food to the dead, eventually warranted reprimand and necessary change: the eucharist was substituted as the funeral meal *par excellence.*[24] When the bones of venerated martyrs were moved or "translated" into church buildings, or when a church was built over the tomb, the burial site was often located in or under the altar, thereby continuing the overt connection of eucharist as a meal shared by the living and the faithful departed.

Whereas in the East the eucharist was generally not customary at funeral rites, in the West the sacrament became a normal part of the Catholic funeral liturgy, though early liturgical texts often do not indicate such. Mass held in conjunction with the funeral was usually at a time separate from the regularly scheduled eucharistic celebrations of the day. Special readings, prayers, and chants that addressed the circumstances of human death were eventually introduced into the form of the mass. Liturgical books containing the proper texts of the funeral mass attest to a rich variety of formulations;[25] and only with the reform of the missal by Pope Pius V (1570) was a normative requiem mass established, derived from the thirteenth-century formulary of the Roman Curia.

Because of the concept that celebration of the eucharist could, symbolically or in actuality, benefit the soul of the departed,[26] mass for the dead was not only offered as part of the funeral liturgy, but regularly repeated thereafter. To this end, small chapels known as chantries were built in churches and as freestanding buildings, and chantry priests were endowed to say mass there for the deceased benefactor and his friends. Reaction against endowed masses for the dead[27] and the theological doctrines associated with the practice resulted in the virtual elimination of the eucharist from sixteenth-century Protestant funerals. The more liturgically conservative 1549 *Book of Common Prayer* included a separate order for "The Celebration of the Holy Communion when there is a Burial of the Dead," but this was removed in the 1552 revision.

As with many matters liturgical in which practices from Christian antiquity are resuscitated, Protestants have begun to reclaim the eucharist as an important component of funerals, in that it provides a liturgical, as well as spiritual, connection between the living and the faithful dead. Even though some Protestant liturgical books include the eucharistic liturgy itself within the funeral ritual text (e.g., the 1993 *Book of Common Worship* of the Presbyterian Church, U.S.A.), while others simply provide appropriate readings for it (e.g., *The Alternative Service Book 1980* of the Church of England), its recovered usage in practice is uncertain, given that celebration of the eucharist itself is an occasional service for many Protestants.

In addition to the service of the word and the service of eucharist, other ritual actions related to the funeral may also take place within the church in certain Christian traditions. Among these, historically and at present, are the use of incense, the final absolution of the deceased following the mass (with accompanying prayers), the commendation of the soul, the sprinkling of the corpse with holy water, and the ritual kiss of peace. Though not prescribed by ritual, the funeral meal, often shared at the church, survives among some Christians as a sign, in the face of death, of the sustaining fellowship between family members and the wider Christian community.

Rituals at the Grave

For some Christians (and at certain periods in a particular denomination's liturgical history), eucharist, sermon, psalmody, scripture readings, and prayers, if not held in the church, may be held at the grave. Selection of the location for these rites may be an optional matter (dependent upon local circumstances), or it may be specified internally within the ritual text by rubric. In spite of the great variability (and sometimes flexibility) in practice, nevertheless at the grave site a necessary action is shared by all Christians: the depositing of the remains in the earth (although it should be noted that today cremation is a common alternative to interment in the earth among many Christian groups: in this case the graveside rite is often performed in a crematorium chapel).

The actions accompanying burial proper, historically and at present, range from the very simple to the elaborate and complex. The body may be interred without any accompanying ceremony, as was ordered in the Presbyterian *Westminster Directory* (1644), or a more elaborate rite may be utilized, as is true in the practice of many eastern Christians such as that in the tradition of the Assyrian Church.[28] Liturgical components for burial are many and may include blessing the grave, singing or chanting (psalms, responses, hymns, or anthems), scripture readings, prayers (including the Lord's Prayer), creeds (e.g., the baptismal Apostles' Creed), and other ritual biddings of farewell. These may be employed at various points in the process of interment: before the placement of the body in the grave, during the lowering of the body into the grave and following, at the covering of the grave, and after the grave is closed or sealed. Custom may dictate that earth is to be sprinkled upon the tomb, either in three castings or in the form of a cross. In some cases, rites of intercession or purification have been provided to continue immediately thereafter in the home of the deceased.

Two commonly shared practices are the placement of the body in the grave with the feet toward the east (in anticipation of the day of resurrection when Christ, the "Sun of Righteousness," will come in glory) and the prayer or statement of committal at the moment of burial petitioning God to receive the soul of the departed. Creation language from the biblical Book of Genesis is often echoed in the committal which asks that even while the deceased is committed to the ground from which life comes, "earth to earth, ashes to ashes, dust to dust," he or she will remain safely in God's keeping until the last day of both judgment and resurrection. This Christian hope has frequently been depicted in cemetery decoration from even before the time of Constantine.[29]

Rites of Remembrance

Christian rituals surrounding death continue after burial, reflecting the presupposition that death does not hold the final word. In general, they focus upon remembering all the faithful dead (including the saints and martyrs) and place recollections of a departed individual within that broader context.

Tertullian, writing in the early third century, attests that, in addition to prayers for the dead, masses for the dead were held each year on anniversaries of death.[30] This practice, which in the Catholic West has continued through the twentieth century, is mentioned in the fourth-century church order, *Apostolic Constitutions,* which enjoins:

> Let the third day of the departed be celebrated with psalms, and readings, and prayers, on account of him who rose in three days; and let the ninth day be celebrated, for the comfort of the bereaved as well as the remembrance of the departed; and the thirtieth day according to the ancient pattern, for so did the people lament Moses; and the year's mind. And let alms be given to the poor out of his goods, for a memorial of him.[31]

The celebration of masses for the dead (or other services) is suggested, in later texts, for the first, seventh, thirtieth, or fortieth day after death or burial.

Special days in the Christian calendar are set apart to mark annually the remembrance of the dead. Many local communities, in antiquity, designated one particular day to commemorate all the faithful departed. All Souls' Day, the origin of which can be traced to the monastery of Cluny in the tenth century, is a direct descendant of the older custom; the Cluniac observance, in turn, influenced subsequent Roman (and western) practice. Dating from the fourth century, the feast of All Saints was developed to celebrate the known and unknown saints and martyrs of the church. For many Protestants, All Saints' Day has been the sole commemoration of all the faithful departed observed.

Local cultural practices or folk customs also shape Christian remembrances for departed individuals or family members. For example, some Orthodox Christians celebrate Radonitsa ("Day of Joy"), held either the Monday or Tuesday of the second week of Easter, when they place red-painted eggs on the graves of their relatives while singing an Easter hymn.[32] In the United States, civil holidays can prompt the visitation of the grave (e.g., Mother's Day or Memorial Day), as can the primary festival days in the Christian calendar (e.g., Easter and Christmas) or in the local church calendar (e.g., the day of "homecoming" celebrated by some—particularly rural—Protestants).

In addition to funeral, anniversary, and special-day rites, many Christians remember the faithful departed through a general commemoration in the eucharistic liturgy, thereby testifying to the resurrection hope that sustains—and connects—all Christians, living and dead.[33]

NOTES

1. Classic studies on early Christian views of death are Albert C. Rush, *Death and Burial in Christian Antiquity* (Washington, DC, 1941), and Jaroslav Pelikan, *The Shape of Death: Life, Death, and Immortality in the Early Fathers* (New York, 1961).

2. Two of these images are contained in the verse *Requiem aeternam dona eis, Domine, et lux perpetua luceat eis* ("Grant them eternal rest, O Lord, and let light perpetual shine upon them"), found in numerous liturgies for the dead from the late eighth century, a time when documentation for death rites becomes more plentiful.

3. One of the earliest known liturgical texts, the so-called *Apostolic Tradition* of Hippolytus, includes in the Sahidic Coptic version instructions regarding cemetery administration and fees; see chap. 40 in G. J. Cuming, *Hippolytus: A Text for Students,* Grove Liturgical Study 8 (Nottingham, 1976), pp. 28–29.

4. For studies of these images, see Bernard Botte, "The Earliest Formulas of Prayer for the Dead," and Adrien Nocent, "Sickness and Death in the Gelasian Sacramentary," in *Temple of the Holy Spirit: Sickness and Death of the Christian in the Liturgy* (New York, 1983), pp. 17–31, 175–89. This collection of essays is particularly helpful regarding eastern Christian funerary practice.

5. See, for example, the eighth-century Sacramentary of Berlin cited in Damien Sicard, *La liturgie de la mort dans l'église latine*

des origines à la réforme carolingienne, Liturgiewissenschaftliche Quellen und Forschungen 63 (Münster, 1978), pp. 8 ff.

6. Prayer 18, in R. J. S. Barrett-Lennard, *The Sacramentary of Sarapion of Thmuis,* Alcuin/GROW Liturgical Study 25 (Nottingham, 1993), pp. 50–51 (slightly adapted); cf. *Apostolic Constitutions* 8.41.

7. See, for example, Martin Luther's 1542 "Preface to the Burial Hymns" in the Weimar edition, *Luthers Werke* 35:478–83, and in the American edition, *Luther's Works* 53 (Philadelphia, 1965), pp. 325–31; and John Calvin, *Institutes of the Christian Religion* 3.25.1–10, ed. John T. McNeill (Philadelphia, 1960), 2:987–1006.

8. The impact of Protestant theological and liturgical changes upon the sentiments of the laity, particularly as they regarded the continuum between the living and the dead, is discussed in Clare Gittings, *Death, Burial and the Individual in Early Modern England* (London, 1984), pp. 39–59.

9. See, for example, the sermons "Death and Deliverance" and "On Mourning for the Dead" by the Methodist John Wesley; cited in *The Works of John Wesley,* ed. Albert C. Outler (Nashville, 1987), 4:204–14, 236–43.

10. For studies on changes in views of death since the Middle Ages, see in particular the works by Philippe Ariès, *Western Attitudes Toward Death* (Baltimore, 1974) and *The Hour of Our Death* (New York, 1981); and by John McManners, *Death and the Enlightenment* (Oxford/New York, 1981).

11. Damien Sicard provides a detailed study of Roman variations of these rites in *La liturgie de la mort,* pp. 33–142. Two sources helpful for surveying the history of Christian rites for the dead, East and West, are Bruno Bürki, *Im Herrn entschlafen: eine historish-pastoraltheologische Studie zur Liturgie des Sterbens und des Begräbnisses* (Heidelberg, 1969), and Geoffrey Rowell, *The Liturgy of Christian Burial,* Alcuin Club Collections 59 (London, 1977).

12. For these, see also p. 167–68 above.

13. E.g., Eusebius, *Historia Ecclesiastica* 7.22.9 (PG 20:689); and Prudentius Aurelius Clemens, *Liber Cathemerinon* 10: Hymnus circa exequias defuncti, "Deus, ignee fons animarum" (CSEL 61:56).

14. Found in several manuscripts, the prayer is cited as no. 4051 in Jean Deschusses, ed., *Le sacramentaire grégorien: ses principales formes d'après les plus anciens manuscrits* (Fribourg, 1982), 3:157.

15. The Penitential of Theodore of Canterbury and the so-called Confessional of Egbert of York allow for anointing the breast of dead

monks and religious men: the Penitential of Theodore 2.5.1, in F. W. H. Wasserschleben, *Die Bussordnungen der abendländischen Kirche* (Halle, 1851; reprint, Graz, 1958), p. 206; the Confessional of Egbert of York 36, in David Wilkins, *Concilia Magnae Britanniae et Hiberniae* (London, 1737; reprint, Brussels, 1964), 1:123.

16. A thorough study of the new Roman Catholic rite and its antecedents is Richard Rutherford, *The Death of a Christian: The Rite of Funerals* (New York, 1980).

17. See, for example, rites or prayers in the service books of the American Episcopal Church (1979), the Evangelical Lutheran Church in America (1982), and the Uniting Church in Australia (1988).

18. See, for example, *Apostolic Constitutions* 6.30 (SC 329: 393–95); Gregory of Nyssa, *De vita Macrinae* 33–34 (SC 178: 249–55); John Chrysostom, *Homiliae in Hebraeos* 4.5 (PG 63:42–44); and Jerome, *Epistola* 108.29 (CSEL 55/56:348).

19. Martin Bucer in his *Censura* (1551) criticized the questionable prayers; see E. C. Whitaker, *Martin Bucer and the Book of Common Prayer,* Alcuin Club Collections 55 (Great Wakering, 1974), pp. 126–29; cf. pp. 50–53.

20. See, for example, the church order for Württemberg, 1536 (where the pastor is instructed to "commend the departed person to the gracious hand of God"), and for Waldeck, 1556 (where the Lord Jesus Christ is indirectly asked to "awaken your body and soul, that you may arise on the last day with the just"); cited in A. L. Richter, *Die evangelischen Kirchenordnungen des sechszehnten Jahrhunderts* (Nieuwkoop, 1967), 1:273; 2:171.

21. Cited in William D. Maxwell, *The Liturgical Portions of the Genevan Service Book* (London, 1931), p. 161.

22. Hermann von Wied, "Vom Begräbnis," in *Einfältiges Bedenken* (Düsseldorf, 1972), pp. 185–92.

23. "An Admonition to the Parliament," in W. H. Frere and C. E. Douglas, eds., *Puritan Manifestoes: A Study of the Origin of the Puritan Revolt* (London, 1954), p. 28.

24. Augustine, *Confessions* 6.2; 9.12 (CCSL 27:74, 150–52); and *Apostolic Constitutions* 6.30.2 (SC 329:391).

25. See, for example, mass formularies for different categories of persons, such as priests, women, and the newly baptized, in an eleventh-century missal from Exeter, England, in F. E. Warren, *The Leofric Missal* (Oxford, 1883), pp. 194–96.

26. This perspective can be found in the writings of Augustine,

Enchiridion 110 (CCSL 46:108–109), and Gregory the Great, *Dialogues* 4.57–62 (SC 265:186).

27. See, for example, the assessment by Martin Luther in "To the Christian Nobility of the German Nation concerning the Reform of the Christian Estate," in the Weimar edition, *Luthers Werke* 6:444, line 22, to p. 445, line 6, or in the American edition, *Luther's Works* 44 (Philadelphia, 1966), pp. 180–81.

28. For the Order for the Burial of Priests (the *Kahneita*), see George Percy Badger, *The Nestorians and their Rituals* (London, 1852), 2:310–16.

29. For photographs of and commentary on early Christian decorations, see Graydon F. Snyder, *Ante Pacem: Archaeological Evidence of Church Life Before Constantine* (Macon, GA, 1985).

30. Tertullian, *De exhortatione castitatis* 11 (CCSL 2:1030-31); *De monogamia* 10 (CCSL 2:1242–44).

31. *Apostolic Constitutions* 8.42.1–5; cited from W. Jardine Grisbrooke, ed., *The Liturgical Portions of the Apostolic Constitutions: A Text for Students,* Alcuin/GROW Liturgical Study 13/14 (Nottingham, 1990), p. 81. "Year's mind" is a traditional English ecclesiastical expression denoting the annual remembrance of a person's death. Cf. the Penitential of Theodore of Canterbury 2.5.2 (Wasserschleben, *Bussordnungen,* p. 206) and the so-called Confessional of Egbert of York 36 (Wilkins, *Concilia,* 1:122–23; cf. Wasserschleben, p. 315).

32. Pierre Kovalevsky, "Funeral Rites in the Easter Season and Prayers for the Dead from Easter to Ascension," in *Temple of the Holy Spirit,* p. 105.

33. For a study of the development of the *memento* of the dead in the Roman canon, see especially Joseph A. Jungmann, *The Mass of the Roman Rite* (New York, 1955), 2:237–48.

Rites of Death and Mourning in Judaism

Lawrence A. Hoffman

Introduction: The Deceased and the Mourners

In the chapter on birth, we saw that traditional rabbinic Judaism does not provide actual birth ceremonies so much as it does a rite that just happens to coincide with the birth of a son: namely, circumcision, which should more properly be understood as a celebration of male initiation into the covenant. By contrast, Judaism does ritualize death. That is to say, since the Rabbis conceptualized human existence covenantally, not physically, they ignored the stages of physical maturation and celebrated instead covenantal partnership: first and foremost, its beginning, but also the deepening familiarity with God's word that accrued through years of Torah study. But however much they chose officially to remain unaware of a person's physical growth, they were acutely conscious of bodily decay, especially when old age reached the point where death seemed unusually delayed in arriving; and they ritualized burial of the dead as well as mourning behavior for those left behind.[1]

But caring for the deceased and seeing to the needs of their mourners are not the same thing; they may even be in conflict with each other. Whether a culture conceives of death as a problem for the deceased or as a difficulty for the next of kin makes considerable difference in terms of what it mandates ritually. To be sure, no culture may easily ignore the physical reality of an actual body requiring burial, but if it attends preeminently to the living, it may choose to dispense with the corpse quickly and without solemnity, whereas if it interprets

214

the crisis as focusing on the dead, it may pay much attention to burial but ignore mourning.

Modern North American culture, for instance, isolates the individual (not the group) as the object of attention; and it defines the individual as a body with a mind (or psyche) that begins functioning at birth and ceases with death. It thus disregards what happens after death, there being no self any more, and hence, no "after death" period worth pondering. As birth is held to be our beginning, so death is considered our end, and what attracts society's attention about that end is how the individual handles its impending arrival and how other related individuals then manage the mourning that follows in its wake. In both instances, the problem is defined as psychological: when the body dies, so too does the psyche, and (therefore) the problem, as far as that individual is concerned.

Not so classical Judaism. Psychology as a religious rationale is distinctly a later overlay of modern interpreters seeking to justify ancient ritual regulations. It plays almost no role in the thinking of the Rabbis who initiated the regulations in question.

Unlike us, the Rabbis did not begin with the idea of a self who disappears at the moment of death. They held instead that despite the body's demise, the essential person housed in the body still enjoyed some beyond-the-grave existence, so that proper burial and continued respect for the deceased were required. Funeral ritual is thus preeminently designed as an act of *kevod hamet,* "honoring the dead." A corpse may not be subject to autopsy, for instance; nor may it be embalmed, except under unusual circumstances where not to embalm would dishonor the dead even more—as in preparing a body for burial far away, by which time if it has not been embalmed, it would putrefy; and even then, the embalming procedure must retain the body intact.[2]

With their attention fastened on honoring the dead, the Rabbis give relatively little explicit attention to the psychological needs of the mourners. Regulations sometimes *seem* to address the pain of bereavement: sumptuary rules that limit exorbitant funeral expenses, for instance. But they are prompted not by the fear that inordinate cost may trouble the living, but by the aversion to the embarrassment that such expense may cause the deceased. They worry that wealthy people will receive a banquet in their honor, but poor people will not. Their rules democratize death, making sure that no one will have a poor funeral repast relative to others, and no one will thereby be dishonored simply because they had the temerity to die without leaving an estate behind.[3] Similarly, the Rabbis passed regulations designed to prevent conflicts of religious responsibility during the time of mourning. But here too, rabbinic legislation worried less about psychic trauma than about the breach of honor due the dead, were mourners to allow the full gamut of daily responsibilities to interfere with the requirements of the recently deceased.

The classic Jewish burial rite should thus be understood as a ritualized interpretive gloss on a rabbinic view of death that focused on the needs of the dead. Rabbis could legislate only for the living, of course; their ritual seems therefore to have the living in mind; but their decisions derive from their dogmatic belief in life after death, and, therefore, their almost axiomatic insistence that customs associated with death affirm the continuing dignity of those who die. In the nineteenth century, this theological hermeneutic came under attack, particularly by German Reform Jews, and Jews today have widely supplemented or even replaced rabbinic attitudes with modernity's ubiquitous psychological justification for burial practices. Still, the notion of honoring the dead is evident, much as it was two thousand years ago.

In terms of the *mode* of burial, rabbinic custom mirrors Greco-Roman practice. Roman Jewish catacombs, for example (first noted in 1602), have turned up Jewish burial vaults not unlike those known for Roman society generally.[4] Second-century Palestine, too, adopted social customs of the prevailing host culture: family vaults for those who could afford them and niches of caves for those who could not. Burial might thus be a two-stage process: laying the body to immediate rest and then, some time afterward, reclaiming the bones for reburial—usually in white limestone or cedarwood chests (ossuaries)—in the fields that belonged to the family holdings.[5] But the latter stage was frequently accomplished by professional "societies for the collection of bones" (*chavurot lelikut atsamot*); it attracted little ritual attention; and in any event, regardless of how widespread the practice became, it ceased without leaving any impact on later Jewish custom. So our attention here is limited to a single burial immediately after death, and to the mourning that followed.

Periods and Terms

The seven immediate relatives of the deceased (as they are known)—mother, father, brother, sister, son, daughter, and spouse—are called "mourners" (*avelim*; sing. *avel*); however, their mourning (*avelut*) begins only with burial. The short interval between death and burial is assigned its own name, *aninut*, during which the bereaved are called *onenim*, from the root *'.n.n*, denoting "oppressiveness," in the sense perhaps of being "grief–stricken."

In rabbinic times, *aninut* began with *keriyah* ("tearing of one's garments"), an act prompted by witnessing death or even hearing about it. *Keriyah* exemplifies the ritualized demonstration of honoring the dead. Originally, attending the death of anyone, not just immediate relatives, prompted the tearing of one's clothes. Exception was made only if the deceased had been a flagrant sinner, who was accorded the right to burial but not to visible signs of honor like *keriyah*. In traditional circles, it is customary still to tear garments for the death of a non-relative who is a Torah scholar,[6] though generally, nowadays, it is performed only by the seven immediate relatives listed above, and it generally occurs as part of the funeral-home ritual immediately preceding interment.

In antiquity, *aninut* usually lasted less than a day, since burial occurred as soon as possible. During *aninut*, the body was ritually washed, perhaps with help from a society established to honor the dead, and a vigil was held to spare the deceased the ignominy of spending its last earthly hours alone.

Avelut (actual mourning) commenced only with burial proper. Lasting seven days, it became known as *shivah* (the Hebrew word for seven);[7] to mourn is thus still called "sitting *shivah.*" Visitors made condolence calls, though their goal was not purely condolence, as it is with us who see the easing of the mourners' psychological duress as our purpose. They came to honor the dead, not succour the living, supplying food and drink to free the mourners from day-to-day worries so that they might mourn the dead honorably. On the other hand, honoring the dead and faith in resurrection did not preclude the open expression of grief. Specially significant was the first meal of *shivah,* the *se'udat havra'ah,* generally rendered nowadays, "meal of condolence," but literally meaning "meal of recovery," from the root *b.r.',* "to be or become healthy." The meal included foods associated with mourning (eggs) and an elaborate Grace, the liturgy for which received more rabbinic attention than did the prayers for interment.

Shivah demanded cessation from work, especially in the first three days, a particularly stringent time[8]—to insist on work would constitute dishonoring the dead. By the eighth day, mourners returned to work, but until the thirtieth day a second stage of mourning prevailed, with ritual strictures being lessened weekly: in the first week mourners did not attend daily synagogue services; the next week, they came but sat separately; the third week, they sat in their usual place, but did not speak; only thereafter did they initiate conversation.[9] The end of mourning is traditionally set now at eleven months from burial, though a minority view from the Middle Ages, now followed also by Reform Jews, rounds the number up to twelve. The traditional number, eleven, reflects the talmudic belief that the souls of ordinary sinners are chastised only that long; to mourn longer would dishonor the dead by impugning their character as having been extraordinarily evil.[10]

The tannaitic funeral featured many liturgical customs that we no longer recognize, though some, such as a *hesped* (a funeral oration) have lasted in some form or other into our own day. Other customs that we now follow were added at various times after the Mishnah was canonized: particularly, the recitation of the mourners' prayer known as *Kaddish* (a practice dated to eighth-century Palestine,)[11] seventeenth-century prayer for the soul, called *El Malei Rachamim* (see below), and the erection of a monument or headstone (called a *matsevah*) in a medieval ceremony called an unveiling.

In sum, we have (1) *aninut* beginning with *keriyah* and ending with burial; then (2) burial itself, followed by (3) *shivah,* including a *se'udat havra'ah*; and finally, (4) liturgical ritual common to the months after *shivah,* especially the unveiling of a headstone. While many of the ritual events in all four categories reflect the human agony of mourning, and hence the psychological needs of the mourners, we can better explain rabbinic liturgy as a reflection of its authors' conviction that the body alone perishes, while the "person" (who remains alive after death) will, upon resurrection, be reunited with the body. The dead thus require special care as long as they remain unburied, and honor ever after.

As we go stage by stage through Jewish death and mourning ritual, we shall draw attention primarily, therefore, to rabbinic eschatology. But as we refer to ritual today, we shall see how psychology has replaced eschatology as the favored paradigm of modernity, with consequences for the way rites of burial and mourning are presently practiced and explained.

Aninut: *Waiting for Mourning*

The Rabbis differentiated between what they called "good news" and "bad news," mandating separate blessings for each. The first ("good news")—calling for the blessing, "Blessed art thou . . . who is good and who does good"—is eschatological, its ultimate hope being resurrection. The latter—accompanied by the blessing, "Blessed art thou . . . who is a true judge"[12]— is the reverse: a recognition of physical death, with the express acknowledgement that it occurs in God's good time. However painful to the mourners, death is thus framed metaphorically as a proper fate meted out wisely and compassionately by an all-just and all-knowing deity. Indeed, the funeral service itself is called *Tsidduk Hadin,* literally, "The [declaration of the] right-eousness of the verdict," a term borrowed from a talmudic ac-count of Jewish martyrs in the time of Hadrian;[13] our version today begins with a string of biblical verses said to have been recited as one of those martyrs, Chaninah ben Teradyon, was expiring, beginning with Deuteronomy 32:4, "The Rock, his work is perfect. . . . Just and right is He."

Keriyah is accompanied by the blessing for bad news. Many Orthodox Jews still follow ancient practice in 1) tearing their actual clothes, not just a symbolic ribbon, and 2) doing so at the moment they become aware that death has occurred. *Keriyah* remains for them a private ritual that initiates *aninut,* the period from death to burial. Most Jews today, however, know that blessing only as part of a public *keriyah* ceremony, the cutting of a black ribbon affixed to the lapel of mourners just prior to the funeral. *Keriyah* and its blessing have thus been moved from the private to the public realm, where they mark the beginning of the funeral, not the beginning of *an-inut. Aninut* for most Jews has thus virtually ceased to exist as anything but an unofficial period of waiting for the burial to get under way.

In traditional circles, however, as in ancient rabbinic society, *keriyah* initiates *aninut* as a period with consequences. In gen-eral, *onenim* (pl.) are exempt from all ritual duties so that they may do nothing but attend the dead, as we see from the eighth-century Palestinian source, *Massekhet Sofrim.*

> As long as the deceased are unburied, an *onen* is exempt from reciting the *Shema* and the *Tefillah* . . . and from all the com-mandments of which the Torah speaks. It is forbidden for such a person to act stringently [by insisting on fulfilling these commandments anyway] *on account of the honor due to the dead [kevod hamet].*[14]

The reason cited to explain ritual exemption matters. It could have been justified on the technical grounds of ritual impurity.

In antiquity, one buried one's own deceased, after all, and for the Rabbis, no form of ritual impurity was so easily contagious as that of a corpse. Merely to lodge under the same roof rendered one ritually unfit to discharge other religious obligations. Reflecting the necessity of risking ritual impurity while preparing a burial, the Babli applies this general principle: "Involvement with one divine commandment [i.e., burial] exempts its doer from other commandments."[15] Our source, however, retains the original theological rationale: not merely the practical obligation of burial but the theoretical notion of "honor due to the dead."

Modern manuals, by contrast, illustrate the triumph of the psychological. Speaking for Conservative Judaism (in 1979), Isaac Klein reinterprets Jewish requirements pastorally:

> Today, when organized groups or commercial firms take care of the burial needs, and the participation of the family is minimal, such exemptions [from daily prayer and the like] are not necessary. Rather *the solace and the comfort derived from prayer and the performance of religious duties would suggest that we should encourage such activities.*[16]

The subjective understanding of burial and mourning customs not to honor the dead but to comfort the living will recur here. I mention it not as a polemic against the pastoral care (which I support), but as a caution against misunderstanding original rabbinic enactment psychologically. We can trace rabbinic ritual accurately, only if we grant rabbinic thought its own autonomy. To the extent that the Rabbis held any notion of a self, that self was far from the mortal creature we moderns take it to be. For the Rabbis, the human self transcended earthly mortality, and, therefore, had a claim on its descendants for the care necessary to ensure life eternal: proper burial, first of all; and during the eleven or twelve months thereafter, when the deceased might expect chastisement for sin, mourning procedures necessary to bring about successful "survival" in the hereafter. "Honor" accorded by the next of kin would redound to the credit of the deceased: heavenly reward for the soul, and resurrection of the body at the end of days.

Burial

Unfortunately, our primary source for tannaitic liturgy, the Mishnah, says little about rites for death and mourning.[17] That it describes tannaitic burial customs at all is due to the peculiar rabbinic conception of sacred time and its halakhic entailments. Jewish cosmology posits a binary opposition between the holy (*kodesh*) and the everyday (*chol*), usually translated incorrectly as "profane," an English word that has negative connotations that the Hebrew lacks. *Kodesh* is the quality of God, who impinges on human experience, leaving behind, as it were, traces of holiness at each such point of entry.[18] But these loci of the holy differ in degree. Thus festival time can be sufficiently sacred as to be fully a holy day (a *mo'ed*) rather than "ordinary" time (*chol*); but it can also be a combination of the two, *chol hamo'ed,* as the intermediary days of the week-long festival are designated: meaning, literally, "the ordinary part of the holy-day period."

We saw above that in rabbinic culture, "honor" due the dead mandates immediate burial wherever possible. But sometimes people die on or so near before a festival that burial prior to it is impossible; in such cases, the biblical command to rejoice on the festivals requires postponing burial until the festival is over and ordinary time begins. But what happens when burial could take place on *chol hamo'ed*? Do we bury then, or do we wait until the entire festival period is over?

This anomalous issue causes the Mishnah's editor to devote a section to explaining which funeral customs may be performed then and which may not. The list thus unintentionally reveals what normally occurred. Given our paltry information, the reconstruction offered here is a necessarily tentative, albeit reasonable, hypothesis of burial practice as of the second century C.E.

To begin with, we see again that bodies were sometimes interred in an earthly grave and sometimes deposited in a tomb, since it is ruled that "On *chol hamo'ed,* they may not hew out [new] niches in tombs [that already exist] or [wholly new] tombs, though they may renovate the tomb, and may make a coffin if the deceased is lying in the courtyard."[19]

Apparently, a corpse was normally taken outside the house during the period of *aninut*. On mid-festival days, burial in an earthen grave would take place as usual, but if the custom was to enshrine the corpse in a vault, such interment might have to wait as long as a week, depending on when the death occurred, and whether the family vault or cave unit was already dug out and required only minor refurbishing or whether it had to be hewn afresh.

If waiting was required, coffins were prepared immediately, so that the deceased would not have to lie outside decomposing in full view. People usually lived in adjoining apartment-like structures surrounding a shared courtyard (the *chatser*); the courtyards led by way of streets to the town square (*rechovah shel ir*). Though the square was public space and each home was private, the courtyard was liminal, neither fully public nor fully private. There the body was deposited and the casket constructed.

Assuming that only the wealthy were so affected, since only they would have used vaults rather than earthen graves, we can say that the normal procedure was to take the body outside the house, and then to proceed immediately to the cemetery where burial occurred not in a casket, but on a board-like bier (like a bed, to judge by the Hebrew term, *mitah*), where the deceased lay wrapped in shrouds.

> They do not tear their clothing [*keriyah*], bare the shoulder,[20] or provide food for mourners, other than [the seven immediate] relatives of the deceased. They feed them only on a bed that is right side up,[21] and they serve food in a mourner's house not in fancy serving dishes[22] but in ordinary wicker baskets. They do not say the Mourners' Blessing [*Birkat Avelim*]. But they stand in a row, offer comfort [*menachamin*] and disperse the multitude.
>
> They do not set the bier down in the square [*rechov*],[23] so as not to occasion a eulogy, and they never put a woman down in the street [even on ordinary days], because of honor [due her].

> Women do not clap their hands on intermediate days of the festival. Rabbi Ishmael says that those near the bier do so.
>
> On the new moon, Chanukah and Purim, they wail and clap hands. On none of them do they sing a dirge. What is a wail? When all sing together. What is a dirge? When one starts, and then all join in together.[24]

What we have is a delineation of how far one may go in enforcing normal burial customs that honor the deceased at the expense of marring the celebration of a festival. The Mishnah compromises: it retains some burial customs, but withholds others so as not entirely to do away with the joy that even the intermediate festival days demand. The account provides us with a glance at what would constitute the normal course of a burial, were this to be ordinary time.

We saw above that when someone died, the corpse would be removed to the courtyard. Normally, the cortege began then and there; it processed next to the town square where the bier was put down while people joined the crowd, offering words of eulogy to the mourners. When the crowd had fully assembled, the cortege continued to the cemetery. From another source,[25] we know that it stopped on occasion, possibly to change pallbearers, at which time other words of eulogy would occur. But eulogies may not have accompanied women to the grave, at least not in the town square,[26] if indeed their bier was systematically secreted so as to avoid their being on view. Rabbinic society regularly passed rules of *peritsut*, modesty regulations that "protected" women from public view. Since even after death the self continues, having a woman lie in state in the town square would be an affront to her honor.

What happened at the graveside remains partly a mystery, largely because the procedure may not be included here in all its detail. On the other hand, there may have been little or no required liturgy to report. It may be that save for clapping, wailing, dirge-singing and the like (possibly as described in the passage from the Mishnah above)—another report provides also "a gesture of praise" [*kilus*], which it defines as "spreading out the arms")[27]—no extensive spoken liturgy was the norm.

From Burial through Shivah

Following the burial, the throng returned to the mourners' home for the required *se'udat havra'ah*. From the Mishnah passage, which describes exceptions to everyday practice, we can infer that this was normally a lavish meal served on beautiful salvers and fancy baskets. Its munificence explains traditions limiting the amount of wine that was served. Details vary, but one *baraita* that appears ubiquitously (albeit differently, depending on recension) describes how and why wine consumption was rationed.

Tannaim taught the following: The sages ordained ten cups of wine for the mourners' house: three before eating, so as to open the intestines; three while eating so as to soak the food in the intestines; and four after dinner—one corresponding to [the first blessing of the Grace after Meals], ". . . who feeds everything"; one corresponding to [the second blessing in the Grace after Meals], "The Blessing of the Land"; one corresponding to [the third blessing in the Grace after Meals], ". . . who builds Jerusalem"; and one corresponding to [the fourth blessing of the Grace after Meals], ". . . who is good and does good."[28] [To these ten cups,] they added four more: one for the *chazanei ha'ir* and one for the *parnasei ha'ir* [two groups of civic leaders], one for the Temple, and one for Rabban Gamaliel. When people started drinking to the point of drunkenness, practice returned to what it had been originally.

Why "one for Rabban Gamaliel?" [the amoraic editor of the Talmud asks, to which he responds with the following.]

Tannaim taught: Once, removing the dead was harder for the relatives than the actual death itself, to the point where they would lay the corpse out and then run away. But along came Rabban Gamaliel, who treated himself lightly [relative to the full respect usually enjoyed by a man of his station. When he died] they brought him out [just] in linen wrappings, so that thereafter, all the people would do likewise.

Rav Papa [fourth-century Babylonia] said, "Nowadays, people customarily bury their dead even in a rough wrap worth no more than two zuz."[29]

Variations on this theme exist, especially with regard to the purpose and symbolic significance of the wine.[30] But the fact that burial was the occasion for a feast that attracted sumptuary restrictions seems certain. We hear of meals held not only in the home of the mourners but also in the town square, with food that includes bread, meat, fish, and vegetables, sometimes cooked in advance, sometimes brought raw and then cooked on the spot.[31]

The meal was accompanied with something called *Birkat Avelim,* the Mourners' Blessing, which sources identify also as *Birkat Rechovah,* the "Blessing of the Town Square."[32] It is usually explained as specified additions to the Grace after Meals that took place in the mourners' home (or in the public square).[33] Such specific insertions (based on a talmudic example) can be found in Amram (c. 860).[34] More likely, however, the additions were not originally "specified," but were ad hoc spontaneous creations offered by guests. As such, the Mourners' Blessing was like the Bridegroom's Blessing discussed earlier in this volume.[35] The locus of both events was similar: in the latter, a bride was delivered to the groom's home, where a seven-day feast was held, accompanied daily by special additions to the Grace after Meals and by impromptu benedictions for the groom and his bride, the equivalent to our modern-day toasts. Assuming with our sources the structural equivalence of the seven-day wedding feast and the seven-day mourning process, and recognizing that the latter too was in many ways just a lavish feast with guests coming and going regularly, and toasts to dignitaries, we are able to attain a better perspective on what probably occurred. As in the wedding feast, guests arrived to pay their respect, but delivered their good wishes in the form of a Mourner's (instead of a Bridegroom's) Blessing.

The main event of a burial was thus the following feast, and its liturgical high point the Mourners' Blessings offered by guests during the Grace after Meals.

We are left, then, with the "comforting" (described in our opening Mishnah passage), known more fully as *Tanchumei Avelim,* the "Comforting of Mourners."[36] The Mishnah presents

it as something that occurred in conjunction with burial—
"They stand in a row, offer comfort [*menachamin*] and disperse the multitude."[37] The Tosefta too describes it, probably in
connection with the Grace after Meals.[38] And finally, we find it
in the Babli: The occasion is the passing of a young child, and
the visit paid to his father by Resh Lakish, an amora who instructs his amanuensis to recite words of comfort.

[Resh Lakish] said, "Get up and say something appropriate to the
occasion."

He cited [Deut. 32:19], " 'The Lord looked on and was vexed
and spurned his sons and daughters. . . .' This means that in a
generation where the fathers spurn the Holy One Blessed be He,
He is angry with their sons and daughters and they die when they
are young."

[An alternative version of the story is given, with an equally
unsympathetic message of consolation, according to which he
cited Isaiah 9:17], " 'Thus the Lord will not spare their youths, nor
show compassion to their orphans and widows; for all are ungodly
and wicked.' "

[The Talmud objects] The Rabbi came to comfort him but
ended up adding to his grief!

[So the Talmud puts the message in what it supposes is a more
sympathetic light:] He must have said to him, "You are important
enough to be held responsible for the [sins of a whole] generation.
. . ."

He [Resh Lakish] said to him, "Get up and say something in
praise of the Holy One Blessed be He."

He said, "God who is enormously great and abundantly strong
revives the dead with his word. He does wonders beyond our finding out and glorious deeds without number. Blessed art Thou, O
Lord, who revive the dead."

He said to him, "Get up and say something with respect to the
mourners."

He opened by saying, "Our brothers, you who are worn down,
crushed by your loss, consider this: This [the fact of death] is
something eternal, a road leading all the way from the six days of

creation. Many have drunk [of it]; many will drink [of it]; as the first human beings drank [of it] so too will the last human beings do so. Brethren, may the Lord of consolation comfort you. Blessed [art Thou] who comfort mourners."[39]

Before turning to this lengthy talmudic account of "comforting mourners," let us recall that in the Mishnah, the "comforting" is paired with the practice of standing in a row and then dismissing the guests from the graveside, a juxtaposition for which at least two interpretations have been offered. In one, it is the mourners who stand in a row, offer comfort [*menachamin*], and disperse the multitude.[40] The more usual interpretation has been that the members of the gathering divide into two facing rows, and the mourners pass between them, receiving consolation.[41]

I think the latter is probable. In sum, normal burial procedure featured short eulogies that were offered on the way to the cemetery, as well as two liturgical items called "Comforting of Mourners," and the "Mourners' Blessing." The latter was part of the Grace after Meals at the mourners' home and the former happened at the graveside before the throng dispersed. But the Tosefta and the Babli texts show us that "comforting" was not limited to the cemetery. It too transpired during Grace; in addition (or perhaps the same thing), it featured guests who arrived to pay their respect by offering comfort in the form of *Tsidduk Hadin,* justifying the death, followed by statements affirming the relatively puny role of death in the grand scheme of life, death and resurrection.

We should understand the Mourners' Blessing as a structural category, a name given to a particular structural element that gets inserted liturgically into a given place in the Grace after Meals. It was omitted during the festival period because too much mourning was inappropriate for the occasion. The "Comforting of Mourners," however, is not structural but topical. It refers to the *content* of things people say to the mourners: Whether at the graveside or later upon visiting the mourners' home, possibly also as part of the Grace, one

offered consolation. Consolation is not psychological, however, but theological, an affirmation of God's just decrees, and
of the promise of resurrection. The deceased is central to the
discourse; the mourners and their grief are secondary.

A particularly poignant account of funeral theodicy along
with the peculiar ideal of comfort that animated the Rabbis
comes from a story purporting to describe the death of Rabbi
Akiba's son.

> A large crowd gathered to bury the son of Rabbi Akiba. He said,
> "Bring a lecturing bench to the cemetery for me."
>
> He sat down and began to preach. "Brothers in Israel, listen. I
> am not that wise—there are others here wiser than I am; nor am I
> so rich—others here are richer than I. People of the south recog-
> nize who Rabbi Akiba is, but how would those from the Galilee
> know me? [Even in the south] the men know who I am, but do
> women and children know me? Still, I know that your reward is
> great, for you have taken the trouble to come here only to honor
> the Torah and fulfill its commands. I take comfort in the fact that
> even if I had seven sons, I would bury them. Not that a man wants
> to bury his own children, but I know that my son will inherit the
> world to come, for he brought merit to the many, and all who
> bring merit to the many are as if without sin.[42]

Though the story's logic is circular, its point is clear. His
son's death accords Akiba the opportunity to deliver a funeral
oration. He establishes the fact that the people in attendance
have come not just for the entertainment implicit in a famous
man's speech (for many who do not even know who Akiba is
have come anyway). Through his own death, therefore, his son
receives credit for bringing others to the study of Torah, an ac-
complishment that establishes him as deserving resurrection.
Ironically, just by giving this homily, Akiba makes it come
true, and thus takes comfort not in the ways that we moderns
might imagine, but in his knowledge that his son has inherited
everlasting life.

Unveiling the Tombstone and Honoring the Dead

I turn finally to the ritual act of laying a gravestone in place, an action known today as "unveiling." Typically, some time before the eleven or twelve months of mourning are out, mourners have a headstone inscribed, and then literally unveil it while reciting a short liturgy made up largely of psalms. The sepulchre or stone vault is ancient (as we saw), but the use of a headstone is not.[43] Better than any other witness, a haunting responsum from the Holocaust sums up the rationale behind headstones, and thus the attitude toward the dead that Jewish burial practices entail.

A man returns to Poland in 1945 to visit the grave of his parents who died before the war. He finds that the Nazis have ploughed under their graves, uprooted the gravestones for use elsewhere as pavement blocks, and taken down even the entrance signs to what was once the cemetery. He asks if he may erect a tombstone somewhere at random in the vicinity, even though he cannot write on it the customary "Here lies . . .", since he can no longer locate his parents' remains.

The rabbi instructs him to put up a stone recording the fact that his parents are buried somewhere near here, but had their remains ploughed under during the Holocaust. He reasons that the dead need markers and so do we. It serves them because it is an eternal recollection of who they are, and therefore a means of paying them everlasting honor. But since the dead live on after they die, a headstone encourages our own praying at the cemetery, where we receive the benefit of intercession by our deceased. Surely this need not occur precisely on their grave site. Both for their sake then and for our own, we need tombstones. They get the honor they deserve, and we get their help if we pray there.[44]

The Jewish Funeral Liturgy Today

Not much of what I have described so far survives. Already in amoraic times, it was no longer clear what the tannaim meant by their localized Palestinian customs, and by geonic days, even less remained. One community asks an unnamed gaon about a cup of consolation:[45] "Where we live, it is our custom that when we return with the mourners from the graveside, we say this blessing over the cup: 'Blessed art Thou . . . compassionate and faithful judge who renders true judgment upon us, as it is written [Deut. 32:4]: The Rock, his work is perfect. Blessed art Thou who comfort the heart of mourners.'" Though *Seder Rav Amram* knows this blessing,[46] the geonic recipient of the note admits, "We have never encountered the blessing that you mention. It is not in the Talmud, and we have heard of no one in the Babylonian academies who says it. Nor have we heard of it from our teachers."[47] Though this may indeed be an old surviving form of the tannaitic Mourners' Blessing, it is more likely a post-talmudic innovation. Another gaon thus surmises, "The Mourners' Blessing is no longer extant."[48]

Of the items mentioned in our opening Mishnah, we have thus only traces:

1. *Aninut* is still practiced (along with *keriyah* initiating it) only by the Orthodox, although for all Jews, Jewish funeral homes arrange a watch over a body until the funeral, and rules regarding the ritual cleansing of the body (as well as an aversion, if not an absolute ban, on autopsies) are observed. Burial still occurs as quickly as possible, usually within twenty-four hours, with postponements only in the interest of heightening honor due the dead, as, for instance, when mourning kin cannot arrive from distant places until a longer period of time has elapsed.

2. Many Orthodox Jews postpone *keriyah* until the funeral; all liberal Jews do so, and instead of ripping actual clothing, they tear a black ribbon which is worn throughout the *shivah* period. Except in certain Sephardic communities in Israel where middle-eastern culture still prevails, the burial liturgy preserves none of the ritualized wailing that marks the Mishnah's account. Modern city life has done away with a communal procession from town square to a local cemetery. The

funeral eulogies, once offered by one and all who stopped to
see the mourners in the square or who participated in the
cortege with its stops and starts along the way, are gone,[49] but
the idea of a eulogy (*hesped*) is basic to Jewish liturgy. The
focus of the service is now a eulogy (or sometimes more than
one), by the rabbi, a family member, or friend, its theological
purpose being *kevod hamet*—honoring the dead.

Otherwise, the standard liturgy for funerals (*Tsidduk Hadin*) is a loose amalgam of psalms and readings, none of it
absolutely mandatory, but usually beginning with Deuteronomy 32:4, "The Rock, his work is perfect. . . ." and featur-
ing Psalm 23, Psalms 144:3–4, and other scriptural selections
popularly or explicitly associated with death. In addition, one
expects to find the *Kaddish* recited at the graveside, as well as
a late prayer dating only from the seventeenth century, *El
Malei Rachamim* ("O God, full of compassion . . ."), which
petitions for the safe care of the deceased's soul.[50] Back
home, *shivah* is observed, though Reform Jews sometimes
limit it to three, not to seven days. People still bring food to a
mourner's home, but one rarely encounters the mourners'
Grace after Meals, even though technically, it still exists in
liturgical manuals.

Above all, however, Jews in North America have largely
abandoned the entire set of assumptions on which the traditional ritual for death and mourning was based. The psychological self has achieved almost universal and uncritical
acceptance. Eulogies thus tend not only to honor the dead
(certainly not for their own sake) but to comfort the living
(who, it is presumed, enjoy hearing of the virtue of their deceased). Prayers affirming resurrection are rarely recited any
more. *Keriyah* may or may not be performed along with the
traditional blessing affirming God's just decrees ("Blessed
art Thou . . . the true judge"). The entire burial rite can no
longer be regarded as an exercise in *Tsidduk Hadin* in its
true meaning, of justifying the death.

Today's burial rites thus combine the ancient motif of honoring the dead with a modern concern for comforting the

mourners, and comfort is psychological, not theological. Except in very traditional circles, we find no assurances that death must emanate from a beneficent and omniscient God who takes us when the time is ripe but rewards us in the afterlife. The rite today features instead a God of compassion whence healing comes. Such a theme is itself theological, but the psychological bias of our times has thus far attracted only pastoral sensitivity, not theological scrutiny. A full theological consideration of the burial rites has yet to be undertaken.

Appendix on Massekhet Semachot
and "The Minor Tractates"

Evidence for Jewish life-cycle ritual is contained abundantly in a series of early medieval works known collectively as the Minor Tractates. The term is modern, reflecting the classical bias in favor of the Mishnah, the Tosefta, and the two Talmuds (second- to sixth-century sources), all of which order material according to treatises known as tractates, but by definition comprise the "major" tractates, as opposed to the "minor" ones that "lesser" rabbinic authors willed to posterity. But "Minor Tractate" is not the designation used for *all* extra-talmudic halakhic work. Rather, it denotes a particular collection of some fourteen such works—their numbering system varies—all of which are technically outside the sixty-three-book "canon" of Mishnah and Tosefta (the tannaitic era) and the Yerushalmi and Babli (the amoraic period). What prompts its comparison with the canonical treatises (which are called "major," by contrast) is the historical accident that European authorities in the high Middle Ages transmitted these ancient works alongside of their canonical Talmud text, until eventually, when standardized printing of the talmudic text became the norm, the "minor tractates" were appended to the "major ones." The term is sometimes applied, however, only to seven of those tractates, which were subsequently (1937) collected separately in a critical form by Michael Higger, whose work in the field deserves special recognition.[51]

Needless to say, whoever the authors of these "secondary" works were, they should not be presumed in their time to have deliberately compiled what they themselves considered only "minor" works, and in fact they are often far from minor as far as their witness to history is concerned. Until the Genizah fragments, a minor tractate known as *Massekhet Sofrim* was our best source for the liturgy of Palestinian Jewry up to the eighth century or so (I have already referred to that tractate as being our first source in which the *Kaddish* is cited as a mourners' prayer).[52] Another minor tractate, euphemistically entitled *Massekhet Semachot,* "The Tractate on Joyous Events" (but known also as *Evel Rabbati,* "The Great Work on Mourning"), presents early mourning customs.[53]

But precisely because they were not canonically controlled, it is unclear exactly when these minor tractates were authored, how many literary strata they contain, or what communities their data describe. By contrast, the Talmuds *purport,* at least, to set off their tannaitic heritage from their own more recent work. Moreover, the date of talmudic canonization is at least roughly known, and is relatively early compared to the minor tractates, which may have grown for centuries before any attempt was made to control what could be admitted to them. Only relatively late, in the geonic time and beyond, were the minor tractates finally edited. The European authorities who passed them along as talmudic addenda, however, treated them as Palestinian, indeed as tannaitic, and often they are correct. We thus find moderns using the minor tractates as evidence for their reconstruction of rabbinic practices in the pre-200 C.E. period with which we are primarily concerned.

But even though the presumption of tannaitic authorship should not be automatically discounted, it cannot be automatically assumed either. I therefore use *Massekhet Semachot* here as supplementary to the Mishnah and to canonically designated tannaitic strata. Even the latter are somewhat suspect with regard to attribution to individual authorities, but at least the date of specific works in which the opinions are embedded is relatively certain, so that even if we cannot say for sure that a given tradition comes from this or that pre-200 individual, we can at least say that it represents the pre-200 era in which that individual lived. Moreover, our goal here is not a strict separation of pre- and post-200 liturgy. We want to explore classic rabbinic culture, especially in Palestine (though to some extent, Babylonia also), whence further rabbinic tradition developed. For our purposes, the reconstruction of liturgy as culture, we thus need not worry overly much about whether a tradition is mid-second century or a hundred years later.[54] But minor-tractate data are best reserved for confirmatory information regarding basic customs already firmly established by canonical evidence, or for illustrations of how such customs were carried out, possibly in the tannaitic period, but possibly also thereafter.

NOTES

1. "He [Judah ben Tema] would say: Five [is the age for] scripture; ten for Mishnah; thirteen for fulfilling commandments; fifteen for study of Talmud; eighteen for marriage; twenty for family responsibility; thirty for the height of one's strength; forty for understanding; fifty for giving counsel; sixty for old age; seventy for ripe old age; eighty for remarkable strength; ninety for a bowed back; and at one hundred, one approximates a corpse who has already passed from the world" (Avot 5:21). Up to age fifty, the categories are all tied to religious commandments, primarily study and *mitzvah,* but also procreation; after that time, creeping old age is the theme.

2. See Isaac Klein, *A Guide to Religious Practice* (New York, 1979), pp. 274–76, and sources cited there.

3. Cf. M. M.K. 3:7, and M.K. 27a, where we are given rules limiting the expense of serving the meal of condolence, because of "the honor due the poor." The "poor" here are usually understood as the surviving mourners *alone,* but that can hardly be right. They did not serve the meal, after all; the community did, using silverware appropriate to the wealth of the deceased and the surviving kin. The issue is the maintenance of class divisions even after death, something to which the Rabbis object, not because they never want to embarrass the poor, but because doing so now is a reflection upon the deceased who may have lived poorly while alive, but deserves not to be dishonored by having that poverty recollected ritually even after death.

4. H.J. Leon, "The Jewish Catacombs and Inscriptions of Rome: An Account of Their Discovery and Subsequent History," *Hebrew Union College Annual* 5 (1928): 299–314.

5. *Massekhet Semachot,* ed. Michael Higger (New York, 1931), 12:5 (henceforth designated *MS*).

6. For modern Jewish law in traditional circles, see Chaim Binyamin Goldberg, *Mourning in Halachah* (Brooklyn, 1991).

7. See M. Meg. 4:3.

8. M.K. 27b.

9. P.T. M.K. 3:5.

10. See Goldberg, *Mourning in Halachah,* pp. 351–55. A twelve-month period for inveterate sinners is derived from M. Eduyot 2:10, but remained limited to northern Europe primarily; the Italian encyclopedic work *Pachad Yitzchak* (s.v. "*Kaddish*") retains a twelve-month mourning period, following the Babli's view that the dead are remembered for that long (Ber. 58b).

11. Mas. Sof. 19:11. For details on the *Kaddish,* cf. David Assaf, *Hakaddish: Mekoro, Mashme'uto Vedinav* (Haifa, 1966), pp. 197–204, and Israel M. Ta-shma, *Minhag Ashkenaz Hakadmon* (Jerusalem, 1992), pp. 299–310.

12. Ber. 9:2.

13. A.Z. 18a.

14. *MS* 10:1; cf. M. Ber. 3:1.

15. Cf. Suk. 25a, 26a.

16. Klein, *Guide to Religious Practice,* p. 274. His references (to *MS* 10:1, Y.D. 341:1) actually cite the ruling banning such activity.

17. The following description makes minimal use of *MS (Massekhet Semachot)*, which claims to reflect the Mishnaic period but is not trustworthy in that regard. For discussion of sources, see the appendix to this essay.

18. Cf. Lawrence A. Hoffman, *Beyond the Text* (Bloomington, IN, 1987), pp. 20–45; "Jewish Spirituality: the Life of Blessing," *Concilium* 229 (1990), pp. 18–39.

19. M. M.K. 1:6. Cf. T. Moed (= M.K.) 1:9, where "renovate" is explained as changing the shape of a space that has already been dug out.

20. Dishevelled clothing, like torn garments, as a sign of mourning.

21. They sat on the hard side of overturned couches, as a sign of mourning.

22. The Mishnah actually enumerates the dishes here: a *tavla* (obviously a flat serving board, apparently made at times, at least, out of gold), *iskutla* (a salver like the Latin *scutella* or the Greek *skoutlon*), and *kanon* (a reed basket, as opposed to an ordinary wicker basket)—see Jastrow, *Dictionary*.

23. *Rechov* can also mean street, in general, not the town square.

24. M. M.K. 3:8–9.

25. M. Meg. 4:3.

26. Cf. confirmatory reports in *MS* 11:2.

27. Cf. T. Moed 2:16.

28. The same blessing as that recited upon hearing good news, albeit in longer form, and associated by tradition with burial of the dead following the Bar Kokhba revolt. Cf. e.g., P.T. Ber. 7:1.

29. Ket. 8b.

30. Cf. *MS* 14:14 and parallel texts cited by Higger, *MS*, p. 209, n. 58.

31. *MS* 14:13.

32. Meg. 23b; B. M. Lewin, *Otsar Hageonim*, vol. 4 (Jerusalem, 1939), M.K. #124, p. 43.

33. Our sources are too incomplete to provide much certainty, but primary evidence for this reconstruction comes from the T. Ber. 3:24, discussed by Saul Lieberman (*Tosefta Kifshutah*, vol. 1 [New York, 1955], pp. 51–52). He sees it as a benediction frequently divided among the various parts of the Grace, including its invitational formula (the *zimmun*).

34. SRA, ed. Daniel Goldschmidt (Jerusalem, 1971), pp. 187–88; cf. Ber. 46b.

35. See above, pp. 136–37, 139.

36. M. Meg. 4:3.

37. See extract above, p. 223.

38. Cf. T. Ber. 3:2–4; Lieberman, *Tosefta Kifshutah*, vol. 1, pp. 51–52.

39. Ket. 8b.

40. Jacob Neusner, trans., *The Mishnah* (New Haven, CT, 1988), p. 328.

41. Classical sources have it both ways, claiming that rivalry between families as to who had the right to pass by the mourners and offer condolence first resulted in having the wellwishers remain stationary while the mourners passed them by (San. 19a).

42. *MS* 8:13.

43. M. Shek. 2:5 refers to some kind of monument as a *nefesh,* a word otherwise meaning "soul." P.T. (Shek. 2:5) explains its purpose as providing *zikaron,* "memorial," but holds that the righteous need no *nefesh* since their words suffice. Medieval commentators know the *nefesh* as a *matsevah*—see, e.g., Bertinoro to M. Shek. 2:5.

44. Ephraim Oshry, ed., *She'elot Uteshuvot Mima'amakim* (New York, 1959), pp. 157–60.

45. Cf. Jeremiah 16:7.

46. SRA, ed. Goldschmidt, p. 186.

47. Lewin, *Otsar Hageonim,* vol. 8, part 1, pp. 32–33.

48. Ibid., p. 32.

49. "Stops and starts," originally understood as a means of resting the pallbearers (M. Ber. 3:1) accompanied by eulogies (cf. Rashi's understanding of Meg. 23b, *d.h. ein osin ma'amad umoshav*) had early on become ritualized into a fixed number (not less than seven times—see *baraita,* B.B. 100b), but was eventually assumed to have occurred only on the way home from the grave side (see Rashbam to B.B. 100b, *d.h. mekom ma'amado*), and had virtually ceased by geonic times (people stopped to rest on the way home from cemeteries that were more distant by then, but did nothing ritually at the time—see Lewin, *Otsar Hageonim,* vol. 7, #123, pp. 42–43).

50. Composed as a response to Chmielnicki massacres. See Eliezer Levi Landshut, *Amudei Ha'avodah* (1857; reprint, New York, 1965), pp. 84–85.

51. Michael Higger, *Seven Minor Tractates* (New York, 1930). Higger dates them as Palestinian, perhaps as early as 400 C.E. (and thus just after the Palestinian Talmud had been completed), but then edited further in Babylon. The preferred early term in midrashic and geonic halakhic works is *massekhet chitsonah,* "Extracanonical Tractate"; but *Halakhot Gedolot* (usually attributed to Yehudai Gaon [eighth century]) identifies "extracanonical" with "minor." See Higger, introduction, pp. 10–11.

52. Also edited scientifically by Michael Higger (but in Hebrew only), *Massekhet Sofrim* (New York, 1937). For English version, see A. Cohen, *The Minor Tractates of the Talmud,* vol. 1 (London, 1965), pp. 211–324. For the *Kaddish,* see Sof. 19:11.

53. Cf. Michael Higger, *MS* (*Massekhet Semachot*); and for English, "Ebel Rabbathi Named Masseketh Semahoth: Tractate on Mourning," trans. J. Rabbinowitz, in A. Cohen, *The Minor Tractates,* vol. 1, pp. 326–400, and Dov Zlotnick, *The Tractate "Mourning,"*

Yale Judaica Series 17 (New Haven, 1966). The title *Semachot* comes from the eleventh century. *Evel Rabbati* is cited as authoritative by the Talmud (e.g., B.K. 24a), where it is identified by Rashi as *Massekhet Semachot.* Whether our version is in fact what the amoraim had before them is the subject of scholarly debate, but positive identification goes back to Natronai Gaon (853–858). Higger's collection assembles other parallel works on the subject also.

54. For a theoretical consideration of this perspective, see Lawrence A. Hoffman, "Reconstructing Ritual as Identity and Culture," in Paul F. Bradshaw and Lawrence A. Hoffman, eds., *The Making of Jewish and Christian Worship* (Notre Dame, IN, 1991), pp. 22–41.

Contemporary Challenges
to Christian Life-Cycle Ritual

Marjorie Procter-Smith

The "life cycle" is a culturally constructed concept. All human beings are born and all die, but the "stages" in between these two events vary widely, depending on such factors as social norms, physical environment, and cultural expectations. Even such apparently biological events as puberty are largely culturally determined: the age of menarche has dropped in this country over the past fifty years, and non-technological societies typically define puberty as the beginning of adulthood, in contrast to industrialized countries in which it marks the beginning of adolescence.[1] Societies have an interest in marking off "stages" in life by constructing their meaning. However, as societies change, the shape or interpretation of certain stages must also change. Since western society is patriarchal in structure, the socially defined "life-cycle" stages represent dominant class male interests and stages.

Contemporary challenges to Christian life-cycle rituals come from two sources. Pragmatic problems unforeseen in earlier centuries may call forth adjustments in existing rituals, even the creation of new ones. Changes in social norms and expectations create a need for changes in the ritual interpretation of traditional stages. For example, the prevalence of second marriages in many Christian traditions has given rise to newer marriage rites which include the possibility of participation by children of the bride or groom in the ceremony.

240

Other challenges are raised by persons and groups previously silenced or marginalized, whose life-stages or special concerns have been ignored or misinterpreted in traditional rituals. These challenges arise not from societal changes but from protest. Many traditional life-cycle stages and the rituals which interpret them function to maintain patriarchal power relationships and roles. Marginalized populations who suffer from attempts to force their lives into these stages are now claiming the right to define their own life images and processes. For example, a significant stage in women's life cycle, menopause, has been ritually ignored by Christian tradition. This absence has been noted by many women, who have created new rituals to celebrate and ritualize this stage of life and to celebrate aging in women, an image which runs counter to society's emphasis on youth, particularly for women. These challenges and protests generally issue in the creation of new rituals, sometimes with roots in traditional Christian sources, sometimes not.

NEW QUESTIONS, OLD RITES

Marriage Rites

Cultural and social assumptions about marriage and gender roles have been changing over the past thirty years, and these changes have been reflected in marriage rites. Older rites, which assumed and proclaimed the submission of the wife to the husband, have in many cases been modified to reflect greater emphasis on mutuality and equality.[2] For example, common to western marriage rites has been the action called "giving away the bride" by the father of the bride, a rite originating in late Roman antiquity which became widespread during the Middle Ages. Although the marriage rites of the Reformation churches have traditionally displayed ambiguity towards this ritual, the recent practice has been to include it, since it is often popularly regarded as a cultural rather than a religious tradition. However, most recent liturgical revisions of mainline churches have either eliminated or modified the practice. For example, *The Lutheran Book of Worship* notes that:

> Because of the nature of the partnership entered upon by the bride and groom, no provision is made for the father giving the bride away. If such an expression is desired, it is appropriate for the parents of each partner to meet the couple as the procession ends and mutually exchange the peace.[3]

The marriage liturgies of the United Methodist Church, the United Church of Christ, and the Presbyterian Church U.S.A. have modified the "giving away of the bride" into a declaration of support by family and congregation. The Episcopal Church also includes a "pledge of support," but it retains the giving of the bride (or "presentation") as an option, although providing for the possibility of the presentation of the man to the woman as well as the woman to the man.[4]

Another cultural change that is reflected in new marriage rites is the presence of children of the couple. As divorce and remarriage have become more common, it has become likewise common for the couple to want to include their children in the marriage rite in some way. *The Book of Worship* of the United Church of Christ includes an optional question addressed to the children who will be part of the new family, and invites the couple to declare their commitment to the children. The children are asked to declare their willingness to give "trust, love, and affection" to their new family, and the couple promises to be "faithful and loving parents."[5] Similarly, the United Methodist *Book of Worship,* a collection of supplementary liturgical services and resources, includes the option of the children of the couple making a brief statement of support at the time of the Declaration of Intention.[6]

Ritualization of divorce is less common, particularly in denominational materials. Only the United Church of Christ includes in its *Book of Worship* an "Order for Recognition of the End of a Marriage," which is a complete worship service. In the general ordering of the book, this service is included among the "Services of Reconciliation and Healing." The introductory notes reveal some discomfort with the idea of such a ritual: "The service is penitential in nature and cannot be construed to be an encouragement of divorce or a deprecation of marriage."[7]

The United Methodist *Book of Worship* includes "Ministry with Persons Going Through Divorce" in a section on "Healing Services and Prayers."[8] It is not a complete service, however, consisting of a prayer that refers to only one person and suggesting possible scripture readings. It is evidently intended for use with an individual, perhaps in a counseling setting.

It is interesting to note that the Methodist service places prayers for divorce in the context of healing, while the United Church of Christ locates its service in the context of penitence and reconciliation. The connection between healing and penitence will be examined further.

Healing Services

As contemporary medicine has become increasingly technological, many people have countered by seeking alternatives that offer more personal involvement and control by the patient. These alternatives include non-western medical practices such as acupuncture or massage, new techniques such as biofeedback, diet, and mental imaging, and recovery of traditional healing rituals, both Christian and non-Christian.[9] In some Christian traditions, of course, healing continues to be an important part of worship practice. For so-called "mainline churches," however, services of healing are sometimes looked on with some suspicion.

In spite of this resistance, however, newer ritual collections of mainline denominations include services of healing. The United Methodist *Book of Services* includes two: one is a full service of worship for use with a congregation and may include communion; the second is briefer and designed for use with an individual or small group in a home or hospital. In addition, there are resources (prayers and scripture) for specialized

situations: a complete "Service of Hope after Loss of Preg-
nancy" and prayers for persons suffering from addiction or substance abuse, persons with AIDS, persons with life-threatening
illness, and persons in a coma. The Presbyterian *Book of Common Worship* offers a comparable array: services of healing
(called "Services for Wholeness") and prayers for the sick
in a variety of specific conditions.[10] The Episcopal *Book of
Occasional Services* also includes an order for a public healing
service.[11]

It is worth noting that all of the denominational healing resources surveyed here link healing with confession of sin in
some way, some more explicitly than others. This connection
between illness or suffering and sin reflects an ancient world-
view of the origin of illness that is being challenged by many,
including feminist theologians and theologians in the disability
community. Their critiques will be taken up below.

Although many current denominational resources include
prayers for those with AIDS, complete rituals of healing, blessing, or memorial for persons with AIDS originated in the gay
community, and will be dealt with in the context of rites for
gay and lesbian life-cycle events.

NEW VOICES, NEW RITES

Challenges of the sort identified above are relatively easily dealt with by the provision of additional or supplemen-
tal resources, leaving the traditional services more or less
intact. Substantial challenges, calling for new rites or radical reconception of traditional rites, are more often found
among marginal groups with little or no access to denominational authorities. Thus many emergent ritual practices
can be documented only in privately published resources, if
they are published at all. I will deal with each of these
challenges in the context of the group in which they arose,
even though many times those groups overlap.

The feminist liturgical movement has long been critical of traditional rituals, challenging not only androcentric language, but also ritual practices and symbols. Women-church groups and feminist liturgy groups have been developing their own rituals for many years now. Similarly, non-white churches often develop their own rituals apart from the white ritual traditions they have received. The gay and lesbian community has claimed the power to create rituals appropriate to their lives and struggles. Persons with disabilities are perhaps the newest voices to be heard, but they offer a powerful challenge to the churches' practice and symbols. These differing voices point up not only the socially constructed nature of life cycles and their ritual interpretation, but also the political function of such construction and interpretation.

Women's Rites

The feminist liturgical movement has criticized the traditional form and content of all Christian life-cycle rituals as being androcentric and designed to serve the interests of powerful men in the church and society. Traditional initiatory rites of the church include both elements of emancipation (such as lack of ritual distinction between male and female candidates), and oppressive elements, such as the implication that baptism in water is a superior birth to birth from a woman's body. Feminist baptism and baptismal catechesis would place women and women's stories, struggles, and experiences at the center of the process.[12] Where confirmation rites function as coming-of-age rituals, they fail to take account of the need of young Christian women to be encouraged to develop their best selves, to resist social pressures to conform to sexist roles, and to challenge church structures which demean or deny them.

The androcentrism of the church and its official rituals has led many feminists to construct rituals which attend to women's life-cycle events in ways that allow them to name specifically female experiences without censure. Out of the feminist liturgical movement and the women's spirituality movement come two groups of life-cycle rituals not found in traditional Christian liturgical resources. One group of rituals commemorates and celebrates the biological stages of women's lives: menarche, menstruation, childbirth, miscarriage, menopause, coming to old age (often called "croning"). A second group of rituals deals with the injuries inflicted by men on women because they are women: battering, sexual abuse, rape, and a host of lesser insults inflicted on women, often by the church or its representatives. The services in this second group sometimes resemble, and may be called, healing services, but they have little in common with denominational healing services.

Christianity's historical distaste for the female body and its functions has prevented it from enabling the development of rituals celebrating women's bodily functions, and feminist groups normally either have to construct a ritual from nothing, or borrow from other religions. Indeed, it could be argued that the whole purpose of rituals that affirm and celebrate women's bodies is contrary to the dominant tradition of Christian ritual, which has circumscribed and prohibited the presence of women's bodies in certain roles. These feminist rituals claim the sacredness of women's bodies and their functions.[13] They often include bathing or anointing of the body, not as means of cleansing or healing (as these symbolic actions would be understood in a traditional Christian context), but as signs of the care and honor we give to women's bodies.[14] Although some of the published versions of these rituals are designed for use in groups—especially the menarche and menopause/croning rituals—others, such as the monthly menstruation ritual, are often done privately, and may be designed by the woman herself. A major influence on the development of these rituals is the recovery or reconstruction of Goddess-centered religions, which, it is argued, value women's bodily functions highly as symbolic of the power of the Goddess. The lack of specific Christian content in many of these rituals leads one to ask whether there are any Christian resources from which to draw in order to affirm women's bodies.

The affirmation of women's bodies is a central emphasis also in services of healing for women. The violence and abuse women experience from men both originate in and result in hatred of women's bodies. Services for survivors of violence often include blessing, anointing, or other ritualized honoring and caring for the body of the one who has been violated.[15] This action intends not only to heal, but also to counter the self-hatred and shame which survivors frequently feel after an attack. Because the cultural message (and often the specific message from the batterer or rapist) is that the woman is responsible for her own victimization, traditional healing services, with their close association of healing with penitence, are not only inappropriate but harmful as well.

The service in Rosemary Radford Reuther's *Women-Church* is typical.[16] In place of a confession of sin there is a lament, mingling the story of a woman's suffering at the hands of her violent husband with the cry of the psalmist in Psalm 22. In place of the reading of scripture the woman who comes for healing tells her story. The anointing with oil is accompanied by words that affirm the goodness of her body; the anointing includes her whole body, particularly its injured parts. The closing declaration commits all present to work to end violence against women. Never does the service state or imply that the woman's suffering is sent by God, that it is somehow "good for her," or that she is responsible for it. Rather, her suffering is lamented, the violence of her husband is named as evil, and the community accepts responsibility to work collectively to bring it to an end.

Some women's healing services include exorcisms, often adapted from medieval Christian rites. In an interesting example of the use of a tradition's rituals of exclusion against itself, these rituals cast out the evils of sexism, battering, sexual harassment, rape, sexual abuse, discrimination, and other forms of insult and injury inflicted on women because they are women.[17]

These rites of exorcism make explicit what the other
women's rites of passage leave implicit: the fact that the Christian tradition's ritual definition of life and its stages ignores,
denies, rejects, or misinterprets most if not all of the central
events in women's lives. Whether done in groups or individu-
ally, including Christian references or not, these are truly examples of what Delores Williams calls "resistance rituals."[18]

Survival Rites

African-Americans, Asian-Americans, Latinos, and Native
Americans in North America who are Christians find themselves attempting to assimilate their racial-ethnic identity with
their Christian identity, often uncomfortably. Frequently the
discomfort arises from the white-western-European character
of the liturgical rituals they have inherited. Amitiyah Elayne
Hyman, writing from an African-American perspective, puts
the problem succinctly: "The rituals developed to give meaning and posit value to the people of America were not created
with Africans in mind."[19] Similarly, Native American Marie
Therese Archambault, a Roman Catholic sister, observes that
Native American Christian women do not "feel good about
ourselves within a Christian setting. . . . Yet we continue to
engage in Christian religious practice without seeing ourselves
included. . . . It is only in a group of native people in ritual or
ceremony that I feel most accepted for who I am."[20] Often what
is experienced as a conflict between ethnic or racial identity
and Christian identity was created by Christian missionary approaches which demanded the rejection of non-white or non-
western culture and religion. This conflict may be resolved
either by rejecting ethnic identity or by attempting some sort of
synthesis.

For example, African-American churches are increasingly
influenced by the Afrocentric movement, which emphasizes
the African origins of western culture and inculcates pride in
the African heritage of African-Americans. The spiritual dimensions of African identity are often emphasized in a way

which Christian churches are able to embrace or adapt.[21] This movement and its acceptance by many African-American Christian churches has combined with a concern for African-American youth to produce "rites of passage" programs. Designed to foster positive self-image and sense of control over the future for young men and women, these programs combine teaching about Africa, about values and commitments, and about entry into adulthood with rituals drawing on African traditions.[22] Not all such programs include specific Christian content, even when offered through churches. They are generally not viewed as opportunities to proselytize or indoctrinate youth, but as rituals to ensure the survival of a threatened people.

Separate "rites of passage" programs are offered to young men and young women. Separation by gender allows the issues specific to becoming adult in the world as African-American man or African-American woman to be central to the process. Amitiyah Elayne Hyman notes:

> In identifying womanist ritual for living that will work for contemporary African-American women and girls, who jump the double-dutch difficulties of race and sex, we look to using ceremonial signs and symbols in repetitive, yet improvisational, ways. We choose those rituals that come out of the past and our common life together in another time and place. The reference to a past life, begun in the Motherland of Africa and continued in the diaspora, helps to reinforce values and ways of being that allow us to transcend the present crisis of our people.[23]

Gay and Lesbian Rites

In *Coming Out Within: Stages of Spiritual Awakening for Lesbians and Gay Men,* authors Craig O'Neill and Kathleen Ritter argue that the dominant "life image" presented by culture and society (and certainly the churches) centers on opposite-sex couples and has no place for the life image of the healthy, mature, fulfilled gay or lesbian person. The result of this absence for lesbian and gay persons is "a condition of incongruence between who they are deep inside and how the culture expects them to live."[24] The churches' emphasis on heterosexual marriage and almost unanimous condemnation of homosexuality create special grief and losses for gay and lesbian Christians. The ritual locus of the absence of gay and lesbian life-cycle events lies in the refusal of churches to bless gay and lesbian identity. In practice, this identity is celebrated in coming-out rituals, in services of blessing a same-sex couple, often called Holy Union, and in rituals of healing, blessing, death, and memorial for victims of AIDS. Few published resources for any of these rites exist.[25]

Services of Holy Union appear to be the earliest of these rituals to be developed in the gay and lesbian community.[26] In a 1984 book on affirming gay and lesbian relationships in a Christian context, Larry Uhrig makes a distinction between a Rite of Blessing and a service of Holy Union. A Rite of Blessing is a simple prayer, "a useful tool that we, as gay men and women, can use to fill the void created when our religious institutions withhold rites of blessing and affirmation of our lifestyle."[27] A service of Holy Union, on the other hand, is a communal event which expresses a contract between two people, intends pair bonding of the couple for life, and creates the union it celebrates. This ritual has consequences beyond those for the couple, however. It is interpreted as a prophetic act in the church: "Rites of Holy Union assault the church at the point of its own internal contradiction; the church's refusal to accept our nature as homosexual persons is in conflict with . . . its central doctrine of incarnation. . . ."[28]

It may also be seen as prophetic, insofar as it challenges gender hierarchy, which is reinforced in traditional heterosexual marriage rites. Robert Goss notes:

> Gay and lesbian unions form a prophetic model of relating for the Christian community. The blessing of same-sex unions represents the basileia practice of solidarity. . . . [It] represents the practice of God's reign in an inclusive discipleship of equals, shared

resources, and service at table. It practices an oppositional basileia model of relationship, contrary to the hierarchical political model of heterosexist marriage. It challenges the inequalities and lack of mutuality found in opposite-sex coupling based on such biblical and cultural injunctions as "Wives be submissive to your husbands as to the Lord."[29]

Not only rites of union but also the "coming out" of a gay or lesbian person illustrate the way in which life-stages are socially constructed. On the one hand, declaring one's sexual identity publicly is something all persons do, perhaps by dating and marrying, or by taking vows of celibacy. But in our society homosexual persons take special personal and professional risks when they do so. As Tom Driver notes:

> The "coming out" that many lesbian and gay persons have enacted in recent years . . . has profound social and political consequences, in addition to whatever it means psychologically and spiritually for individuals. . . . The idea of going public with one's sexual identity is in most cases an explosive one, for the risk is high. It is not only the likelihood of being punished and shamed by society, friends, and family: It is also the risk of losing one's present identity, losing self-esteem, giving up a known way of life without the reassuring experience of another.[30]

Obviously, for many lesbian and gay persons, "coming out" to friends, family, and colleagues is a critical "life-stage," with its own processes and needs. Although this process is often informal and private, some lesbian and gay Christians are attributing religious significance to coming out, and working to create appropriate religious rituals to help mark the stage, and to enable the church to aid persons moving through this critical life passage. One "Celebration of Coming Out" introduces the service in this way:

> This celebration provides the opportunity for a lesbian, gay, or bisexual church member to ask for and receive support from her or his congregation. This may be done as a part of the Sunday morning worship service or as a special private ceremony.

The service includes scripture reading, the declaration of coming out by the individual, witness by the individual and others, a congregational declaration of support, laying-on-of-hands with prayer, and a blessing. The declaration of coming out is adapted from Psalm 139:14:

> I praise God for I am fearfully and wonderfully made. Wonderful are the works of God: that I know very well. Therefore I am proud to say, "I am a (lesbian/gay/bisexual/transgender) child of God."

The response is begun by the presider and continued by the congregation:

> (Name), we are humbled by your courage which testifies to your faith in the Liberating Christ.
>
> (NAME), YOU ARE WONDERFULLY AND FEARFULLY MADE AND WE GIVE THANKS FOR YOUR FAITHFUL PRESENCE IN OUR MIDST. MAY WE BE WORTHY COMPANIONS ON YOUR JOURNEY.[31]

From the same source, a eucharistic "Great Thanksgiving for National Coming Out Day" appropriates the religious significance of gay liberation symbols:

> Because of your grace and justice, we are no longer a people of the closet but a people of parades, rainbows, and quilts called to lead your church in a march for liberation. . . . In his [Jesus'] journey to heal wounds of estrangement and silence, to cast out demons of fear and hatred, Your Spirit anointed him to act-up against all forms of oppression, bigotry, and enslavement.[32]

Like the feminist use of exorcism rites against the church, these rituals use the church's own language about and theological claims for baptism to charge the church with its Christian responsibilities and to make room for lesbian and gay Christians in the church's central rituals. Rituals of coming out and Holy Union mark significant moments in the life cycle of gay and lesbian Christians; but as the Great Thanksgiving just cited demonstrates, the symbols and experiences central to this marginalized community must be moved from

the realm of the forbidden into the central rites of the church
in order to place the Christian observance of these life-cycle
events in a meaningful context.

The AIDS epidemic has taken a particularly heavy toll on
the gay community, and it is out of that community that services of healing and blessing for persons with AIDS grew, as
well as memorial services for those who have died of AIDS.
Where the religious communities have withheld blessing and
even—in many cases—basic pastoral care, the gay community
has offered prayer and ritual as well as physical care. The pre-
dominant symbol of the care of and loving memory of those
with AIDS is the AIDS quilt, made up of squares created by
family, friends, and lovers of persons who have died of AIDS.
Although AIDS is not a "gay disease," its symbolic value is
often claimed by the gay community. The condemnation and
alienation often suffered by those with AIDS, as well as the
courage of those living with the disease, are claimed by the gay
and lesbian community as part of their story, particularly their
religious story, as the Great Thanksgiving for National Coming
Out Day demonstrates.

Traditional healing and memorial services fail to recognize
the particular suffering of persons with AIDS, not only from
the terrible forms of the disease, but also from ostracism and
bigotry, often including rejection by churches and family.
Given the not uncommon religious interpretation of AIDS as
judgment from God, traditional healing services that include
confessions of sin by those seeking healing are not appropriate. A service included in an Episcopal AIDS curriculum for
youth allows the confession of sin to be optional, and makes
the following suggestion about hymn selection: "Hymns that
are joyful and strong are recommended; those that are overly
concerned with sin should be avoided."[33]

As Robert Goss says about Holy Union service, all of these
rituals centered on the lives and struggles of lesbian and gay
Christians are prophetic. They are prophetic in that they place
the lesbian and gay body at the center of ritual; the gay and lesbian life cycle is blessed and confirmed.

Disability Rites

Persons with disabilities have long been marginalized by the church. Their marginalization ranges from building designs which prevent access to the church buildings, and therefore to worship, to denial of access to the sacraments and other spiritual services of the church on the assumption that persons with certain disabilities would not understand or benefit from them.[34] It is not uncommon, for example, for children with developmental or learning disabilities to be excluded from rites of baptism, confirmation, and eucharist, as well as from the general worship and educational life of the church.[35] Nancy Eiesland, in *The Disabled God: Toward a Liberatory Theology of Disability,* makes a comment about eucharistic celebrations that is probably generally applicable to all Christian life-cycle rituals:

> For many people with disabilities, the Eucharist is a ritual of exclusion and degradation. Access to this celebration of the body is restricted because of architectural barriers, ritual practices, demeaning body aesthetics, unreflective speech and bodily reactions. Hence the Eucharist becomes dreaded and humiliating remembrance that in the church we are trespassers in able-bodied dominion.[36]

While none of Eiesland's proposals focuses directly on life-cycle rituals, the issues of access and acceptability have wide-ranging implications for Christian initiatory and life-cycle practices, as does her concluding eucharistic liturgy addressed to the disabled God.

The life-cycle issue most directly affecting persons with disabilities is healing. Medical healing rituals and religious healing rituals sometimes are experienced as congruent, sometimes as dissonant. Eiesland notes:

> I, like many people with disabilities, have experienced the negative effect of healing rituals. Healing has been the churchly correspondent of rehabilitation medicine in which the goal was "normalization" of the bodies of people with disabilities. . . .

Failure to be "healed" is often assessed as a personal flaw in the individual, such as unrepentant sin or a selfish desire to remain disabled.[37]

At the same time, Eiesland goes on to say, healing services including laying on of hands have on occasion been for her "restorative and redemptive."

As in the case of rituals of healing for women who have been raped or battered, the traditional (and false) association of sin with illness or suffering is harmful for persons with disabilities. Yet most denominational published healing rituals make just this connection, either explicitly or implicitly. For example, many services incorporate a reading of James 5:14–16, which includes the text, "Therefore confess your sins to one another, and pray for one another, that you may be healed."[38] Healing services in the United Methodist *Book of Worship* the Episcopal *Book of Occasional Services,* the United Church of Christ *Book of Worship,* and the *Book of Common Worship* of the Presbyterian Church include prayers of confession. The assumption of an association between sin and illness is made clear in the commentary of the United Methodist *Book of Worship*:

A Service of Healing is not necessarily a service of curing, but it provides an atmosphere in which healing can take place. The greatest healing of all is the reunion or reconciliation of a human being with God. When this happens, physical healing sometimes occurs, mental and emotional balance is often restored, spiritual health is enhanced, and relationships are healed.[39]

While the distinction between healing and cure is appropriate, persons with permanent disabilities may find in the suggestion that reconciliation with God brings about healing the implication that their disability is a result of separation from God. By suggesting that sin is a kind of disease, these liturgies invite the idea that disease is a kind of sin. Persons with disabilities are no more and no less in need of reconciliation with God than temporarily able-bodied persons, but they combat both stereotypes constantly. Persons with disabilities are seen at times as being especially sinful, and under God's judgment, or, paradoxically, they may be seen as being especially close to God because of their suffering.

Services of healing are often designed with the temporarily disabled or ill person in mind. The purpose of many of the prayers and rituals is to restore "wholeness," as shown in examples from three denominations:

> As your holy apostles anointed many who were sick and healed them,
> so pour out your Holy Spirit on us and on this gift,
> that those who in faith and repentance receive this anointing may be made whole. . . .[40]

> N., may the God of all mercy
> forgive you your sins,
> release you from suffering,
> and restore you to wholeness and strength.[41]

> Lord, grant your healing grace to all who are sick, injured, or disabled, that they may be made whole.[42]

It is true that the prayers do not specify what type of wholeness is asked for; but since the services are designed for persons with physical illnesses, physical wholeness seems to be implied as the norm for blessing. The disabled body, not being "whole," thus becomes problematized, requiring some further theological explanation. Also missing from these services and prayer resources are prayers and blessings that celebrate "speaking without a voice," "celebrating without hands," and "dancing in the dark."[43] In other words, missing is the experience of the whole, disabled person.

CONCLUSIONS

Probably no rituals are more reflective of and subject to cultural context than life-cycle rituals. Their inevitable particularity leaves room for adaptation and inculturation to express the life of the individuals for whom they are celebrated. Birth, adulthood, marriage, illness never happen in the abstract or to universal people, but to individuals in particular social locations. In practice, the rituals surrounding these experiences are always personalized (no two marriage ceremonies are alike). At the same time, life-cycle stages also reflect society's and church's expectations for these particular individuals; these institutions have an interest in defining the meaning of these stages in lives of individuals, and in urging individuals to conform to expectations. No two marriage ceremonies are alike, but all heterosexual marriage ceremonies reinforce the norm of opposite-sex pairing, and many also reinforce (either explicitly or implicitly) asymmetrical gender relationships. Contemporary challenges from those who either do not fit into the "standard" life-cycle stages or who reject the prevailing interpretation of a given stage sound a prophetic voice in the church. Women, non-white communities, lesbian and gay people, persons with disabilities are claiming their own liturgical authority, taking seriously the church's dictum that liturgy is indeed the people's work.

NOTES

1. See Jeanne Brooks-Gunn and Edward O. Reiter, "The Role of Pubertal Processes," in S. Shirley Feldman and Glen R. Elliot, eds., *At the Threshold: The Developing Adolescent* (Cambridge, MA, 1990), p. 35.

2. For a brief review of some of these changes, see Kathleen Fischer and Thomas Hart, "The Contemporary Setting for Marriage: Sociobehavioral Insights," in Bernard Cook, ed., *Alternative Futures for Worship,* vol. 5, *Christian Marriage* (Collegeville, MN, 1987), pp. 15–32.

3. *Lutheran Book of Worship,* Minister's Desk Edition (Minneapolis/Philadelphia, 1978), p. 36. The "exchange of peace" is a gesture of reconciliation, generally expressed by a kiss, handshake, or other greeting.

4. *The United Methodist Hymnal* (Nashville, 1989), p. 865; *The Book of Worship: United Church of Christ* (New York, 1986), pp. 332–33; *The Book of Common Worship* of the Presbyterian Church U.S.A. (Louisville, 1993), p. 844; *The Book of Common Prayer* of the Episcopal Church (New York, 1979), pp. 425, 437.

5. United Church of Christ *Book of Worship*, p. 332.

6. United Methodist *Book of Worship* (Nashville, 1992), p. 118. The suggested statement is, "We love both of you. We bless your marriage; Together we will be a family."

7. United Church of Christ *Book of Worship*, p. 289.

8. United Methodist *Book of Worship*, p. 626.

9. For an example that connects rituals (but not necessarily religious rituals) specifically with healing, see Jeanne Achterberg, Barbara Dossey, and Leslie Kolkmeier, *Rituals of Healing: Using Imagery for Health and Wellness* (New York, 1994).

10. Presbyterian *Book of Common Worship*, p. 967–1022.

11. Episcopal *Book of Occasional Services* (New York, 1979), pp. 147–54.

12. On the development of feminist baptismal catechesis, see Marjorie Procter-Smith, *In Her Own Rite: Constructing Feminist Liturgical Tradition* (Nashville, 1990), pp. 144–60.

13. For a discussion of the importance of embodiment for feminist ritual, see Marjorie Procter-Smith, "The Marks of Feminist Liturgy," *Proceedings of the North American Academy of Liturgy* (1992): 69–75.

14. For examples, see Rosemary Radford Ruether, *Women-Church: Theology and Practice* (New York, 1985); Diane Stein, *Casting the Circle: A Woman's Book of Ritual* (Freedom, CA, 1990); Barbara G. Walker, *Women's Rituals: A Sourcebook* (San Francisco, 1990).

15. For published examples, see Mary D. Pellauer, Barbara Chester, and Jane A. Boyajian, "Resources for Ritual and Recuperation," in their book, *Sexual Assault and Abuse: A Handbook for Clergy and Religious Professionals* (New York, 1987); Mari West Zimmerman, *Take and Make Holy: Honoring the Sacred in the Healing Journey of Abuse Survivors* (Chicago, 1995); and Jane A Keene, *A Winter's Song: A Liturgy for Women Seeking Healing from Sexual Abuse in Childhood* (Cleveland, 1991); as well as the rituals in Ruether, *Women-Church*.

16. Ruether, *Women-Church*, p. 153–58.

17. See Diann Neu, *Women of Fire: A Pentecost Event* (Silver Spring, MD, 1990), p. 30.

18. Delores Williams, "Rituals of Resistance in Womanist Worship," in Marjorie Procter-Smith and Janet Walton, eds., *Women at Worship: Interpretations of North American Diversity* (Louisville, 1993), pp. 215–23.

19. Amitiyah Elayne Hyman, "Womanist Ritual," in Lesley A. Northrup, ed., *Women and Religious Ritual* (Washington, DC, 1993), p. 175.

20. Eileen King, "A Lingering Question: What is Feminist Prayer?" in Procter-Smith and Walton, *Women at Worship,* pp. 228–29.

21. For example, see Dona Marimba Richards, *Let the Circle Be Unbroken: The Implications of African Spirituality in the Diaspora* (Trenton, NJ, 1980); Sterling D. Plumpp, *Black Rituals* (Chicago, 1987).

22. For example, see Mary C. Lewis, *Herstory: Black Female Rites of Passage* (Chicago, 1988); Paul Hill, Jr., *Coming of Age: African American Male Rites-of-Passage* (Chicago, 1992).

23. Hyman, "Womanist Ritual," p. 175.

24. Craig O'Neill and Kathleen Ritter, *Coming Out Within: Stages of Spiritual Awakening for Lesbians and Gay Men* (San Francisco, 1992), p. 2.

25. *Equal Rites: Lesbian and Gay Worship, Ceremonies, and Celebrations,* ed. Kittredge Cherry and Zalmon Sherwood (Louisville, 1995), came out too late to be considered in this review. It is a collection of Christian liturgies and liturgical resources including coming-out rites, healing services, and funerals and memorial services, and convenant rites, among others. In addition to the references mentioned here, see also the publications of Chris Glaser, *Coming Out to God: Prayers for Lesbians and Gay Men, their Families and Friends* (Louisville, 1991), *Uncommon Calling: A Gay Man's Struggle to Serve the Church* (San Francisco, 1988), and *Come Home! Reclaiming Spirituality and Community as Gay Men and Lesbians* (San Francisco, 1990).

26. Cherry and Kittredge in *Equal Rights* refer to such services as "Covenant Rites for Couples."

27. Larry J. Uhrig, *The Two of Us: Affirming, Celebrating, and Symbolizing Gay and Lesbian Relationships* (Boston, 1984), p. 88.

28. Ibid., p. 90. For a sense of the great diversity among ceremonies of Holy Union, see also Becky Butler, ed., *Ceremonies of the Heart: Celebrating Lesbian Unions* (Seattle, 1990). The examples narrated here include Christian, Jewish, pagan, and non-religious

ceremonies. It remains to be seen what influence, if any, John Boswell's historical study, *Same-Sex Unions in Premodern Europe* (Villard Press, 1994), will have on the further development of rites of Holy Union. A draft experimental liturgy prepared by a group of Episcopal clergy, laity, and seminary faculty, "An Illustration of a Rite for The Celebration of Commitment to A Life Together, Suggestions for Education Regarding Such a Rite, and Theological Reflections on the Need for Such a Rite" (Cambridge, MA, 1994), proposes the use of a single rite for same-sex and opposite-sex couples. So far as I have discovered, this is a unique approach. The document is proposed for consideration by the Standing Liturgical Commission of the Episcopal Church.

29. Robert Goss, *Jesus Acted Up: A Gay and Lesbian Manifesto* (San Francisco, 1993), p. 140.

30. Tom F. Driver, *The Magic of Ritual: Our Need for Liberating Rites that Transform Our Lives and Our Communities* (San Francisco, 1991), p. 115.

31. From Marilyn Bennett Alexander and James Preston, *We Were Baptized Too: Claiming God's Grace for Lesbians and Gays* (Louisville, 1996), p. 116.

32. Ibid., p. 114.

33. Gene Robinson, ed., *You(th) and AIDS: A Curriculum* (New York, 1989), pp. 26–27. For another example of AIDS-related liturgical resources, see Louis F. Kavar, *To Celebrate and to Mourn: Liturgical Resources for Worshipping Communities Living with AIDS* (Gaithersberg, MD, 1989).

34. For a general introduction to the issues and suggestions for change, see *That All May Worship: An Interfaith Welcome to People with Disabilities* (Washington, DC, 1992).

35. See Edward Foley, ed., *Developmental Disabilities and Sacramental Access* (Collegeville, MN, 1994).

36. Nancy Eiesland, *The Disabled God: Toward a Liberatory Theology of Disability* (Nashville, 1994), p. 113.

37. Ibid., p. 117.

38. United Methodist *Book of Worship,* Presbyterian *Book of Common Worship,* Episcopal *Book of Occasional Services.*

39. United Methodist *Book of Worship,* p. 614. The United Church of Christ *Book of Worship* includes the services for reconciliation of penitents and healing services in the same section. The distinction between cure and healing is also made by Helen Betenbaugh

in "A Theology of Disability" (unpublished paper); she makes a distinction between moral evil and natural evil in order to interpret the suffering of persons with disabilities.

40. United Methodist *Book of Worship,* p. 620.

41. Presbyterian *Book of Common Worship,* p. 1013.

42. Episcopal *Book of Occasional Services,* p. 148.

43. See Valerie Jones Stiteler, "Blessing the Darkness: Toward a Feminist Hermeneutic for Worship which Is Inclusive of Women with Disabilities," unpublished paper. See also Kathy Black, "Beyond the Spoken Word: Preaching as Presence," on preaching in the deaf community, *Quarterly Review* 14, no. 3 (fall 1994): 279–93.

Contemporary Challenges to Jewish Life-Cycle Ritual

Yoel Kahn and Lawrence A. Hoffman

Inclusion, Representation, and Authenticity

Completely at home in modern American society, contemporary Jews wrestle with many of the same issues that plague their Christian contemporaries. Marjorie Proctor-Smith's analysis of the challenges to Christians occasioned by changing cultural norms are therefore closely paralleled among Jews as well. Changes in Jewish practice, too, involve either the adaptation of received rites or the creation of new ones—what Proctor-Smith describes as "radically reconstructed" rituals. But despite significant common ground that Jews and Christians share, the Jewish case bears its own uniqueness as well.

To begin with, Judaism is simultaneously a religion and a culture. Many contemporary Jews who look to Jewish tradition as the vehicle for expressing the significance of important moments in their lives find themselves attracted to Jewish culture but uncomfortable with the traditional religious language in which Jewish ritual is couched. While affirming absolutely their Jewish identity (culturally speaking), they are able, at best, to nod assent in a very tentative way to the personal, imminent, and confident divinity invoked in the traditional liturgy. Rabbis may share their congregants' ambivalence. But they feel obliged also to retain those same congregants' loyalty to the Jewish people past and future, and to the Jewish community as it exists in the present—both of which may be seen as cultural and theological *realia* by rabbinic officiants.

Contemporary Jews, rabbis included, place great emphasis on making ceremonies "meaningful" to those Jews who opt to celebrate them. It is this assumption of a rite's potential "meaningfulness" that proves most nettlesome. What celebrants mean when they declare that they want a "meaningful ceremony" is that the public ritual should embody the meanings that they themselves bring to the ceremony. But the meanings the celebrants bring are not the only ones present. Following Hoffman,[1] we can say that every rite has at least three different meanings, what Hoffman labelled (1) official, (2) public, and (3) private. A more precise delineation, preferred by Kahn, might be meanings that are (1) authorized, (2) shared (but unauthorized), and (3) private.[2]

The *authorized* (*official*) *meaning* is what the liturgy itself, the religious tradition and the authorized interpreters say it is.[3] The *shared* (*public*) *meaning* is what the majority of people who participate in the rite believe it to be.[4] The *private meaning* is the personal interpretation that some or all of the participants or observers bring to any given performance of it.

Thus, for example, while the authorized meaning of *brit milah* (circumcision) is that it is a rite of covenant initiation for boys, its shared meaning is primarily a celebration of a new birth and a chance to welcome a new baby boy into the family or social group. The private meaning for a specific family might also include the *brit* as "the time when all the in-laws and extended family are gathered together in one place," or "the occasion when grandpa's name finally gets passed on to the next generation."[5]

Contemporary rites come with clerical interpretations of the authorized meanings; participants may have nothing to say about them, and may or may not acquiesce to what they hear when they get there. But they expect at least to find some nodding acceptance of their own shared and private meanings as well. It happens, therefore, that in their efforts at revision and reimagination, contemporary Jews (including the rabbis who speak for the tradition but also for the Jews who come to celebrate it) try to include within the reconstituted rite the unauthorized but shared meanings that are widely assumed as important, and the private meanings that belong to particular participants on hand at a given occasion.

Vesting the determination of meaning in more than the inherited ritual script and its authorized interpreters (usually the clergy) implicitly empowers others, by saying that the ordinary people who attend a rite matter. Ritual conflict nowadays arises from this implicit claim that meaning derives from the agenda of participants, not just officials or the real or perceived authorized interpretations. We shall consider challenges to the meaningfulness of life-cycle rituals under three overlapping rubrics, *inclusion, representation,* and *authenticity,* all of which derive from the same underlying expansion of the notion of who matters.

Inclusion is the challenge of creating ceremonies for members of the community who were previously not even recognized as attending, let alone mattering. Women have generally been cited as the prime example of a group whose inclusion has only recently been acknowledged. But attention today is expanding to include others as well, for instance, gay and lesbian people, who receive attention specifically later in this chapter.[6]

Representation is the challenge of creating rituals which move beyond mere inclusion to actually integrate within the ritual script the needs and values of those who are newly included. If a *brit milah* is deliberately scheduled to accommodate the presence of the mother who is recovering from a difficult delivery, we have a case of inclusion. If, in addition, the ritual is designed so that the mother *qua* mother has a role, we have representation.[7]

Authenticity is the challenge of including the various private and shared meanings that participants bring to the ritual, but doing so without sacrificing the traditional meanings that the rite conveys, no easy task given the conflicts that the former may have with the latter. The traditional symbols and meanings will actually authenticate the private and shared meanings that are novel to the occasion.

In this age of personalism, issues of inclusion generally arise first, as participants see themselves, rather than the formal rite as objectively given by tradition, as central. To some extent, their demands can be met without changing the rite at all. But they then feel newly empowered to bring their own agenda of meaning to bear upon what the rite has to say. At this point inclusion expands to become representation and authenticity as well. Only then do proponents of the rite as it "has always been" raise objections of authenticity. Authenticity is thus the usual battleground on which fights occur whenever a received ritual is changed.

But even the individuals for whom the ceremonies are designed want more than a chance to voice their own agenda of meanings. They opt for Jewish ritual precisely because over and above their own meanings, they want a ceremony that meets their expectations of what an authorized rite looks like. When the ceremony strays too far from its authorized format, it does not feel historically or communally authentic.[8] However, the desire to modify the ceremony in the first place emerges from the perception that the "authorized" ceremony does not adequately convey the meanings brought by the participants. The challenge is then to create a ceremony which preserves the historical features of the rite enough that it is perceived as authentic to the tradition, while simultaneously integrating the modifications necessary for the ceremony to be personally authentic as well. Authenticity for the celebrants entails the public acknowledgement that their new or modified ceremony is rooted in the historical tradition.

As traditional religious ceremonies, every Jewish life-cycle event is a statement of participation in and commitment to the covenant. The covenant, as developed and understood by the Jewish tradition, is not just a relationship with God; it also encompasses a relationship with Torah as the Jewish People's historically binding tradition, and with the Jewish People itself. But covenantal loyalty is implicitly present whenever people choose to include a particular ritual element or a rite as a whole, if their choice derives from their own perceived loyalty to the historical or communal dimension of being Jewish. They may not use the specific language of "covenant" the way a theologian might, but their existential decision to honor historical Jewish practice because (as they may put it), "This is the way Jews 'do' weddings [or births or deaths]" is itself an act of covenantal loyalty of the highest order. They may not even know the official meanings of the rite in question, but they yet may prize the authenticity of the rite as a whole and their own participation in it.

Insofar as they assume that the ancient rite does not convey their own modern meanings, they seek to surround it with additional words or gestures that do. These are the informal things they tell each other about what the rite means to them. Eventually, however, they may ask that their marginalized ritual glosses be integrated into the liturgy itself. That is the point at which representation occurs. Only then does the newly integrated meaning system vie with the old official one, so that from the perspective of the theological or communal gatekeepers, issues of authenticity emerge.

One further distinction is important here. We have been speaking so far of challenges to the *authorized* life-cycle rituals passed down by tradition. But besides revising existing ceremonies, many Jews wish to mark significant moments in their lives for which no Jewish liturgical precedent exists. They seek, therefore, to create new ceremonies which are both personally and Jewishly authentic, i.e., ceremonies which not only convey the personal meanings of the rite brought by the participants, but which invoke as well the covenant as understood by the celebrating community. Ceremonies where issues of inclusion, representation, and authenticity arise thus tend to be either *revisions* or *innovations*: modifications of an existing rite or creation of a new one for a previously unritualized occasion.

To be sure, this simple binary typology is not rigid. For example, new ceremonies ("innovation") usually mark an occasion which has not yet been liturgically recognized (e.g., the onset of menopause), but they may also displace an existing rite when the participants find the received liturgy unacceptable—a novel wedding rite, for instance, that may effect marriage the way the old one did, but be rooted in an entirely different conceptual scheme, and not at all look like the old one in terms of the prayers and ritual actions that one normally expects in the inherited rite. Rachel Adler, for example, finds the historical foundation of Jewish marriage to be the legal category of *kinyan* (bridal acquisition), so replaces the usual rite with a new one which she entitles *brit ahuvim,* the "covenant of the beloved."[9] Similarly, one might point to marriage ceremonies of gay and lesbian couples, which to some extent are entirely innovative, but at the same time can be seen as revisions of heterosexual marriage ritual in Jewish tradition. Depending on the Jewish legal and religious perspectives of the participants, initiation rituals for daughters too may be imagined as a variation on the *brit milah* ceremony, in which case it will be designed to look as similar as possible, or it may be conceived as something entirely *de novo,* and therefore be imagined and celebrated as an entirely new rite.

Bar/Bat Mitzvah and Funeral Liturgy

The official Jewish life-cycle events that most Jews mark are bar/bat mitzvah, wedding and funeral—and to a lesser extent, *brit milah.* Although once controversial, at least among Reform Jews from Germany who replaced it with confirmation, the bar/bat mitzvah ceremony particularly has become a standard of American Jewish religious life. In some Orthodox circles where egalitarian demands are not honored, bat mitzvah (if it occurs at all) is deliberately differentiated from bar mitzvah, being held, for instance, only on Friday nights, when no official reading of Torah is mandated, so that bat mitzvah retains its character as something a girl and her parents opt to do, but not something that has official legal standing in Judaism; by contrast, bar mitzvah remains on Saturday mornings, when the boy's reading of scripture is officially required;

alternatively, bat mitzvah may be limited to a group ceremony, a whole cohort of young women being inducted into Jewish adulthood together, again only as part of a totally elective ceremony from the viewpoint of Jewish law.

But by and large, bar/bat mitzvah is an accepted feature of the North American liturgical landscape, for girls as for boys. To be sure, much controversy exists regarding the conflict between the inherited official meaning which retains religious significance in the eyes of the clergy, and the publicly shared meaning that individual families bring to the event—they may see it only vaguely as religious at all, preferring some inchoate cultural explanation of what they are about, or even explaining their investment in the rite as something they are doing just because Jewish parents have to do this sort of thing whether they like it or not. A relatively recent (1992) book accurately reflects the reality of bar/bat mitzvah in its title: *Putting God on the Guest List: "How to Reclaim the Spiritual Meaning in Your Child's Bar or Bat Mitzvah."*[10] But whatever their reasons for doing so, Jewish parents overwhelmingly subscribe to the importance of this rite, to the point where they will do practically anything their clergy demand to make sure it takes place appropriately in a synagogue setting.

They add their own interpretive glosses at occasions within the rite where they are allowed to bless their children or otherwise to address them or the assembled guests; and they make their own statement regarding the cultural significance of this occasion in the life of their family at the evening "mandatory party" which has become the norm, usually in rented halls complete with catered dinner and rock band, and accompanied by lavish decorations and a cake-lighting ceremony borrowed from the American culture of birthday parties. The evening festivity thus constitutes almost a rival ritual to the daytime religious one. But clergy and laity have effected a truce of sorts whereby the day belongs to the former and the evening to the latter, and whatever one may think of the arrangement from a religious perspective, it at least has the salutary result of erecting privatized domains of influence, and thereby buffering each from the potential conflict that might be sparked by the guardians of the other.

Funeral liturgy too avoids contemporary controversy, albeit for different reasons. There is more than sufficient cause to believe that Jews do not in large part subscribe to the theological perspective of the traditional funeral prayers. They probably do not believe in resurrection, for instance, and they surely do not accept traditional Jewish notions of theodicy. They are unlikely to think this life is merely a preparation for the afterlife of the world to come, and they may bristle at the notion of a God who personally might have intervened to postpone or to soften the blow of their loved one's death, but who chose not to do so for His (*sic*) own inscrutable reasons. They may also be surprised to discover that Jewish law does not permit eulogies at certain occasions (days with a semi-festive quality, for instance, such as the intermediary days of the festival of Sukkot), since eulogies have become the popular centerpiece of the rite, to the point where even Orthodox ritual usually finds some way to circumvent Jewish legal demands when they prevent a full eulogy, in the interest of making funerals meaningful to grieving families. The rite, moreover, is usually conducted in Hebrew that most people do not understand, or at least, do not interpret literally, while English translations and inclusions omit or paraphrase theological passages that might prove difficult.

But funerals differ from other life-cycle ceremonial, in that they are generally unplanned far in advance. Mourners have little or no chance to think through what the liturgy will be. They just show up at it, usually preoccupied with their sorrow, and in a frame of mind that allows them to pardon anything liturgical on the grounds that funerals ought to be done "right," out of honor to the deceased, and the rabbi knows best what Jewish funerals look like.

The rest of this article thus omits any further conversation regarding bar/bat mitzvah and funerals. They are not the frontier on which the liturgical wars of change are being fought. Instead, it examines rituals of covenant initiation for boys and girls, and the innovation of union ceremonies for homosexuals, both being today's preeminent examples of the challenges of inclusion, representation and authenticity.

Covenant Initiation

Brit milah, the Covenant of Circumcision, is the best known, distinctively Jewish life-cycle ceremony. Since biblical times, Jews have ascribed great power and significance to what has always been seen as a primary act of Jewish commitment.[11] As its traditional liturgy reveals, the Rabbis who designed it did not conceive of the *brit milah* ceremony as an occasion to celebrate a new life or successful birth per se, but instead, sought to create a ceremony for "welcoming a new member into the [male] covenant community."[12] Insofar as women were treated as covenanted through their fathers and husbands rather than as directly covenanted members in their own right, no rite of covenantal initiation for baby girls existed. By contrast, the modern shared understanding of *brit* is that it is a birth celebration to welcome the arrival of a new life (male or female) into the community, and that, in any event, women are as much members of the covenant as men. Participants look to the liturgy to express these alternative meanings which they automatically assume the rite is all about. The gap between these modern meanings and those conveyed by the authorized liturgical text presents a challenge in ritual authenticity. At times, the conflict is not resolved. Instead of integration,[13] we may get, side by side, a proper "traditional" ceremony and an unacknowledged personalist celebration by parents and community, in what emerges as a mixed and even syncretistic ceremony.

This dual rite comes about because traditionally speaking, circumcision requires a surgical expert called a *mohel,* whose background or training may prohibit his being open to the changes in traditional script that a proper integration of meaning requires. Typically, he is invited to a home whose owners (the parents) he has never met, to perform what they perceive as a mysterious ritual, entirely in Hebrew, not one word of which either they or their family and friends comprehend.

They put up with him, because he is the acknowledged expert in the "authorized" rite, and their very decision to go through with it is intended as their conscious act of validating the authenticity of tradition. The assembled guests accompany this undecodable rite, however, with impromptu personal remarks to each other about the significance of this birth and child, and these observations serve as the informal means by which they make the rite their own. What they say has nothing whatever to do with the rite as officially passed down through tradition, but it reflects their own sense (shared and/or private) of why they are there. In addition, though the gathering may thus neither understand nor follow the specific prayers and actions of the *mohel,* the meaning of his actions as a whole is perceived as a widely shared meaning to the effect that the parents are handing over their newborn to the temporary care of this representative of the tradition and folk; this is their expression of continuity to Jewish tradition and commitment to the Jewish people. They thus want it both ways. Though primarily invested in their own personalist statements and rituals over which they have exclusive control,[14] they care also that the authorized rite take place, despite the fact that the only element in it that they comprehend is the surgical expertise of the circumciser.[15]

If the conflict thus far is between tradition and modernity, between what the rite has traditionally been and the personalist nature of contemporary celebration, a second source of contention is the fact that circumcision celebrates the covenantal citizenship of males only. The secondary status of women, in traditional Judaism, is best illustrated by the absence of any parallel rite of initiation for baby girls.

Orthodox Judaism has generally addressed the problem by offering a blessing in the context of a regularly scheduled synagogue worship service, along with a public announcement of the child's name. The naming occurs as part of the special honor by which the father is summoned to stand alongside the reader at the public reading of Torah (usually the first Sabbath after his daughter is born). Neither mother nor child is expected to be present at the time, but even if the naming is postponed to an occasion when they can attend, they do not accompany the father to the pulpit, which is viewed as the exclusive domain of the men. In Orthodoxy too, therefore, as well as in the more liberal branches of Judaism to which we will turn, pressure has mounted for a welcoming ceremony for girls that parallels in some way the historical rite of *brit milah* for boys.

The failure to resolve this challenge is part and parcel of a broader conflict for halakhicly committed Jews: the demand by women for greater access to Jewish ritual recognition, despite the fact that the *halakhah* clearly and firmly distinguishes ritual roles along gender lines to the point where an egalitarian liturgy within the boundaries of the *halakhah* may be considered impossible. Over the last two decades, Orthodox practice has thus increasingly sought to create parallel but separate alternatives for men and for women, as in the instance mentioned earlier by which some congregations celebrate a bat mitzvah but only by allowing girls to chant a prophetic reading on Friday nights, while boys read Torah on Saturday mornings.[16] Similarly, some Orthodox Jews give their daughters rituals of welcome which do not resemble the *brit milah* liturgy, but which take place (like the boys' ceremony) in the home rather than in the synagogue, and are at least halakhicly acceptable. But like other women's parallel tracks, they are not halakhicly demanded; they may thus be separate but by no means equal, as long as Judaism is defined solely in halakhic terms. This compromise remains the standard within most Orthodox and a minority of Conservative communities today.

Reform Jewish practice in regard to baby girls has been shaped by two conflicting forces. There is first of all Reform's long history of emphasizing the covenantal dimensions of the rite and deemphasizing the actual physical act of circumcision.[17] This approach encouraged the creation of identical ceremonies for boys and girls, since the operation itself, now seen as secondary, could be separated off from the naming and covenant aspects of the rite.[18] Reform Jews thus often removed actual circumcision from its public and religious location to a private and secular one, asking a physician to circumcise their sons without any religious attention at all, and then celebrating a separate religious event of baby-naming publicly. This option amounted in effect to removing physical circumcision altogether, and merging what was left of the rite—covenantal prayers of initiation—with the public synagogue liturgy where it could be celebrated for boys as for girls, without distinction.

But at the same time, modern Reform Judaism has made a concerted effort to reclaim the physical act of circumcision as a religious rite, not just as a surgical procedure that most other American boys go through. Wanting also to provide circumcisors who are medically trained, religiously committed, and open to liturgically revised liturgies, the Reform Movement has begun certifying Reform Jewish doctors as *mohalim* and *mohalot* (male and female circumcisers). The availability of spiritually motivated, Reform-affiliated, and medically trained *mohalim/ot* has made a religious circumcision ceremony more appealing to many marginal Jews. Reemphasizing the physical aspect of the rite has also suggested an alternative strategy to solve the gender inequality, namely, the creation of ceremonies for girls that include a ritual action that approaches the emotional intensity of boys' circumcision. Unwilling to initiate actual female circumcision (which is widely regarded as barbarous), Reform innovators of rituals for daughters have mostly used water, including foot washing, immersion in a real or symbolic *mikvah* (ritual bath), and anointing with oil. Far from universal or even widely normative, most of the examples of such rituals are still evolving oral traditions.[19] Also, despite the principle of equality that underlies them, these alternative covenant ceremonies for daughters do not usually take place on the eighth day, as biblically mandated circumcision must, and as in fact, virtually all religious circumcisions do. At any rate, new ceremonies continue to be created by those knowledgeable and committed enough to compose them, even though in most congregations, daughters are still merely welcomed at a brief naming and prayer at Sabbath services.

We could say that the failure of covenant ceremonies for daughters to assume the same time-specific urgency that *brit milah* holds for sons (i.e., being limited to the eighth day) shows that the religious valuation of daughters' births is still second to that of sons. Alternatively, we could argue that the reluctance to insist on the eighth day is evidence for an accessibility conflict contained in the traditional practice, a possibility that deserves its own attention.

Circumcision specifically on the eighth day has been an important dimension of the traditional rite, allowing it to take place on festivals, the Sabbath and even Yom Kippur. But the insistence on the eighth day as the time for public entry into the covenant has become problematic today, as mothers point out that they may be in no position to participate fully in a public ceremony so soon after giving birth, especially if there are complications of labor. They see the timing of the *brit* ceremony as a question of access, in which continued insistence on the eighth day presents an unintended (perhaps) but nonetheless a very effective modern extension of the historical exclusion of women. While women are no longer legally excluded, the organization of the rite in such a fashion excludes birth mothers from actively planning and fully participating in it. In addition, a secular but still significant source of pressure comes from grandparents and other relatives who want to purchase plane tickets in advance and therefore ask that the ceremony be scheduled when "convenient" rather than on the eighth day. While of different religious weight, these two concerns about access reflect a conflict between the goals of full and meaningful ritual participation, on the one hand, and of loyalty to historic and communal practice, on the other.

Moreover, the very return to circumcision among Reform Jews has become a matter of debate. A generation ago, hospital circumcision of infant boys was routine. Jews took pride in modern medicine's validation of Jewish tradition, defending circumcision as one more example of the wisdom of ancient Israel. But as contemporary American medicine has gradually moved away from recommending routine circumcision, it has tended either toward neutrality or outright opposition. Fears that without any medical rationale to justify it, circumcision may amount to sexual mutilation have here and there given rise now to a Jewish backlash against it.[20]

Conflicts over circumcision are thus played out according to the different interests of nuclear and extended family members, often between "modern" parents and "traditional" grandparents, the former describing the rite as atavistic and harmful, the latter wondering aloud how one can even consider not circumcising a Jewish boy. Despite isolated authorities from within the Jewish community who have spoken out against it,[21] circumcision still remains the official norm. Most boys are still circumcised either religiously or privately in the hospital, and the overwhelming majority of rabbis will not agree to officiate at a covenant liturgy for a boy who is not or has not already been circumcised as well.[22] The conflict is likely to grow in the future.

Weddings

The wedding ceremony in non-Orthodox circles has been transformed over the last generation, as a newfound desire for a distinctively Jewish wedding has led to the reclamation of traditional practices that were once abandoned, especially within the Reform movement, where standing under the *chuppah* (a canopy), breaking a glass as the ceremony ends, and signing a *ketubah* (the marriage contract) are now common practice. At the same time, concerted effort has been made to guarantee gender equality: where once the groom was the sole active participant and the bride a passive recipient of the consequences of his action, language and gesture have been revised so as to include both parties equally; once a conditional promissory note reflecting damages owed the bride should her husband wrongfully divorce or maltreat her, the *ketubah* has been reconstituted as a broader statement of mutual love and obligation; a single ring given to the bride as a remnant of the bridal purchase price has become a double ring ceremony taken to symbolize parallel marriage vows.[23] Gender issues are

thus largely perceived as solved, after many years of heated debate and experimentation. By contrast, gay and lesbian questions of inclusion, representation, and authenticity are just now
entering the arena of public discussion.

Gay and lesbian weddings are only part of the larger question of the authenticity of homosexual Jews, which the rise of
gay rights activism across North America has pressed upon the
North American Jewish community. Reactions vary across a
wide spectrum that correlates with movement identity. By and
large, Orthodox Judaism still opposes homosexual behavior
as sinful. The Conservative, Reform, and Reconstructionist
movements, however, have all gone on record in support of gay
and lesbian inclusion in the life of the community. Only the
Reconstructionist movement has gone so far as to endorse rabbinic officiation at gay and lesbian union ceremonies. The
Conservative movement officially opposes officiation and, as
of 1996, the Reform rabbinate was still uncertain as to where it
stood.[24] Anecdotal evidence, however, suggests that more and
more rabbis are officiating, some with the endorsement, others
over the objections, of their congregants.

Even among rabbis who officiate, there is no unanimity as to
the Jewish legal status, and thus the ritual form, that such ceremonies should take. Some rabbis (ourselves included) argue
that since the relationship is a sacred commitment equal in
weight to heterosexual marriage, the proper Jewish rubric for it
is *kiddushin,* Jewish marriage proper.[25] Others, who identify
kiddushin inextricably with heterosexuality, or who want to
privilege heterosexual marriage for other reasons, create new
ceremonies which depend on elements of the traditional rite, but
are denied the designation, "*kiddushin,*"[26] and may not, therefore, be accorded Jewish legal status.[27] Gay and lesbian Jews
(and their allies) are themselves divided on the issue. Rabbi
Janet Marder, for many years the rabbi of a gay- and lesbian-
outreach synagogue in Los Angeles, sums up the tension by
commenting, "These relationships are no less valid or worthy
than heterosexual ones and therefore deserve no less. Yet they

are not exactly the same, and therefore we do not need to do everything exactly the same."[28]

Like their heterosexual equivalents, gay and lesbian couples expect their ceremonies to symbolize certain ends normally associated with weddings: the affirmation of mutual commitment; the aspiration to establish together a Jewish home and family; and the transformation of two "single" people into a couple, in the eyes of each other and of the community. But the cases differ. Because the homosexual relationship and ceremony lack legal standing, and often, alas, familial acceptance as well, it is impossible to overestimate the significance of the accepting community, the use of traditional rituals and symbols, and the presence of a rabbi. In heterosexual weddings, the religious ceremony is a reenforcement of and inseparable from the larger institution of marriage in general. For gay and lesbian unions, it is more: the ceremony must bear the heavy burden of being the key element in the creation of a counter-normative narrative that flies in the face of the way people's stories are "supposed to turn out." In Jewish categories, it thus becomes a prophetic act as much as a priestly ritual.

The Jewish authenticity of the ceremony—and of the union that the ceremony celebrates—is conveyed through the recognizable incorporation of elements from the traditional Jewish rite, while the specific representational concerns of gay or lesbian people are best effected by adding new layers of meaning to the already established structure. Here, where the marriage rite may be the only public act of recognition available, ordinary ritual acts like witnessing, blessing, and promising to create a covenantal Jewish home within the community of Israel assume deeper significance. The breaking of the glass, for instance, may now go beyond symbolizing its authorized (but rarely invoked) meaning as a reminder of the destruction of Jerusalem,[29] and beyond its shared folk symbolism as the marker of the end of the wedding and the *sine qua non* symbol of the Jewish wedding itself. In addition to these meanings, it has also been invoked as a reminder of grief for the loss of friends and community members to AIDS, or sadness at the absence of family members who refuse to attend.[30]

In lieu of the traditional betrothal formula, "You are consecrated unto me according to the religion of Moses and Israel," many substitute such things as "in the spirit of Moses [or: Moses, Miriam] and Israel," or "before God and these witnesses." While the precise legal formulation is of major concern to the *officiant's* sense of authenticity, the couple and community usually consider the recitation of any formulaic phrase in Hebrew and English as sufficiently authentic, and are not distressed by the change in wording, which they may not even notice, since they may not know what the usual phrase would have been otherwise. Other liturgical issues of authenticity involve the traditional *Sheva Berakhot* (the Seven Benedictions), which may evoke opposition because of their explicit emphasis on "bride and groom" and procreation; or even their reference in general to "brides" or "grooms," for that matter. Once "loving friends," "committed companions" or a similar expression is substituted (in Hebrew and English), the recitation of the traditional text is no more inappropriate at a gay or lesbian union ceremony than it is at a wedding for a couple which is past the age of child-bearing or otherwise does not have procreation as a goal. On the other hand, many lesbian and gay couples consider becoming parents their prime motivation for having a union ceremony in the first place.

Whether or not the ceremony is technically called *kiddushin,* it usually combines recognizable elements of the Jewish wedding ceremony, and of gay and lesbian source material, whether biblical, historical or contemporary, thus guaranteeing not just inclusion but actual representation and authenticity as well. The desire of the participants to mark their union as authentic is primary. Since the option of a religious ceremony is relatively new, and because there remains no civil recognition of these relationships, the union ceremony often has as much of a retrospective dimension as a forward one. Moreover, given society's marginalization of homosexuality, the gay and lesbian community itself becomes extraordinarily important to its members. Gay and lesbian couples thus frequently see their own relationship intrinsically embedded in the nexus of friends, and the ceremony expands to include full recognition of friends and community, not just the two nuclear families (usually the parents) from which the two participants hail, as is the case in most heterosexual weddings.

Adult Life Passages

With the exception of funerals, the most commonly observed rites of the Jewish life cycle—*brit milah,* bar/bat mitzvah, wedding—are normally clustered toward the beginning of life. The majority of adult years thus have no traditional life-cycle ceremonies at all. In recent decades, many new rituals have been created to fill the void. Most of these derive from the *chavurah* movement, a loose federation of grass-roots groups that began in the 1960s as part of the counter-culture, and evolved into a very participational, highly democratic, and exceptionally egalitarian mode of Jewish community.[31] In 1981, the Reconstructionist Movement expanded to include a broad swath of *chavurah* Jews who had themselves come together in an official body two years prior, and since that time, new rituals have frequently appeared especially, though not exclusively, in Reconstructionism's official publications.

Some of these new rites began as efforts to include people denied traditional rites—for example, bar/bat mitzvah ceremonies for women, Jews-by-choice, or others who did not have a Jewish education as a child. Other rites are completely new, a rite to celebrate menopause, for instance. The creators of these rites face a particular challenge: How can a ceremony whose authenticity is grounded in the life-experiences of contemporary men and women be made to look and "feel" Jewishly authentic when there is no precedent for it in the Jewish religious tradition? The solution seems to lie partly in the fact that Jewish authenticity is bestowed by the ritual invocation of the three dimensions of the covenant. That invocation is achieved not only by actual cognitive content within the new prayers that people recite, but in more subtle ways as well. The covenant can be obliquely suggested through the replication of familiar words and gestures that denote aspects of God, Torah, and Israel in their original contexts. This borrowing of ritual language and form makes the new rite resonate with traditional associations, even if the actual meaning of the phrases in question never become explicit; if, for instance, only the Hebrew is used, the rite nonetheless echoes with an aura of familiarity by virtue of the Hebrew expression that is known to all present from their prior association with the traditional rite whence the Hebrew comes.

Examples include ceremonies for growing older ("Recognizing an Elder" or "A Celebration of Wisdom"), which include being called to the Torah, an act that resonates with recollections of coming of age, since it is the central symbolic gesture of bar/bat mitzvah.[32] In addition, this specific ritual action evokes covenantal authenticity, since the symbol of rising to stand by the Torah as it is formally read connotes Sinai and Jewish peoplehood. The use of recognizable elements in turn legitimates the inclusion of new ritual gestures which may have no prior Jewish history but now begin to assume Jewish authenticity through their use in what has already become a recognizable Jewish context.

Other stages of adulthood on the way to old age have also emerged as common landmarks in American culture, and therefore called forth new ritual in Jewish circles. One woman explained the purpose of her midlife rite of passage by saying, "I am creating my future. I am choosing the road I will follow during the rest of my journey through life."[33] This contemporary, personalist language is then recast in spiritual, and specifically Jewish covenantal terms: the ceremony's purpose is to "reaffirm [her] relationship with God [and her] purpose in life. . . . Midlife is the fruitful time for new beginnings." While ordered in an entirely original sequence, and including several original prayers and ritual gestures, the ceremony includes six of the "seven blessings" from the traditional wedding liturgy, the recitation of the *Shema,* and the citation or invocation of several different Torah narratives about transformation and blessing. This ceremony, and others like it, merge personalist language and traditional symbols. The newly defined ritual moment thus becomes a vehicle for expressing the personal spirituality of the participant. It conveys religious meaning to what would otherwise be an entirely secular transition. In similar fashion, feminist circles have initiated rituals for abortion, still births, weaning a child, first menstruation, menopause, and the like, while elsewhere we find new rituals for changing a name, moving, reaching middle age, and encountering various stages of illness. These exist in no officially recorded collection of ritual; they are recognized as official by no movement. But they are grass-roots attempts by individual Jews to mark personalist moments in Jewishly authentic ways.

A primary challenge for the Jewish community will continue to be how to acknowledge ritually the authenticity of the life experiences of contemporary Jews while maintaining the integrity of the Jewish religious tradition. The only more or less certain prediction is that the celebration of new ritual will probably continue, as the boundaries of authentic Jewish observance broaden still further in the years ahead.[34]

NOTES

1. Lawrence A. Hoffman, "How Ritual Means: Ritual Circumcision in Rabbinic Culture and Today," *Studia Liturgica* 23, no. 1 (1993): 78–97.

2. Discussion of the different types of meaning is based on Hoffman, "How Ritual Means." Changes in the original formulation are indicated below.

3. Hoffman in "How Ritual Means" conflates the meaning assigned by the religious tradition itself with the scholarly, external interpretation, e.g., "Passover is the commemoration of the Exodus" and "Passover is the remnant of an older spring fertility celebration." Here, we use "official" to refer to the interpretation given by the tradition itself and the tradition's authorized interpreters (clergy, texts, etc.), so that scholarly exegesis is included only if it has entered the

religious lexicon of interpretation as well as the academic one. This caveat was intended in the 1993 formulation, but was not explicit. It is important to note, though, that the tradition's own self-understanding, and therefore "official" meaning, may change over time, with new meanings being added but not necessarily displacing the prior ones. Thus, meaning is multi-vocal not just across these categories but within them as well.

4.   Hoffman's "public meaning" is replaced here with "shared meaning" to emphasize that the shared meaning(s) is/are common to the celebrating community but may be more or less congruent with the "normative" shared and official meanings. See Hoffman, "How Ritual Means," p. 82.

5.   Depending on the flexibility of the liturgy, the officiant and the participants, these various meanings may be integrated (appearing serially or in parallel), glossed over, opposed or ignored.

6.   See, e.g., Lawrence A. Hoffman, "Non-Jews and Jewish Life-Cycle Liturgy," *CCAR Journal* (summer 1990): 1–20, and responses thereto.

7.   The movement from inclusion to representation is parallel to the movement from first-order to second-order feminism. See Lawrence A. Hoffman, "Blessings and their Translation in Current Jewish Liturgies," *Worship* 60, no. 2 (March 1986): 139–40.

8.   In the decentralized American Jewish community, it is difficult to speak with confidence about "authorized" rites. For this essay, "authorized rite" means the liturgy as presented in the "Rabbi's Manual" of the various movements and subsequently interpreted or modified by the respective decision-making groups of the rabbinic bodies. Many "mainstream" rabbis guided by the values implicit in this essay do not uniformly follow the official liturgy. This is not to claim that every rabbi's definition of covenantal authenticity is equivalent to the authors'; rather, that the goal of authenticity—however understood—is what motivates dissent from the authorized rite. From the rabbi's perspective, the very decision to make a change may in itself bring up issues of personal authenticity.

9.   See Rachel Adler, *"Brit Ahuvim*: A Marriage Between Subjects," in her forthcoming volume.

10.   Jeffrey K. Salkin, *Putting God on the Guest List* (Woodstock, VT, 1992).

11.   See Hoffman, "How Ritual Means," and Lewis M. Barth, ed., *Berit Mila in the Reform Context* (New York: Berit Mila Board of Reform Judaism, 1990).

12. Hoffman, "How Ritual Means."

13. A similar virtual syncretism to that described above is the "ritual for saying good-bye" included in the Reform movement's *A Time to Prepare* (Philadelphia: UAHC Committee on The Synagogue as a Caring Community, n.d.), p. 37. In the "Suggested Ritual for Saying Goodbye," a personalist and contemporary introduction precedes an unmodified presentation of the halakhic rite for the end of life.

14. In some circles, it is presumed that creating an original ceremony is simply what one does. See Ellen Umansky, "What's in a Naming Ceremony?" *Genesis* 2 (autumn 1989): 10–13.

15. This is not to say that having the ceremony is not important. If the rite were not meaningful at all, then the circumcision would occur only in hospitals without any attendant Jewish recognition.

16. In virtually all Conservative synagogues today, the bar and bat mitzvah ceremony is identical. Where this is not the case, as in Orthodox congregations, the official meaning of the ceremony has been changed. The shared meaning of bar and bat mitzvah—a public statement of Jewish identification and commitment—is the official meaning of bat mitzvah in these Conservative communities. Although it borrows from the name of the halakhic ceremony, the bat mitzvah ceremony is halakhicly marginal so long as bar mitzvah remains the time when men are first authorized to read publicly from the Torah, and women are still not authorized to do so at all. Sometimes the halakhic conflict can be finessed. For example, the Conservative *Rabbi's Manual* includes a ritual for the bride to present the groom with a ring at the wedding ceremony. While the groom effects the wedding with his presentation of her ring, and recites the traditional legal formula, the bride is invited to simply declare that the ring "is a sign of my love." In this case, the gesture is physically parallel but religiously irrelevant. Some couples no doubt find this level of visibility acceptable; others surely find it representationally inadequate. If a double ring ceremony is requested, the bride may now say: 'This ring is a symbol that you are my husband, and a sign of my love and devotion.'" Jules Harlow, ed., *A Rabbi's Manual* (New York: Rabbinical Assembly, 1965), p. 43.

17. Reform Judaism never suggested that circumcision should be stopped; the surgery moved from a religious home ceremony to a hospital medical procedure.

18. See Simeon J. Maslin, ed., *Gates of Mitzvah* (New York: CCAR, 1979), pp. 14, 17.

19. Texts which are photo-copied and passed on from one person to another, but not widely published, are the functional equivalent of "oral" in our culture.

20. The counter-feminist, so called "masculinist" movement has taken up the anti-circumcision cause, sometimes employing an anti-Semitic argument. Having already been blamed for killing the matriarchal goddess (See Plaskow, Judith, "Blaming the Jews for the Birth of Patriarchy" and Daume, Annette, "Blaming the Jews for the Death of the Goddess" in *Nice Jewish Girls: A Lesbian Anthology,* Evelyn Torton Beck, ed. [Boston, 1982] pp. 298–309), Judaism is now in danger of being charged in the death of the "Ur-Wild-Man."

21. See Lisa Braver Moss, "Circumcision: A Jewish Inquiry," *Midstream* 38, no. 1 (January 1992): 20–23; Daniel Landis, Lisa Braver Moss, and Sheryl Robbin, "Current Debate: Circumcision Decision," *Tikkun* 5 (September/October 1990): 50–74.

22. Some might officiate at a separate naming ceremony in the synagogue. The halakhah firmly declares that circumcision should not occur if the infant's health would be compromised in any way, and modern liberal *responsa* have commonly expanded the boundaries of "health" to encompass mental and social health (most notably in the context of when abortion should be permitted). This reasoning has been applied to the case of adult converts who fear circumcision; see "Prospective Convert Who Fears Circumcision" in Walter Jacob, ed., *American Reform Responsa* (New York: CCAR, 1983), p. 239; some would make the same arguments on behalf of parents.

23. See Adler, "*Brit Ahuvim.*"

24. At its 1993 convention, the Reform Central Conference of American Rabbis convention had a closed session on why rabbis should or should not agree to officiate. In 1994, a leading Reform rabbi called for formal recognition of gay and lesbian union ceremonies as *kiddushin.* See Mark Winer, "Our Vision of the Future: Personal Status and K'lal Yisrae," *CCAR Yearbook 104* (New York: CCAR, 1995).

25. The earliest public piece we are aware of is Jeffrey Perry-Marx, "The strangers in our midst" (student senior sermon presented at Hebrew Union College-Jewish Institute of Religion, New York, 1983). Also see Yoel H. Kahn, "The *Kedushah* of Homosexual Relationships," *CCAR Yearbook 99* (New York, 1989), pp. 136–41, and

Yoel H. Kahn, *Kiddushin: A Guide to Officiation at Gay and Lesbian Union Ceremonies* (San Francisco: Congregation Sha'ar Zahav, 1993).

26. The significance of this nomenclature debate cannot be underestimated. The question of the rubric under which gay or lesbian union ceremonies will be organized in liberal synagogues is directly parallel to the conflict in Orthodox synagogues about how to liturgically celebrate the birth of daughters without conferring upon the new rite a status equivalent to the traditional rite it seeks to imitate.

27. The range of responses to this conflict can be illustrated by the actions of the board of a Reform synagogue, which recently voted to permit its rabbi to officiate at union ceremonies for gay and lesbian Jews but would not permit the public acknowledgement of the anniversary at Sabbath services.

28. Oral communication to authors.

29. Following Psalm 137:5,6 (NRSV): "If I forget you, Jerusalem, let my right hand wither . . . If I do not set Jerusalem above my highest joy."

30. Without knowing about the Jerusalem association, many people are familiar with the breaking of the glass as a symbol of "sadness at happy times." These new meanings which are added on are consistent with the shared understanding of the symbolism of the glass. At the same time, the glass never gives up its primary assocation as an essential distinguishing marker of a Jewish wedding and its inclusion further validates the rite's message about its own Jewish legitimacy.

31. See, e.g., Riv-Ellen Prell, *Prayer and Community* (Detroit, 1989).

32. While the new name of the ceremonies sets them apart as different, they often resemble the traditional bar/bat mitzvah more than most adult bar/bat mitzvah ceremonies do. Adult bar/bat mitzvah is not identified as a life-transition time, for instance; its scheduling is arbitrary.

33. Bonnie Feinman, "Midlife Celebration" in Irene Fine, *Midlife and its Rite of Passage Ceremony* (San Diego: Woman's Institute for Continuing Jewish Education, 1983), p. 43.

34. See, e.g., Debra Orenstein, ed., *Lifestyles: Jewish Women on Life Passages and Personal Milestones* (Woodstock, VT, 1994), which was published after the completion of this essay.

Conclusion

Life Cycle as Theology

PAUL F. BRADSHAW AND LAWRENCE A. HOFFMAN

Our introduction suggested that the overall shape of a human life is theologically constructed by our life-cycle liturgies. The foregoing chapters were arranged without immediate regard for Jewish or Christian theologies; we divided this volume instead into chronological units that correspond to the way modern western culture conceptualizes human existence, that is to say, the individualistic experience of moving steadily through time from birth to death, with adolescence just the other side of childhood, and sickness just this side of death. To be sure, our religious traditions are not impervious to that course, but they do not correspond entirely to it either. Rather, they skew that simple temporal scheme so as to emphasize some points and ignore others, giving us what amounts to a ritually engaging theological commentary on life's meaning at the appropriate stopping points along the way. To go through life as Jew or Christian is to say something profound about what matters in the mystery of life and death to which we are all subject.

Life Cycle as Theology: The Christian Example

At first glance, it may appear that Christianity possesses an integrated set of life-cycle ritual intentionally designed to cover all the significant stages of human life from the cradle to the grave, and to do so equally moreover, without special attention paid to one point in human development rather than another. However, as the historical studies in this volume reveal, this is not the case; the various rites emerged at quite different times and for quite different reasons, generally having little or nothing to do with biological processes per se.

Both sickness and death had a direct and intimate connection with the core of the Christian message, so from the beginning, Christians had theological convictions that they wanted to express ritually in relation to these two conditions. First, they proclaimed that before long Jesus would return and bring the consummation of God's kingdom. What would happen to those who died before this event took place was thus of immediate concern to them, and indeed this question is faced and answered in the New Testament itself: Christians who had died would be raised up to share in the kingdom with the living, and so the bereaved should "not grieve as others do who have no hope" (1 Thess. 4:13). If Christianity was to be true to itself, therefore, it was imperative that there should be specifically Christian funeral rites reflecting the hope of resurrection. Yet, while this may have been the motive behind the original emergence of Christian funeral ritual, the note of joyful expectancy would largely be lost in later centuries and the rites would increasingly become conformed to cultural influences around them. It was not until the advent of the process of liturgical revision in the late twentieth century that they began to recover some of their former distinctiveness.

Second, Jesus was remembered not merely as a teacher but as a healer of the sick, and the canonical Gospels contain a large collection of healing stories. Once again, therefore, the idea of the healing power of Christianity was something that was integral to its central message, and this could not but give rise to a Christian liturgical and pastoral ministry towards the sick. As in the case of death, however, the original message of healing embodied in the rites gradually gave way to other influences, especially in the West, where the ministry came to be seen as preparatory for death and has only recently begun to reclaim its earlier focus.

The development of a specifically Christian rite of marriage was slower, and undertaken only with some reluctance. At first, Christians were content to be married in the traditional manner of their native cultures, to which was added a further but tangential desire to receive God's blessing on their union from their own ministers. The lack of adequate supervision over the process of marriage by the secular authorities, however, led to frequent abuse. Clandestine, illegal, and forced unions often took place, and so with the emergence of Christendom the clergy were more or less compelled to take some responsibility to try to regulate matters, since they were often the only people in a position to be able to do so. Once they had taken this step, they naturally tried to express a Christian theology of marriage in the nuptial rites that they created. However, since a Christian approach to marriage was by no means as clearly defined in the New Testament scriptures and Christian tradition as were the attitudes to be taken towards sickness and death, Christian wedding liturgies display some variety in their understanding of the character of the institution. For example, some view the process of marriage as essentially a mutual and equal act by both the man and the woman, while others see it more in terms of a change in the bride's status. Similarly, some rites articulate a very positive concept of the role of marriage in God's purposes, while others view it more as a way of avoiding the sin of fornication.

It was yet a different story again with regard to birth and adolescence. While rites for the purification of the mother and for the naming of the child, based on biblical examples, sprang up at an early date in some places, primitive Christianity knew of no universal birth rite nor of any rites at all in connection with adolescence, and there was nothing in the Christian faith that strongly encouraged their development. The eventual extension of baptism to infants everywhere and the emergence of a separate rite of adolescent confirmation in the West were not the result of human biological need, but they did not arise out of careful theological reflection either. While the former may have arisen out of some inchoate desire on the part of parents to enable their offspring to share in the theological benefits of baptism while they were yet young, confirmation came into existence largely as the result of a series of non-theological circumstances. Both of them may aptly be described, therefore, as originally rites in search of a theology. While in time official explanations did appear for the two rites which related them to the Christian faith, in popular culture they assumed the function of rites of passage for birth and adolescence as two crucial points in human life. This development has made it very difficult for liturgical reformers today to disentangle their cultural role, as markers of stages in the biological cycle, from their theological role as markers of points on a spiritual journey to full Christian faith which may be completely unrelated to physical birth and maturation.

But the very chronological pattern in which the rites developed demonstrate the theological overlay that Christianity enforced upon human experience. Drawn from the outset to the promise of a life beyond the grave, and interested primarily in Christ's passion, death and resurrection, the Christian ritual repertoire very quickly adopted rites of sickness and of burial, both of which were the most apt theological markers for the Christian message. As a rite of initiation, baptism was central also, but for spiritual rebirth as a Christian, not for biological birth as a human being. It was rebirth as a believer, a child of God, that beckoned to the early Christian liturgical imagination. Life-cycle liturgy thus demarcated a life, but not what we consider the human life of womb to grave. Only eventually did Christian culture expand to include marriage, hitherto just a secular ceremony with legal consequences but largely outside the church's purview; and only with the triumph of Augustinian thought did baptism extend to all Christian children, and confirmation develop as the moment for the bestowal of further grace to combat the challenges presented by adolescence and adulthood.

Life Cycle as Theology: The Jewish Example

If the death and resurrection of Christ was the model narrative for Christians, Exodus, Sinai and entry to the Promised

Land proved determinative for Jews. Both communities thereby celebrated covenant, but the covenants were different in type and leaned toward different facets of human experience.

Funeral liturgy, so central to Christians, remained relatively subsidiary to Jews—unlike other events, it was never even fixed with mandatory sets of blessings such as we find for circumcision and marriage, for instance. No less than its Christian parallel, Jewish burial too pointed the way to a life after death, but in Judaism, that promise did not eclipse the primary covenantal stance that Judaism celebrated, a covenant that demanded the fulfillment of the Torah's commandments throughout the period we call life. Judaism therefore focused on those life-cycle rites that emphasize Torah and commandments: *brit milah* (circumcision) most of all.

Circumcision mattered to the Rabbis because they believed that it was men who were primarily covenanted, first in their flesh as eight-day old boys, and second in their obligation to study Torah and then to direct families where a life of the covenant was the norm. Judaism thus celebrated a sort of male life-line that began not at birth but at circumcision time. The popular birth celebrations called *Shavua Haben* and *Shavua Habat,* go practically unrecorded in rabbinic literature, and certainly have no religious significance attached to them. But circumcision is the occasion for little boys to be admitted into the "covenant of Abraham our father." Images of Torah study thereafter are ubiquitous in rabbinic literature, culminating (in the high Middle Ages) in a rite of beginning Torah education for boys. The age when boys reached their majority had all along been known as the moment of bar mitzvah, but bar mitzvah was originally just a status: the age of adult responsibility. Only relatively late in time (again, the high Middle Ages) did that moment too attract a ritualized demonstration of adult Torah competence for boys becoming men. Finally, there was marriage, the end of the male life-line in a sense, in that its purpose was to father children and start the process all over again.

People did die, so funerals were held. Other rites, too, were once common—a celebration of virginity for instance, that the

Rabbis ignored officially and Maimonides protested actively, but which retained at least some popular support nonetheless. Above all, officially speaking, *Pidyon Haben,* like burial, was a necessity, though for a reason completely unrelated to biological processes—redemption had been mandated by the Torah. But redemption and burial, even though universally followed where called for, never became central to the theological focus that makes Judaism what it is. They are not central the way circumcision and Torah rites are. Even marriage remained somewhat a private matter, as it had been in the Roman empire at large and as it became in Christianity as well, but marrying a boy off was part of the father's Torah-obligation, so marriage received its due share of religious commentary in a rite called *kiddushin*—a rite that affirmed the covenantal status of a woman through her husband to whom she had been conjoined.

As living religions that must eventually take cognizance of biology as well as theology, both Judaism and Christianity therefore came eventually to outfit human life from birth to death with a variety of rites. But each retained its own theological version of life's ultimate meaning, and coded that meaning into the way it skewed the pattern of life-cycle events. Classical Christianity emphasized the new covenant through adult baptism and then burial. Judaism underscored the covenant with Abraham and at Sinai, giving attention above all to circumcision and to Torah.

Biology, Theology, and Culture

If life could be adequately captured as a biological process, life-cycle rites would be relatively unchanging. Our life expectancy expands with time, but people are born and they die nowadays much as they did centuries past. Considered merely as biological processes, the mystery of new life and the profundity of death shake us to our foundation neither more nor less in one century rather than another. But the whole point is that taken merely as biological processes, they probably would not shake us at all. It is culture that encodes events as earth-shaking or as ordinary, and then decides in what manner they are so. It is culture that bids us not to dispense with the remains of our loved ones without a proper ending; and to celebrate rites of passage along the way toward our final demise. The rites we adopt depend on the culture we see ourselves as inhabiting, and the cultural world-view that we accept as an adequate explanation of the world around us.

It is culture then, not biology, that changes; and if our religious rites of passage demonstrate evolution, it is because religious communities too evolve, being influenced by nonreligious cultural events like the opening of the trade routes during the Crusades and the rise of science in the seventeenth century. Religious culture is thus always in dialogue with its host environment, even in those periods of time when Christianity so informed the environment as to make it possible to speak of European and Christian culture as if they were the same thing. Certainly in our age the dialogue between Judaism and Christianity on one hand, and secular society on the other, is abundantly evident. That Jewish and Christian cultural constructs would be challenged by modern scientific alternatives is to be expected; and along with that challenge, we ought to anticipate major transformations in the life-cycle theologies that our rites of passage confer upon reality.

The most evident challenge in the Jewish camp has been the egalitarian temper of our times. No longer is a male life-line sufficient; *brit milah* can hardly mark the central covenantal rite if there is no covenant–ceremony parallel for girls. Marriage as a male act of taking a wife and covenanting her through her husband is similarly suspect. But in an age when free choice is more evident than ever as part of the human condition, the underlying Jewish theological concept of a covenant has, if anything, only increased its hold on the Jewish imagination. The covenantal theology implicit in the Jewish rites of passage thus serves moderns as well as it did their ancestors, as long as allowance is made for the inclusion of all men and women equally.

In Christianity too, a cultural critique is being felt. Modern Americans who find the severity of Augustinian theology unappealing find also that baptism can again mark the free choice of adults who elect the Christian promise. At the same time, the generally life-affirming ethos of modern America celebrates births (and birthdays) more than death and martyrdom. Predictably, American Christians will be attracted also to baptism as a rite for infants—not to protect them against the possibility of dying in a state of sin, but to welcome their arrival into the world.

Both Judaism and Christianity find themselves increasingly wrestling with other issues too. The rise in feminist consciousness raises questions about the extent to which religious traditions ought to value the experience of women *qua* women— providing rites of weaning, for instance. Increasing individualism calls religion to celebrate birthdays and anniversaries more than we used to. To what extent religion should accede to popular demands is perhaps the most significant question that faces us. On the one hand, it can be argued that if religion does not confer religious meaning upon life as people genuinely know it and live it, it draws an artificial boundary between faith and experience. If today's experience includes a first date or a college graduation within its repertoire of landmark events, then so be it—let religion provide a sanctifying vehicle that transforms pure secular celebration into a moment of transformative personal meaning. Let the life-cycle celebration expand endlessly to include the events of American culture in its ritual umbrella. On the other hand, it can be said with equal cogency that it is not religion's task to proclaim the religious centrality of every event that secular culture draws to our attention. It should instead insist on its own priorities, the message of Sinai and covenant, or the good news of the gospel. If that be so, religion will resist the temptation to expand into every nook and cranny of modern life. It will be satisfied with making its age-old message timely, fine-tuning its inherited rites so that the theological message that it sees as transcending cultural change speaks as clearly as ever to adherents who must conceptualize their lives now, no less than in the past.

Either way, life-cycle ritual plays a theological role of incalculable importance. We learn to see our world by attending to the things we celebrate. What we celebrate in life and what we choose to ignore, how we choose to demarcate the things to which we attend, and the passion that celebration alone evokes, go a long way toward overlaying biology with interpretation. In the end, Aristotle may be wrong: more than rational animals, we may be interpretive animals, and life-cycle ritual is a large part of our interpretive apparatus.

Contributors

DEBRA R. BLANK teaches liturgy at the Jewish Theological Seminary in New York City. She is completing her dissertation there on Massekhet Sofrim, one of the so-called "minor tractates of the Babylonian Talmud."

PAUL F. BRADSHAW, an Anglican priest, is Professor of Liturgy at the University of Notre Dame and editor-in-chief of *Studia Liturgica*. Among his recent books are *The Search for the Origins of Christian Worship* (SPCK/Oxford University Press, 1992), *Two Ways of Praying* (SPCK/Abingdon Press, 1995), and *Early Christian Worship: An Introduction to Ideas and Practice* (SPCK, 1996/Liturgical Press, 1997).

LAWRENCE A. HOFFMAN is Professor of Liturgy at the New York campus of the Hebrew Union College—Jewish Institute of Religion. His books include *The Canonization of the Synagogue Service* (University of Notre Dame Press, 1979), *Beyond the Text* (Indiana University Press, 1987), *The Art of Public Prayer: Not for Clergy Only* (Pastoral Press, 1988), and most recently, *Covenant of Blood: Circumcision and Gender in Rabbinic Judaism* (University of Chicago Press, 1995).

YOEL KAHN is a doctoral candidate at the Graduate Theological Union, Berkeley, California. Ordained at the Hebrew Union College—Jewish Institute of Religion in 1985, he served as rabbi for eleven years at Congregation Sha'ar Zahav, San Francisco, California, a Reform congregation with a special outreach to gay and lesbian Jews, their friends, families, and communities.

STACY A. LAVESON was ordained as a rabbi from the Hebrew Union College—Jewish Institute of Religion in 1993, and is now Associate Rabbi of Congregation Rodef Sholom in San Rafael, California.

RUTH A. MEYERS, a priest of the Episcopal Church, Diocese of Western Michigan, obtained her doctorate in liturgical studies from the University of Notre Dame and is now Assistant Professor of Liturgics at Seabury-Western Theological Seminary, Evanston, Illinois.

MARJORIE PROCTER-SMITH is Associate Professor of Liturgy and Worship at Perkins School of Theology, Southern Methodist University, Dallas, Texas.

KAREN B. WESTERFIELD TUCKER, a Methodist minister, is Assistant Professor of Liturgical Studies at the Duke University Divinity School. She is also the editor of the *Proceedings of the North American Academy of Liturgy.*

Index

297